Emergency Broadcasting
and 1930s American Radio

Emergency Broadcasting

and
1930s
American
Radio

Edward D. Miller

 Temple University Press
Philadelphia

Temple University Press, Philadelphia 19122
Copyright © 2003 by Temple University
All rights reserved
Published 2003
Printed in the United States of America

⊗ The paper used in this publication meets the requirements of the
American National Standard for Information Sciences–Permanence
of Paper for Printed Library Materials, ANSI Z39.48-1984.

Library of Congress Cataloging-in-Publication Data

Miller, Edward D., 1960–
    Emergency broadcasting and 1930s American radio / Edward D.
Miller.
       p.   cm.
    Includes bibliographical references and index.
    ISBN 1-56639-992-0 (cloth: alk. paper) – ISBN 1-56639-993-9 (pbk.:
alk. paper)
       1. Radio broadcasting–United States–History.   2. Radio broadcast-
ing–Social aspects–United States.   I. Title.

PN1991.3.U6 M55   2002
302.23'44'0973–dc21   2002020418

Contents

	Acknowledgments	vii
1	Introduction: Thrown Voices	1
2	The Uncanny Home and the Transmitted Voice	14
3	The Recital of the *Hindenburg* Disaster	48
4	Radio and the Voice and Body of the President	77
5	The Case of the "War of the Worlds"	106
6	Echo's Broadcast: Desire and Disembodiment	141
7	Body and Space in the Radio and Internet	179
	Notes	207
	Bibliography	229
	Index	241

Acknowledgments

I AM VERY GRATEFUL that the Museum of Radio and Television (New York, N.Y.) has the wisdom to maintain a Scholar's Program, which enabled my listening to all sorts of radio programs.

I thank Dean David Podell and the Office of the Dean of Humanities and Social Sciences at the College of Staten Island/CUNY for a summer stipend in 2001, allowing me to complete this manuscript, and for funding that allowed me to hire a research assistant.

I thank Nathalie Baginski and Laura LaBega for their research assistance, Carol Berman for alerting me to writings on Capgras' Syndrome, and Michael Quadland for his responsive listening. This project has been made better by comments on an earlier version from Richard Schechner, Mark Roberts, May Joseph, Martin Spinelli, Toby Miller, and, most especially, Allen Weiss. Also, I am lucky to have worked with a skilled editor with a real dedication to radio scholarship, Micah Kleit at Temple University Press. My fortune continued with Elizabeth Yoder as copy editor.

I have great colleagues at the College of Staten Island, particularly in the Department of Media Culture. It is a privilege to work alongside George Custen, David Gerstner, Jason Simon, Valerie Tevere, and Cindy Wong. I also thank the maestro in the office, Janet Manfredonia.

I want to thank those people whose maverick intelligences, startling wit, and loyal friendships have sustained this project–most notably Beth Nathanson, Guillermo Castillo, Jeffrey Stephens-Prince, Richard Collin Green, Mark Seamon, Frances Sorensen, John McGrath, Suzannah Clemitson, Marck O'Connell, Sumitra Mukerji, Kathryn Tannert-Niang, Wade Ehle, Scott Ferguson, Peter Wing Healey, and Hugo César Andrade. I thank my family, particularly Eric, Jake, Jon, Myriam, Ruth. Most especially, I express gratitude to my parents, Jean Baker Miller and Mike Miller.

1

Introduction

Thrown Voices

Premise of the Project

RADIO BROADCASTING in the United States began in 1920. By the 1930s broadcasting was popular, commercialized, and important to the life of the nation. The industry had a definite structure to it, and the medium played a key role in mass communication systems. Although radio has continued to be important, one could argue that in no other decade did it have such cultural influence. Thus, this book, which is about the radio and the radiovoice[1]–and may, indeed, be more about the meaning of thrown voices themselves–focuses on programs from the 1930s. As radio became structured and the medium rendered seemingly ordinary, extraordinary events served to reveal the dynamics of listening to voices with an unseen source.

I focus here on specific programs that reveal the more everyday relationship between transmitted voices and listener. By studying some of the sounds of American popular radio in the 1930s, I move to new understandings of how such voices resound differently than other forms of speech.

My understandings are concerned with the politics and aesthetics of radio as a cultural force.

This project is informed by my background in performance studies and my use of cultural studies in teaching media. The book takes an interdisciplinary approach, reflecting both my training and my current research. My close readings of radio thus move in two directions at once, treating radio both as *text* with meanings and as *event* with theatricalities. These readings are also distinctly influenced by ideas from the fields of psychoanalysis and film theory, particularly those that discuss the significations of the voice.

Following J. L. Austin's distinctions in *How to Do Things with Words* (1962), I view the mediated act as an utterance that is not necessarily "constative" but also poised to enact what it announces. For Austin, the *performative utterance* is an event in language when words match action–or rather, words *are* action. The often-cited example of this is when a bride or groom at a wedding ceremony utters the words "I do." In saying those words, the person has become married; the words have simultaneously performed the action. A performative utterance is spoken in the "War of the Worlds" broadcast because the program is itself the invasion that Welles's narrative depicts. It lays bare the action of the medium. It is a performative utterance that enacts the contract and contact between the medium and the listener.

Electric speech and the performative utterance produce an overlay that pronounces not only the speech or the utterance but also the devices and the characteristics of the medium. It matters greatly through which means one communicates, and the medium itself is also always communicating in these messages. Thus, this project follows Marshall McLuhan's insistence that each medium is not neutral but develops a seeming personality with different characteristics (1995). This insistence is a crucial one. McLuhan, writing in an era saturated by television, insisted that reality becomes "televisualized." Likewise, I suggest that the 1930s were a time when the radio and the importance of the transmitted voice permeated all aspects of life in America and elsewhere. It dominated the imagination of the culture, connecting and severing the nation from itself.

Radio had distinct characteristics in the 1930s that informed its structures for decades. It removed voices from visible bodies and brought them into the homes of the listeners. It provoked a kind of seeing through voice, an envisioning inside the head, that required a focused listening.

Many of the characteristics of radio remain, yet the placement of the medium in the cultural life of Americans has changed. Radio has in large part left the home. Many users listen to radios in cars or through headphones in personal stereos; increasingly, radio stations are on-line, and users tune in via the Internet. Listening to the radio via a multitasking home entertainment center or in a vehicle (or while walking or running) changes the dynamics of the medium. Radio becomes one of many activities involving the body and psyche or the immediate technology. In the 1930s, by contrast, radio had a central place in the life of the nation and in the nation's homes. It was a domestic object plugged into the walls, receiving traveling voices. This aspect is key to my particular reading of the medium.

Bodies and Disembodies: Media and the Medium

Communications historian Carolyn Marvin writes that "the body is the most familiar of all communication modes"

(1988:109). In her view, the body is used to send or receive information. Also, each communication medium involves the activity of at least one region of the body intensely as part of the act of transmission and the process of operation. Although it is understood as part of the process of mediated communication, the body itself is often configured as a communications medium and not just as a "mode." Judith Butler suggests that the body is configured as a medium on which "cultural meanings are inscribed or as the instrument through which an appropriative and interpretive will determines a cultural meaning for itself" (1990:8). In other words, the body is not used neutrally, but its usage and appearances are related to larger cultural meanings. The body–or a particular configuration of the body–is interpretable and mediates between self and sociality. Since it is deemed responsible for the operation of the apparatus needed for transmission of bodily productions, the body is seen as speaking or heard as making an appearance.

In the last twenty years, much theorizing has focused on "the body" and its social construction, cultural meanings, and modes of communication. This work follows upon this emphasis, but it is offered as a discussion of *the disembodiment*. By making this distinction, I do not mean to infer that the latter term is only in the shadow of the body or only the lingual expressivity of the body. The disembodiment gains a relative coherence differently via electric media, and I stretch the word's usage so as to use it as a noun. It is set apart from this "theoretical" body of recent inquiry.

Much insightful work has also been done on radio disembodiment, and media history has been invigorated by recent reconfigurations of gender and performance theory. Yet I aim to reconfigure much of this thinking on the body in order to understand the particular expressivity of *vocal* disembodiment. I write of this disembodiment in its early electric and vocal appearances because the proliferation of Internet disembodiment–although of a different construction and with a vastly divergent background–has a strong relationship to radio disembodiment and echoes some of its aspects. In many ways, I use radio in the 1930s as a way to address contemporary media.

My use of the word *disembodiment* in this endeavor is particular. To disembody means "to divest of the body, of corporeal existence." In order to be a disembodiment, one has to have been once encased in a body; one has to have emerged from some original carnality to which one may or may not be reunited.

For example, Kaja Silverman notes that in classic Hollywood cinema virtually all examples of the female voice-over are embodied at some point during the film (1988:49–50). A female voice may narrate a scene and may be heard as originating from another perspective than that of the camera, but this voice "does not transcend the body" (50). The female voice is affixed to a body from which it originates and to which it will return; the camera will reunite voice and image.

Gender and disembodiment are articulated differently on radio. In radio, voices are always what Michel Chion–following Pierre Schaeffer[2]–calls an *acousmêtre*. Radio voices are discernible entities without a corresponding fixed visual aspect, hence they are "sound-beings." Male voices were predominant in 1930s radio: in classic Hollywood cinema the vocal disembodiment is virtually a male voice.[3] Yet what I want to avoid in this project's usage of the term *disembodiment* is the assumption that I am referring to the spirit or the essence of what was once comfortably bounded within a human frame. Neither does this disembodiment within the medium of radio gain access to the transcendental by virtue of its acoustic entity in the ways in which it might in cinema. The vocal disembodiment in radio, simply put, is not a narrative device that involves a search for the corresponding body; it is the aberrant norm of the medium.[4]

Another meaning of *to disembody* found in Webster's Dictionary is "to free from the body." However, my sense of the noun form, *disembodiment*, is not that it is without incarnation. Rather, I argue that there is a body in the disembodied voice itself. I mean this in two ways. First, this voice is itself an entity that can be thought of as having texture and consistency. Second, the listener, in hearing the vocal disembodiment, imagines a specific body. Depriving an auditor of the source of the voice provokes a fantasy of the originary body. This is part of our cultural training; as beings that hear, we always look to see what occurrence has produced a sound. When the occurrence is outside the visual field, we imagine the origin of it. We conjure up a body we don't get to see.

Thus, my use of the word *disembodiment* foregrounds its production and the willingness of the listener to participate in this production. Disembodiment suggests a body, but it is not necessarily the *original* or the remainder of what was once–or will become–the actual body.

Contemporary sound artist Gregory Whitehead's work examines "the schizophonic double" of the radiovoice. In his essay "Who's There: Notes on the Materiality of Radio," Whitehead describes radiophonic space as

> *a public channel produced by an absent other entering into a private ear.* The material specific to radio inscribes itself within the thoroughly libidinal circulations internal to a

ménage à trois. The language of radio is thus constructed not from a series of applied techniques, but from a series of fragile complicities. (1989:11; italics in the original)

The vocal disembodiment enabled by radio production is estranged from its speaker as soon as it enters radiophonic space. This voice operates within this space independently of the disc jockey, performer, or reporter. The body of the speaker, needed to initiate the sound, is no longer required for its transmission into the private ear. The absent other is this source, which, due to the processes of the medium, becomes an "other," deprived of presence but able to affect listeners never seen. For Whitehead, radio is an intimacy of strangers, with voices entering ears via the public channel. Whitehead foregrounds the notion of the ears as organ *and* orifice. The process of listening to radio–that is, hearing a disembodied voice received and projected by a machine running on electricity–requires an affection toward the unseen voice that is also made possible only by the tacit agreement of the listener. The disembodied voice enters into the corpus of the listeners. This is an anonymous and intimate interaction, a backroom of sound.

The production and dynamics of the disembodied radio voice, which provides an opening for a philosophical and aesthetic questioning and appreciation of the medium, also serves to create a precarious situation for the listener. This situation could be called the "Oz Effect."[5] As in the Walter Fleming film classic, *The Wizard of Oz* (1939), the transmitted voice creates a booming, commanding voice, rich with missives and instructions. This voice's sonority anticipates and encourages the complicity of the listeners. The disembodied voice becomes a ruling voice through the auditors' involvement with the broadcast.

President Franklin D. Roosevelt used his disembodied voice to gain support for his policies. Although he was handicapped and his actual corporeality could be viewed by the populace as frail, the voice he transmitted became a key way to show strength, confidence, and reliability. The voice thus becomes a *representation*[6] amongst many other key representations of the power and ramifications of the person.

The disembodied voice desires its listener. This listener, even if deemed inactive or rendered laconic by the broadcast's command, is never exactly passive. As Roland Barthes writes: *"Listening speaks"* (1985:259). Listening is a posture and a form of utterance–a way of accepting sound into "a hole in the head" (Whitehead 1991), but it is also an embodied production that enters into a relationship with the enunciator and with the auditor's context. Listening, which may appear to be silent, is not a silence. Listening speaks, then, not only through the speaker's interpretation of the listener but in the responsive modes the listener uses, all of which might escape the speaker's consciousness but are crucial to understanding the event.

In the realm of radio, Whitehead suggests that the speaker engages and imagines the listener he cannot see as part of the pleasure of sending out a voice (1989). The listener looms large; the audience's posture is audible. The experience of the listener to the disembodied radiovoice of the 1930s is multifarious (described as hysterical, for example, after responses to the "War of the World" broadcast). I argue that the newness of listening to so many unseen voices produced an uproarious connectedness. This experience of connectedness was not always welcome–even as the radio as object became ubiquitous, with its dial always switched to on. By this I mean that even as radio became familiar, it retained a strangeness in the home. In fact, I believe radio still retains this strangeness and has the potential for creating hoaxes in a way that television, for example, could not. This potentiality resides in depriving the listener of the source of the sound and the body of the speaker. Radio keeps its poker face.

The word *medium* is the singular form of the word *media*, but it also suggests spiritualism. A medium is a person one visits in order to contact the beloved dead, a person who enables an interchange between the living and someone who has been revivified. This medium is also able to transfer (or appear to transfer) the whims and activities of the deceased. The medium is someone who goes between the dead and the living and transmits messages back and forth. The medium was a very prevalent figure in the nineteenth century. I argue that the medium also has a great impact on conceptions of twentieth-century media.[7] This spiritual medium uses his body in order to transmit in ways that the character in *The Shadow* does. Such a medium is at once radio-like and yet never totally evacuates all sites of corporeality.

Lamont Cranston's alter ego in *The Shadow* becomes disembodied as a tactic to expose and transmit truth. He is able to enter into the heads of the villains. In turn, as a specter, he is able to transmit–in a booming voice–to these villains (and via radio waves to his girlfriend, for they share a frequency to which she can tune in). Not exactly a telepath, he is more of a radio transmitter and receiver. He personifies the medium in its haunting omniscience. The medium never completely disappears from the place of interaction. Rather, when completely possessed and transformed by the interaction between human parties, the medium itself extends and is enlivened.

In this aspect, my stance is different from that of Marshall McLuhan, who argued that media are the extensions of humans and suggested that media are analogous to (or literally) prosthetics. I view media, and radio in particular, as a separate terrain–in between, but able to interact. I view "radiospace" as a breeding ground and a graveyard for the disembodiment, not as an attachment to the human frame. I acknowledge this space's autonomy. When voices are thrown into the medium, they are severed and resound virtually independently of their origin. The intent of the speaker does not guide how the voice is heard.

The word *medium* also has the meaning of "middle" or designates that which is neither small nor large but "in between." For me, this between is expansive and peculiar. Influenced by the parties on all sides of this middle, it also keeps its distinctiveness. Radio is an "in between" that seems to forget that which is around it. It begins to appear as if it were a distinctive space.

Medium in its verb form also refers to intervening between two conflicting parties so as to lessen the effects of the clash. In this way, the word suggests a cultural healing– to mediate in order to resolve. Yet much of the discussion of the medium of radio here foregrounds the more menacing aspects of the medium. My premise, then, is indebted to Catherine Covert's argument in her essay on the popularization of radio "We May Hear Too Much" (1984). She shows that although radio became popular during the 1920s–and was being hailed as way to unite geographically and culturally diverse Americans, creating a common American culture–this did not mean that the medium was unequivocally and universally loved. In fact, she argues that by the late 1920s the radio became a dread necessity as much as a beloved fireside companion.

Yet at the risk of contradicting myself, I do not want to entirely repress the more curative meanings of reconciliation that the word *medium* suggests. Although broadcast disembodiment can sound creepy or haunting at times and in each instance involves an operation (in the medical sense of operating–removing a voice from a body), this voice also creates pleasure. It can connect listening and speaking publics, producing a space of dynamic interaction energized by a seduction. Yet when the ether is increasingly run by corporate forces that delimit interaction and encourage censorship, the harsher aspects of the radiovoice are emphasized.

Radio as Identity

A subculture of "radio boys" during the teens in America used the medium of radio as a way to communicate with each other across great distances.[8] They were inspired by Thomas Edison and by Jack London–adventurers and inventors. With homemade receivers and transmitters, they quickly became more proficient at navigating the airwaves than was the Navy. "Narrowcasters," as opposed to broadcasters, some of them believed their communication was circumventing the encroaching monopoly of the Bell company. Amateur radio users organized into groups of radio operators (such as the American Radio Relay League), later becoming a lobbying group that vied with the Navy for control over the airwaves.

This struggle–over commercialism, modes of usage, and military versus civilian (and then corporate- versus community-oriented) applications–has been repeated with the Internet. As before, it is clear that the large corporations–now Microsoft and ATT, then General Electric and NBC–are winning. This project does not focus on the takeover itself, but rather emphasizes the ramifications of this corporate victory and its trickle-down effect on how voices on the radio are heard.

Broadcasting is always, in part, a potentially disastrous endeavor, not because it serves to turn the public into a passive listening mass, kept in the home tuned to strange voices from a box but because the circumvention of distance has the capacity to become troublesome, a magic performance of technology with all sorts of possibilities. Radio gives voices to eyewitnesses. Yet they transmit only sound; the speech of the eyewitness is made up of "word-pictures," a term used to designate an attempt to relay what the reporter sees. Their access to the visual puts such voices traveling along all sorts of psychic borders. For the eyewitness and his listeners, risk is involved in this transmission because the eyewitness can get too close and become subsumed into the event.

Radio voices are thrown. Their sound is often enjoyable: erotic, captivating, enlivening. Seemingly customized to each listener, they connect each to the story. The corporate structure of radio, though, is an estranging one, turning the voice into something potentially more nebulous. American broadcasting is concerned with particular strategies of covering events that are deemed disaster, tragedy, catastrophe, crises, and so forth, rather than focusing on presenting the news from a variety of viewpoints, contextualizing what is happening locally, nationally, and globally. Indeed, it is not involved in telling stories in either innovative or time-proven ways.

Of course, the world of the 1930s was filled with the need to report on occurrences of disaster. But the burgeoning communications industry was linked to the threat of malfeasance. This was not only to ensure that listeners stayed tuned, but also because the industry was affixed to the circumvention of distance and the ability to place a voice near the edge of the horrid event.

For the listener, the presentation of the event and the capability of the medium itself to describe far-off events can be framed as "entertainment" or even as "info-tainment" or just plain old "containment." Yet by the 1930s, this also pointed to the power relations of the industry. The amateur radio users and broadcasters of the first two decades could claim mastery over an event and the medium. But the dynamics were different for the listener to the commercialized broadcasts of the 1920s and 1930s. Listening may speak, as Barthes asserts, but with the advent of the broadcasting industry, the speech of the listener may be drowned out. Catherine Covert suggests, referring to this audience, that it "may hear too much" (1984).

Perhaps the hope of American isolationism is for a story that is not interrupted by the reporting of a crisis. But reports of crises have their own bizarre reward: Tales of survival are held so dear and seem so real; first person accounts encourage vivid picture-making in the minds of the listener.[9] The Internet, which is often touted as providing information, also repeats modes of storytelling that emphasize being there.

Even so, homespun conspiracy theories circulate, and all sorts of rumors run rampant on the Internet. Such missives reveal a relationship with the medium and its management. With media under corporate control, aided by the complicity of the government, fantasies and falsehoods gain credence. In this structure, a strange yet familiar voice can sound quite harsh and haunting, telling unfathomable stories, warning of monstrous invaders from Mars. The monsters stand in for corporate forces that dominate the medium.

2

The Uncanny Home and the Transmitted Voice

Voices of the Dead

In her essay "Radio from Beyond the Grave" (1994), Carola Morales reports on the activities of the American Association of Broadcast Voice Phenomena. This association collects tapes from people who have heard and recorded voices of the dead on the radio. Listeners hear dead speakers in between stations (a region of the radio spectrum where, appropriately, dead air "blows"). Rising above the static and hum, the voices of luminaries such as Freud, Descartes, and Hitler have been heard as well as those of loved ones who have died more recently.

Morales notes that the inventors of electric technology also imagined their objects as connecting with the dead: Marconi and Tesla "realized the possibility of using the radio as a wireless telephone to the dead," and Edison "invented the phonograph during his search to record voices of the dead" (331).[1] Modern technology was envisioned—and is still experienced—as having mediumistic capabilities. To turn one of these objects on or to respond to its call or ring (Bell and

14

Watson's telephone) is to initiate and experience a potential séance. (No doubt Internet users will soon start to profess to receiving e-mail from the dead.)

In his essay "A Gramophone in Every Grave," Steven Connor argues that new technologies became part of the séance in the early part of the last century:

> The flourishing of the direct voice[2] during the twentieth century was undoubtedly encouraged by the developments of acoustic technologies–the telephone, the phonograph, the gramophone, the microphone, the megaphone, the radio, and the tape-recorder. These kinds of acoustic technology supported the development of the dramaturgy of the séance in two ways. First of all, they plainly supplied the technical means for achieving various vocal and acoustic illusions.... But the technology was also crucial in supplying explanations for the new manifestations. (2000:366)

New scientific developments thus aided belief in the supernatural rather than dispelling such myths. Instruments like the telephone became part of the séance and also served to justify what occurred during the performance. Connor reports that a leading voice medium, writing in the journal *The Direct Voice* in 1930, urged her readers, "Be your own psychic radio station" (2000:369). Clearly, the inference is that radio is already a link-up between visible and invisible forces.

Relatedly, Gregory Whitehead writes about radio in ways that conjure up images of the séance: "Every living speaker is enveloped by airspace riddled with the dead" (1990:60). Airspace is for Whitehead where disembodiment involves a seeming dissection of the corpus, voice from body; "radio-bodies" roam the vast pseudo-enclave of radiospace. Writing on the ontology of radio, Whitehead adds, "My strengthening suspicion is that the life of radio is in fact an *after*life, that the cave [of radio] is most vibrant *when the air is most dead*" (1989:11). Radio is experienced as haunted–or enchanted, even enlivened–by the dead. The radio artist or announcer is akin to a medium channeling voices that may or may not have an origin from inside his own body.

Technology's Haunting

The word *technology,* as Heidegger indicates in the essay "The Question Concerning Technology" (1977), is derived from the Greek word *technē:* "the name not only for the activities and skills of the craftsman, but also for the arts of the mind and the fine arts" (13). In Heidegger's emphasis, technology not only refers to tools made for a means but more importantly names a process, "a way of revealing" (12). Technology is an activity related to truth-seeking. The Greek use of the term *technē* also indicates technology's connection to artisanry. Yet in the twentieth century, technology is viewed as developed only by those involved in science and industry. Even as technology affects the methodology of the artisan or the consumer, technological objects are not usually made by them. Rather, technology is developed by industry.

In *High Technē: Art and Technology from the Machine Aesthetic to the Posthuman* (1999), R. L. Rutsky uses Heideggerian concepts to discuss technology and its relationship to aesthetics:

> Heidegger's point ... is not that technology's close relationship to art in ancient Greece has simply been lost. Rather, he argues that the relationship between art and technology, so visible in the Greek *technē,* has always been basic to technology, to its "essence," even when the conception of technology has been explicitly posed (as it has in the modern,

instrumental conception of technology) in contrast to art, to the aesthetic sphere. (1999:4)

For Rutsky, high tech signifies a return to the aesthetic emphasis in *technē*. Contemporary technology is not only concerned with usefulness but with its look and stylishness; this signifies an end to a modern conceptualization of technology. In modern uses of the word *technology,* as Rutsky indicates, art and technology are seen almost as opposite.

David Nye points out in *Narratives and Spaces: Technology and the Construction of American Culture* (1997) that *technology* as a term was introduced by Harvard professor Jacob Bigelow "as early as 1828 as an all-encompassing word for systems of mechanical improvements" (3). Yet the term did not become popular until the end of the century, and Americans continued to use the terms *the mechanic arts* or *the arts,* until the word *technology* become more widely used "during the rapid expansion of engineering education." Currently, Nye argues, the use of the term "tends to obscure human action and to represent machines as an abstract force in history" (3) instead of part of a series of systematic interactions involving objects that are man-made.[3]

With the popularization of technology in everyday usage, the concept once designated by "mechanical arts" became associated with the sciences and not the arts. In addition, the term *technology* became related to the finished product (the machine) and not to the dynamics of developing new processes and techniques (how the machine is made and operated by users, and the aesthetics involved). Thus, the artistry of mechanical activity is removed from the definition of mechanical innovation.

Even as I nuance this modern use of the word *technology,* however, I want to suggest that this Anglo-American use of the word is "haunted" by its past. It bears traces of its more process-related meanings expressed by the Greek word *technē*.

On the surface, it is puzzling that the American relationship to new technological objects could be fraught with panic and fear. After all, progress was seemingly a national religion, and an embrace of the new was a documented and celebrated national trait. Indeed, at the beginning of the twentieth century, inventors replaced explorers and pioneers as national heroes. With this rush to settle the airwaves, why did once-nascent technological forms remain–or become– so connected with the dead? How did the radio become a place where both the work and the denial of mourning seem to take place, a vivified space of the deceased, creating a revolutionary medium where, perhaps, the old regime returns bodiless? It appears that the shock of new technology is mediated by more "primitive" presences.

Hamlet and the Ghost of Technology

Hamlet's father is one of the most famous literary ghosts. This ghost appears first to Hamlet's friends Horatio and Marcellus, who relay his appearance to Hamlet. He does not believe their tale of witnessing the dead king's return but goes to meet the apparition nevertheless. Initially, Hamlet distrusts his own sighting of the apparition, yet he follows the gesturing ghost. Only when he *hears* it speak to him, does he believe that the specter could be his returned father. The ghost's harsh words of revenge then become verifiable, trustworthy. Whereas the image of the ghost could be a shared hallucination, his voice was familiar. Hamlet–the sole auditor of the speech of the ghost–believes that the ghost's voice is a familiar one. The ghost becomes less an apparition and more of a disembodied sound. Later in the play, he doubts this belief.

In other words, the fatherly voice reaches Hamlet in a way that the image does not. Images deceive more than words do. Here, the ghost's utterances remind him of his own unsaid thoughts. This familiarity is uncanny for him.

Furthermore, as a stage piece, the appearance and sonority of the ghost is itself a working of technology, a feat of craft. (In Elizabethan stages, the ghost would emerge from a concealed door at the bottom of the stage.) The revealing of the stage-ghost is a technological feat (in both modern and premodern meanings of the word) even as it is deemed a supernatural occurrence within the play itself. In nonstage settings, the revealing of the ghost for the reader is technological (in both Heideggerian and premodern terms) as well: it is an effort of artisanry, a *technē* of narrative; it is a way to reveal the past that will not leave the present alone.

Hamlet's ghost, the specter of his father, is then also the ghost in the machine, a haunting of "harshness" beyond but including patrilineal mandates. The ghost is a revealing of the machinations of representational devices. It is not uncanny due to its ghostliness per se. Rather, it is uncanny because of the familiarity of its message in a recognizable voice, a message that has been repressed by Hamlet.

Hamlet's ghost is the spokesperson of the technology of theatre, exposing its wirings. At the scene's end, the ghost has returned to its place beneath the stage, but its voice is heard urging Horatio and Marcellus to "swear" upon Hamlet's sword to speak nothing of the occurrence. And the ghost is also reminding Hamlet of his own pledge to commit murderous revenge. Thus, the voice of the ghost from beneath the visible frame urges Hamlet to fulfill a deathly and dangerous swearing. To stretch my analogy, the underbelly of technology's promise is deathly. The ghost is the voice of technology. Technology's promise is lethal as well as reviving.

Danger and Friendliness

For Hamlet, the revealing of technology's work is fraught with danger.[4] In some uncanny way it is also like the workings of his family and his kingdom. Much lurks beneath the surface in Denmark; it is only revealed in moments. These moments do not expose the truth in its entirety but rather hint at an entire network beneath the stage or the surface of an event. The sense, both theatrically and psychologically, is that danger can enter at any moment, but via technology, via the wiring in the walls and the piping underfoot. Surveillance and danger seem constant.

In the marketing of contemporary technology during the 1990s, particularly with the home computer, there was a decided emphasis on the object's "friendliness." Manufacturers of personal computers and software programs repeatedly promised that their product was "user-friendly." What could this possibly mean for a machine? How does this extend or expose the meanings of the word "friendly" when it describes a mass-produced object, even if it is also deemed a "desktop" or a "gateway"?

Of course, the word choice here is meant to convey that the product is easy to use and has been adapted to the user. Furthermore, the product does not require that the user adapt to it–the manufacturer swears that its instructions and its day-to-day operations are made understandable and fathomable to the consumer. The computer wears this friendly disguise securely, and the disguise has been sutured on, remaining in place until its warranty expires.

Yet the term used by manufacturers is not "easy to use." Instead, the product is "friendly." The promise, then, is not only that it is easy to use but also that the product itself is not hostile; rather, it is a suitable and amiable object of the home, one that has a personality. The object is thus essentially comforting and amicable, behaving in a manner akin to an intimate, a confidant, or a friend. However, the underlying assumption here is that technology also has the ability to be hostile, unruly, and unsuitable in the home. These products have been tamed and exorcised of their ability to be nasty.[5] For example, Microsoft's ad campaign for Windows 95 emphasized its warm, almost embraceable utility. Unfortunately, the product was released with many "hostile" bugs in it, and an affiliated industry emerged for software to correct, or make polite, the inherent unsociable aspects of the initial software. Thus, the friendliness of the product had been betrayed by "bugs" that the company failed to remove before product release. The proclamation of friendliness is hence also perhaps a suggestion that there is something less than congenial inherent in its operations.

The Uncanny and the Ghostly

In his essay "The 'Uncanny'" (1919), Freud devotes much space to unraveling the meanings of the German words *heimlich* and *unheimlich* (translated into English as "canny" and "uncanny"). The German words, unlike the English translations, convey the meaning of belonging to the home (or not belonging to the home). Freud also notes that the meanings of *heimlich* are various. One meaning is synonymous with what might be perceived as its antonym and hints at something secretive and potentially threatening. Freud quotes Schelling's nuance of *unheimlich:* "[It] is the name for everything that ought to have remained ... hidden and secret and has become visible" (129). Freud also quotes Grimm's dictionary entry on *heimlich:* "The notion of something hidden and dangerous ... is still further developed, so that 'heimlich' comes to have the meaning usually ascribed to 'unheimlich'" (131).

Freud realizes that there is a correlation, not an opposition, in the meanings of these two words. Their meanings bleed into each other. He writes: "Heimlich is a word the meaning of which develops towards an ambivalence, until it finally coincides with its opposite.... Unheimlich is in some way a sub-species of heimlich" (131). For Freud, the tale of *heimlich/unheimlich* is a story that begins with *heimlich.* He explains: "This uncanny is in reality nothing new or foreign, but something familiar and old–established in the mind that has been estranged only by the process of repression" (148).

The uncanny, then, is distinguished not only by its effect but also by a process whose result serves to conceal the canniness at the start of the process. In order to experience the uncanny, to experience it as unfamiliar, one has repressed a history. The canny is originary, but its familiarity (its friendliness or intimacy) is tinged with a potential hostility that will necessitate a repression. Freud suggests that the menace of the intimate object begins the process of estrangement. Uncanniness is always a return, and the prefix *un-* is the "[linguistic] token of repression" (153). In the Freudian relationship of *heimlich/unheimlich,* there is shrouding. The *heimlich,* in its most secretive element, wears a disguise. The *unheimlich* response also disguises, but in its outbreak, it provides clues to a history that involves the *heimlich* at its outset. These are the attributes of the uncanny that distinguish it from other forms of fear: a horror of the mask revealed as mere mask, but with the sense that there is another mask beneath.

For Freud, the uncanny also involves a substitutional logic. For example, severed heads, dismembered limbs, and so forth, are uncanny because they relate to "an association with the castration complex." The uncanny fear of being buried alive is not a fear of death per se, but the transformation of "another fantasy which had originally nothing terrifying about it at all, but was filled with a certain lustful pleasure–the fantasy ... of intra-uterine existence" (151).

One can transpose this substitutional logic to an event more contemporary and less overtly about castration anxiety. When a computer user is watching a document becoming scrambled by an unforeseen virus, an uncanny feeling may arise. But this would not be due to the horror of losing work. (Losing work is horrific, but it is not uncanny.) Rather the event's eeriness would be related to how this experience stands in and repeats another (repressed) fantasy or experience in the past. The computer user may connect this experience with a surmounted childish belief in spells and incantations and may feel that such a spell has been directed against him as a punishment. He may believe an encoded message from a dead friend or a vengeful ghost is in the machine.

For the listener who believes he hears a dead relative on the air, this is only uncanny if he also believes (as an adult who has consciously rid himself of primitive fear) that it is not possible for the dead to speak via an electric medium. It is uncanny if this occurrence reminds him of a fantasy of a voice that he once experienced as pleasurable. Indeed, it is uncanny if it reminds him of the sound of his own voice severed from his own body.

Although it may be impossible to do a history of the uncanny, it is clear that twentieth-century technologies of the home have served, not to eliminate the return of surmounted primitive beliefs or infantile neuroses, but rather to extend such beliefs into burgeoning regions, enabling new mani-festations and inviting a frenzy of diagnoses and patholo-gizing. The uncanny idea that objects (such as dolls or ven-triloquists' dummies) can come to life is invigorated by the notion of electric objects that speak and always seem to behave with mystery. Such objects seem to be able to tune into the vast enclaves of the dead with the ease of an Ouija board without even having the specific software program.

Derrida (1994) notes that even though Freud brings up haunting by the dead as penultimate examples of the uncanny, he refrains from a full discussion of the subject matter (173). Freud explains his own omission with two reasons: his "orig-inal emotional reaction to it" (ghosts bring up the terrible and fearful, which disrupts research), and "the insufficiency of our own scientific knowledge" (1958, 149). He acknowledges that biology has not discerned whether death is the ultimate fate of existence. As Freud is more concerned with fictional renderings of the uncanny, he does mark case studies of ghostly haunting as a topic he ignores. Yet he concurs that these hauntings are the penultimate setting of the uncanny.

Freud writes that the term *ein unheimlische Haus* is trans-lated into "a haunted house." Hauntings have a place, reside in a dwelling, and pronounce the return of a repressed act (for example, Hamlet's ghost in the house of Denmark). The ghost reverts to technology to make an appearance. And the ghost speaks of death, which for Freud (as Derrida notes) is not the province of the uncanny. Furthermore, Freud is sus-picious of the uncanniness of uncanny effects in fictive realms. He suggests that audiences treat specters as if they were just like other conjurings on the stage or in the text, even though Freud almost exclusively uses examples from literature to explicate his usage of the uncanny (see Derrida 1994:195–96, n. 38).

In *Strangers to Ourselves* (1991), Julia Kristeva questions Freud's distinction of the actual and the representational in the workings of the uncanny. Whereas she agrees that the uncanny involves the return of a familiar repressed, it also requires "just the same the impetus of a new encounter with an unexpected outside element." Furthermore, Kristeva writes, uncanniness "occurs when the boundaries between imagination and reality are erased" (188). Her emphases serve us well in applying the uncanny to 1930s radio. I am framing radio at this time as an almost new-encounter (an outside element within the *heimlich haus*) filled with voices of the dead that serve to provoke a return for the listener, where facts instigate fantasy. I am also asserting radio as a place where stories based on fact replace factuality itself.

Radio as Stranger than Human

The English words *canny* and *uncanny,* unlike their German equivalents, are not so expressly connected with the home. Yet one meaning of *canny* is "cozy" (conveying a "homeyness"); other meanings are "shrewd" and "gentle," suggesting an intelligence that is intimate. *Uncanny,* like the German *unheimlich,* is not the opposite of *canny.* It is more a subdivision of *canny*'s sense of knowledge. That is, *uncanny* does not mean unintelligent or wild; rather, it conveys a particular kind of horror that is also smart: eerie, mysterious, suggesting superhuman or supernatural powers.

The radio, particularly as a new object in many homes in the 1930s, is especially primed as uncanny: its powers surpass the human, transmitting and receiving voices far beyond the amplification of the human voice. Its canniness is found in its coziness, its placement in the home as a shrewd object. It is canny because the spectrum is well administered by a federal government complicit with corporate networks. Despite this order–and perhaps energized by the failure of this order–the radio retains these supernatural qualities.

In the 1930s, the supernatural became a popular theme of the (superhuman) radio dramas. Shows like *The Witches Tale, Suspense, Lights Out, Inner Sanctum, The Black Museum, Black Curtain,* and *The Shadow* all depict the inexplicable as part of their lure to listeners. *The Witches Tale,* which began airing in 1930, was one of the first horror shows. Each episode started with this introduction: "The fascination of the eerie–weird, blood-chilling tales told by old Nancy, the Witch of Salem, and Satan, her wise black cat." Old Nancy, 117 years old, serves as narrator, spinning yarns of disembodied spirits, ancient curses, and evil spells. The show uses heavy sound effects and a meowing cat as percussive backdrop. With her creaky voice, Nancy is an omniscient narrator, exploring terrain that science has not yet explained and new technology has served to refertilize. If these stories of sorcery, magic, and creeping hands seem quaint or overacted today, they seem so because they are taken out of context. To the listener of the 1930s, these stories were popular and spine-chilling encounters with the unnatural.

Shows like *The Witches Hour* reveal and make literal the uncanny, mediumistic aspects of the radio. Their depictions of the unfathomable (with clear resolutions) continually situate the return of the dead as retributive, as if they are able to speak via radio dramas. The programs place in a representational frame an aspect of the medium of the radio itself, for as Morales notes, the radio is a chatty graveyard where the dead appear as voices.

Lights Out, which began in 1934, was considered so scary that it came on the airwaves after midnight. It began with a commandment to the audience: "Lights out, everybody." Then a mechanical-sounding, slow, staccato voice uttered: "It is later than you think." Special sound effects included the very real-sounding ripping and burning and pulsating of flesh, urging audiences to imagine a disembodiment. Again, radio drama made literal what the radio itself as medium accomplishes phantasmagorically. As Whitehead suggests, radio severs bodies, ripping voice from body, returning it as strange, placing it in a realm where it interacts with other estranged voices. Voices are spliced onto other imagined bodies. Bodies are left speechless. In the darkness of *Lights Out,* the declaration that "it is later than you think" is also an admission. The disembodiment has already occurred. Not only the narrative but also the daily operations of the radio deprive the subject of voice.

The popular hero of *The Shadow* also participated in this "literalization" of the unseen properties of radio. Originally played by Orson Welles, The Shadow was able to transform himself supernaturally from Lamont Cranston (an embodied socialite) into a booming voice with no apparent body.[6] Through hypnosis he clouded the minds of his adversaries into being unable to see his physical frame. Instead, they heard his voice, which was put through a filter, so that when Welles switched to his Shadow persona, his voice sounded as if it were emanating from a telephone speaker—suggesting that he was at once both there and far away (Sterling 1978:122). This voice was able to observe and scare criminals with The Shadow's ability to be an absent presence, with laughter framing his enunciation of the famous line "The Shadow knows." Clad in the darkness of a shadow, he chilled wrongdoers with his capability to survey, to laugh omnisciently; he scared criminals into confession. Uncanny with a vocal disembodiment enlisted against evil, "a subject who knows," The Shadow and his adversary reenact the relationship between the radio and its listener. The listener never sees the speaker, and the radiovoice can be "harsh." The listener, in this sense, is listening to a shadow already, whenever the radio is on.

To his enemies, The Shadow appears only as a voice. This voice is threatening and powerful. It enters into bordered spaces easily. The Shadow's enemies become panicked trying to find the source of the voice within the darkness as their only form of resistance. The listener, like the outsmarted wrongdoer, cannot master distance like The Shadow, who is one step ahead. The Shadow is seemingly always en route to the scene of a crime and is able to send and receive messages telepathically as if he were a telephone as well as a radio. Moreover, he can enter into a mind filled with evil without turning evil. If The Shadows knows, he knows because he has mastered the medium and becomes a medium himself.

When his girlfriend Margo tunes her shortwave radio to The Shadow's frequency, he can transmit to her by only using his voice, circumventing great distances. The Shadow, as a voice that hears interiority, renders psychic borders porous. It lays bare the mastery and the eeriness of the disembodied voice. The show makes apparent the fantasy that broadcast radio can be two-way; it listens in while it is being heard. It is a "bug" in the home; when it speaks, it also listens to unspoken thoughts.

As noted above, one of the meanings of the word *canny* is "coziness." Radio design in the 1920s mimicked other objects in the home. This was done, I believe, to make the radio seem as familiar and appropriate in the home as a piece of furniture. Print advertising emphasized the "friendliness" of radio, and when a radio craze began in the early 1930s, the design of the radio became more "radio-like." Thus, the radio was presented as canny, shrewd, intelligent, and replete with smart human (mostly male) voices.

Broadcast radio, although seen as the latest in a series of technological advancements, was also structured to appear via an object that had its ready-made familiarity securely attached. Of course, this canniness was but a patina; other aspects of the object could reveal itself as disguised in uncanny experiences. (Specific examples are explored in Chapters 3 and 5.) These experiences suggest the shock implied all along in letting such a stranger into the home. In the 1930s, unexpected occurrences made the object seem as if it had, uncannily, come to life with secret "Shadowlike" powers.

The Friendly Voice and the Hostile Object

In *The Writing of the Disaster* (1995), Maurice Blanchot distinguishes between the relationship of the writing self to the other, and the imagined relationship of the other to the writer. In the former, the other is unfathomable, exceeding the grasp of the self, securely strange. However, in the imagined relationship of the other to the writer, "the distant becomes the close-by, this proximity becomes the obsession that afflicts me, that weighs down upon me, that separates me from myself ... dis-identifying me, abandoning me to passivity, leaving me without any initiative and bereft of present. And then the other becomes rather the Overlord" (19).

In my discussions of radio in the 1930s, I am at once describing the radio as an (animated) object and as a (stationary) actor in the home. As a domestic object with a certain amount of autonomy in its relationship to the listener, as in Blanchot's depiction, it brings the far-away to the intimate sphere of the ear. The radio–as exemplified in the reporting of the *Hindenburg* disaster and the simulated invasion in the "War of the Worlds" broadcast–appears to cancel out geographic distance, rendering the witnessing of disaster into the experience of panic, blurring borders between transportation and communications media. Disaster moves ever nearer; it gains velocity via the media. Disaster announces the possibility of inexplicable death due to the chance of location, of being too near almost anywhere at that unpredictable moment.

The perceived control of the other, here the other that is given voice through technology, was an obsession of the 1930s. Reproduced, recorded, or transmitted voices were heard and depicted as controlling agents. They were able to define and patrol the borders of nation-states, invoking the forgetfulness of passivity. These disembodied voices rendered the human machine-like in its obedience and its attention to detail.

In his discussions of sound and cinema, Michel Chion uses the terms *acousmatic* and *acousmêtre* (1993; 1994). Radio is an acousmatic medium: the listener hears sound without seeing its originating source. (Telephones as well as record albums, compact discs, and cassette tapes are also acousmatic.) In film, a sound that is heard but not linked to an object on-screen is also acousmatic. For example, the sound of a gun going off in a room that is without a gun indicates that in a neighboring room a murder is occurring. Such sounds are called "off-screen" even when it is not the sound that is "off." The sound is indeed "on" (audible); it is the object producing the sound that evades the visible frame.

Acousmêtre is a compound word, combining *acousmatic* with the French verb *être,* meaning "to be." As suggested by these roots, *acousmêtre* is "a kind of voice-character specific to cinema that in most instances . . . derives mysterious powers from being heard and not seen" (1994:221). Chion explains that this being, who "speaks over the image but is also forever on the verge of appearing in it" (129), has three powers: seeing all, knowing all, and having all power to act upon the visual.

Using Chion's terminology, we can see that when Lamont Cranston becomes The Shadow, he also becomes an *acousmêtre.* The Shadow sees all, he is omniscient, and he can enlist this omniscience in action (solving the crime). As a show broadcast on radio, *The Shadow* is from the outset operating in an acousmatic medium. Yet the character of The Shadow becomes an *acousmêtre* when his voice is responded to by all characters with a panic derived from their inability to see the source of the voice but their knowing that it is near, that it has impact. The Shadow wears a sonic mask that grants him secret power—one that is only effective if the correlation between The Shadow and Lamont Cranston remains a secret.

As Chion notes, the *acousmêtre* can be "de-acousmatized" by revealing "the face that is the source of the voice"

(1994:130). For Chion, this de-acousmatization (also an embodiment) always occurs as the camera shoots the speaking face. This embodiment as the talking head is a testament to the proper placement of voice to character to body, thus humanizing the character (and stripping it of the supernaturalness or omniscience). For The Shadow, this de-acousmatization (occurring only when the face of Lamont Cranston becomes visible to his antagonist in the darkness) could only happen if it were narrated by another character as an event of de-masking and the witnessing of embodiment.

In Fritz Lang's 1933 exploration of the *acousmêtre, The Testament of Dr. Mabuse,* the mad, criminally genius doctor appears in a variety of sonic masks. This film depicts the allure that a voice can attain in the 1930s when severed from a physical body. Dr. Mabuse exists beyond his death, on phonograph and loudspeaker. He also exists in the textual testament he has left behind that has detailed instructions for industrial sabotage. When the Inspector, hot on the trail of the mad doctor, views the dead body of Dr. Mabuse and questions if this is, in fact, the real corpse of the doctor, the audience knows that the dormancy of the doctor's body is a ruse. Death does not deter the spirit from his plan. In fact, this dormancy will enable the doctor's expansive mind to continue controlling his gang of criminals via technology that he can master.

The ex-convict Paul, who is part of Dr. Mabuse's gang, gets recorded instructions from an unseen source. When he is captured by Mabuse's gang for not being loyal to the mission, he and his girlfriend are thrown into a room with theatrical curtains along one wall. They hear a voice that emanates from behind the curtain announcing to them that there is no escape. Paul shoots at what he perceives to be the source of the voice behind the curtain. They race behind the curtain only to realize that the source of the voice is a loud-speaker and not the body of Dr. Mabuse, who is always else-where. This transmitted voice was staged. It is not connected to a body when the curtain goes up. A ghost has spoken—again, through the technology of the theatrical scenario, through a staged use of technology that casts objects as actors.

Similarly, when Paul and Inspector Lohmann knock on the office door of Dr. Baum (who is believed to be the dead Mabuse's living proxy), they hear a voice saying, "I am not to be disturbed." At each knock, the voice repeats this patri-cian command. Paul and the Inspector charge through the door, only to find an office with no body. Instead, they find a gramophone record set up to play when anyone knocks. They also find the papers of the testament of the mad dead doctor atop the desk of Dr. Baum. Dr. Mabuse exists absently, but omnisciently, away from his pursuers.

Dr. Baum is possessed by the evil doctor through trans-missions of the text from Mabuse's testament. When Dr. Baum reads the testament, the specter of the dead doctor appears to him. On screen, Mabuse is ghostly, faint, with huge pupilless eyes set in an impossibly white face. The specter moves to Dr. Baum, and his outline merges into the frame of Dr. Baum. The spectral image of the dead and the living image of the body become united, conveying that Dr. Baum is no longer just himself. He has no will and is con-trolled by another. This is a secret that the audience knows. It is up to the Inspector and Paul to unravel the mystery of the bodily source of this *acousmêtre*.

Dr. Mabuse rules through rendering his body invisible and projecting and extending the purview of his voice through recordings and speakers. His hypnotism occurs via the rep-etition of his voice. Through technology his voice reaches into other spheres—and particularly into the criminal mind eager for plots. His listeners lose autonomy. They receive instructions from a possessed and animated machine.

An American example of the *acousmêtre* in sound film is *The Wizard of Oz* (1939). The Wizard is a feared vocal entity in the city of Oz, tyrannical in his kingdom, but without a body. Of course, his body is eventually revealed to be that of a diminutive, anxious guy who rules via the microphone that amplifies and transports his voice into all rooms of his kingdom. The Wizard's normally meek voice rules acousmatically, even as his body seems unfit for the job. The voice instructs and surveys, encouraging listeners to imagine a matching body.[7]

Fleming's *The Wizard of Oz* is barely mentioned as a paradigm or as a warning against authoritarian rule (although the film is laden with the treacherous and the threat of the uncanny). Yet Lang's *acousmêtre* Dr. Mabuse is viewed (in hindsight) as a parable about the rise of fascism and the method that authoritarian figures came to rely on increasingly—the amplified and transmitted voice. This emphasis is indeed important, yet it is key to approach the role played by the body of machines and the disembodiment of the human voice. There are crucial similarities in the machines of Mabuse and the influencing machine described by the schizophrenic patients of Victor Tausk as well as in the memoirs of the "paranoid" Schreber and the writings about him described in the next section. Technology is implicated in these scenarios because it is at times seen as consisting of controlling and persecutory speaking objects. Technology is also implicated because patients often feel that they are becoming mechanical and losing their humanity, being transformed into machines.

Influencing Machines

In Blanchot's description of the relationship of the other to the self (1995), he foregrounds the menace of the other so that the other comes to deprive the self of "initiative" and of the "present." In the frame of the disaster, the other takes over and is authoritarian, not through its actual operation, but in its imagined ability. In Victor Tausk's article "On the Origin of the 'Influencing Machine' in Schizophrenia" (1948 [1919]), he discusses the importance and recurrence of machines in the descriptions of schizophrenics in the early part of the last century. These patients (both male and female) felt persecuted by a machine operated by enemies (who were all male). Tausk relays their various descriptions of the machine into a conglomerate: Patients are able to give only vague hints of its construction:

> It consists of boxes, cranks, levels, wheels, buttons, wire, batteries, and the like. Patients endeavor to discover the construction of the apparatus by means of their technical knowledge, and it appears that with the progressive popularization of the sciences, all the forces known to technology are utilized to explain the functioning of the apparatus. All the discoveries of mankind, however, are regarded as inadequate to explain the marvelous powers of this machine. (33)

The patients, while able to describe its workings and sketch its unseen but imagined visual form, are unable to explain how and why the machine works—despite all attempts at gaining technological knowledge. Tausk explains that the "influencing machine" has five main effects on the patient:

1. "It makes the patients see pictures" (33). These pictures are one-dimensional, cinematic, projected onto a flat surface.

2. "It produces, as well as removes, thought and feelings by means of waves or rays or mysterious forces" (33). The machine transmits or removes thoughts and feelings perceived as originating outside the patient.

3. "It produces motor phenomena in the body, erections and seminal emission, that are intended to deprive the patient of his male potency and weaken him" (33).[8] These phenomena are done either by psychic suggestion or the use of air-currents, electricity, magnetism, or x-rays.

4. It causes inexplicable body sensations that are deemed as "electrical, magnetic, or due to air currents" (34).

5. The influencing machine is also "responsible for other occurrences in the patient's body" (abscesses, skin eruptions, "and other pathological processes" [34]).

Tausk notes that the machines are usually operated by physicians who have worked on the patient. Even though patients are unclear about how the machine operates, they are sure of its existence. In some instances, invisible wires connect the machine to the patient's bed, rendering the patient virtually passive to the workings of the machine.

My purpose in discussing the influencing machine is not to suggest that the public's response to technology is akin to that of the schizophrenic. Rather, I am demonstrating that the hostile other in such case studies is a *technological* other. Or at least the antagonist in these narratives has mastery over technology that the patient (or the public) lacks. Technology becomes a puppet that accomplishes the antagonist's cruel task.

Tausk's influencing machine is a historical object. Its description is related to the new forms of technology that render the supernatural into mass-produced objects. The influencing machine drains the patient of will and autonomy. In Blanchot's terms, it deprives him of initiative and of the present. Moreover, although Tausk wrote just before the popularization of radio, the machines he describes are undeniably radio-like. The influencing machine transmits, works via "unseen wires," and consists of boxes, batteries, and buttons.[9]

For Tausk's schizophrenic, the other is granted power due to his proximity and usage of the technical as an accomplished puppeteer. Its hostility is enacted almost magically, through its virtuosic navigation over unseen machine-terrains that the patient can not exactly discern. In the fantasies of the schizophrenic in the teens of the last century, the other has become machine-like, treacherous, deathly, technocratic. The other rearranges the organs of the body. Man's double takes on a technological whirr–a static. This double plots sabotage.

Tausk notes that although the influencing machine is operated by a hostile foreign power, it is also constructed "with some or all of the pathologically altered organs [of the patient] projected outward" (59). The machine is made from the body of the schizophrenic, enlisted against him. Tausk posits that "among these organs the genitals take precedence in the projection" (59). The patient's body–especially the sexual organs–is involved in a conspiracy against him.

Deleuze and Guattari (1983), however, disagree with Tausk's reading. They argue that projection "enters the picture only secondarily" (as a form of counter-investment against the repressive mechanism and that the machine is "an avatar of the desiring-machines" (9).[10] The influencing machine is a representation of harsh sociality and as such is purely a box at first. The schizophrenic's projection of his own features onto it could be seen as a defensive tactic of self-preservation.

Tausk's patient Natalija, for example, imagines an influencing machine that is akin to a doll or a puppet. It seems to represent herself, constructed with her body parts projected outward. Like the imagined properties of the relationship between a voodoo doll and the victim of its curse, "all effects and changes undergone by the apparatus take place simultaneously in the patient's body, and vice versa" (42). As a result, the machine, which can suggest a human form, loses its genitalia "following the patient's loss of her genital sensations" (42, 43). In Tausk's retelling of the progression of Natalija's machine, the apparatus loses its three-dimensionality gradually. Limbs are replaced by drawings of legs and arms atop the lid of the machine. The genitals disappear altogether without representation. The machine becomes less like what Tausk views is its origin, appearing more like a machine, taking on a substitutional logic. For example, the apparatus's "batteries" stand in for intestines. For Deleuze and Guattari, the box becomes a visual literalization of a desiring-machine.

Importantly, the machine is not perceived as an organism or as a living thing, even as it may be constructed from projections from the organs of the patient's body. Whereas Tausk's universal emphasis on the role of genitalia in the influencing machine may ill serve Natalija's particularity (due to the schizophrenic's renunciation of the genitals, the machine represents the genitalia), his interpretations may suggest other readings of her machine. For Tausk, the machine's body represents an intrauterine fantasy, and the batteries within are the fetus (previously described as intestines). Yet, Natalija does not describe the machine then as becoming-human, but instead herself as within the apparatus, as becoming-machine, as batteries. In her symbolic identification with her feared schizophrenic production, she has allied herself, to some degree, with the batteries of the machine. This does not convey utter powerlessness, even as it implicates her as fueling the production. Rather, it implies an ability to perform magical transformations. As battery, she is the form of energy within the radio box that transmits to her.

Interestingly, Tausk notes that the conspiracy involved in schizophrenia is different than that of paranoia. With his patients there is a conspiracy among the persecuted, not a conspiracy involving the persecutors organized against the paranoiac. For the schizophrenic, there is a "passive conspiracy": love objects—mothers, close friends, ex-physicians—are "compelled to share his fate in being subjected to the influencing machine" (60). Whereas Tausk explains this via identification with narcissistic object choices that are nearby and well-known, it is clear that these individuals are "compelled" to become passive to the control of the influencing machine as a way to identify with the patient. The patient perceives that those who love him are involved in the conspiracy, subjecting themselves to the torment that he experiences without choice in order, simply, because of love, to know.

Blanchot also remarks on this conspiracy of passivity: "In the patience of passivity, I am he whom anyone at all can replace, the nonindispensable by definition, but one for whom nonetheless there is no dispensation: he must answer to and for what he is not. His is a borrowed, happenstance singularity—that, in fact, of the hostage" (1995:18).

Compelled to join this conspiracy, the loved objects around the schizophrenic are held hostage by the schizophrenic's machine. Such a machine is made perhaps by the doubling of his body organs and controls him due to the skillful operation of the faraway hostile other. The schizophrenic's body receives

messages via an automated medium, and his enforced passivity is contagious, compelling. Also, since the machine is
made of the body of the schizophrenic, he has gained a kind
of power over the loved one in this conspiracy of the persecuted; they join together, passively, to be the subject to this
machine. Whereas the machine may not be owned and operated by the schizophrenic, it is produced, in part, by him.

The schizophrenic's influencing machine exercises power
not only against the patient but also against his family. The
schizophrenic is an exploited worker of the economy of the
psyche. He makes or visualizes a box that works efficiently
but also against him, even as the box is made from his labor-
ing and yet passive body. The influencing machine, like
Mabuse's recorded incantations, is introjected as well as
becoming a screen onto which fantasies are projected. I
argue that the popular response to radio in America bears a
resemblance to this process: it reworks this crisis–the drama
of inside and out, of control and autonomy, of action within
passivity.

Canetti asserts that "paranoia is an illness of power"
(1963). Schizophrenia in Tausk's exploration is, however, in
broad terms, related to power and sociality: the ruled are
implicated in securing the place of the ruler. The ruler gains
access to the interiority of the ruled, enabled by a conspiracy of the persecuted. This conspiracy involves the mechanics of the *acousmêtre*. It involves a machine that reproduces
and projects voices.

Hearing Other Voices

Freud's work on Daniel Paul Schreber is based on his reading of Schreber's text, *Memoirs of My Nervous Illness* (1988

[1901]).[11] Schreber was a textual analysand; he has become perhaps the most discussed figure in the history of psychoanalysis. He came from a long line of accomplished, prominent German men. His father was a renowned orthopedist and promoter of mental and physical fitness whose writings are still referred to today in contemporary Germany. His son rose to become a judge, but after losing an election to the Reichstag, he was committed for six months to the Psychiatric Clinic at the University of Leipzig. In 1885 he resumed his career as a judge. Shortly thereafter, however, his anxiety and insomnia returned, and he was placed under the care of Dr. Fleichsig once more; this time for eight years. While institutionalized, he developed an elaborate, exacting cosmology, which centered on his own body as the focus and object of divine forces.

"Schreber Studies" has had many factions, and the iconography of Schreber has suited many agendas. For example, Elias Canetti in *Crowds and Power* (1966) used Schreber's writings as a paradigm for the inner workings of the ruler and as a precursor and foreshadowing of fascist ideology. More recently, Eric Santner (1996) has argued that Schreber's memoirs consist of resistant strategies and in-depth critiques of emerging German political and psychic actualities. My own engagement with the Schreber material is intended to be akin to that identified in the collection *Psychosis and Sexual Identity: Toward a Post-Analytic View of the Schreber Case* (Allison et al. 1988). The editors write that after Lacan's work on psychosis in 1955–56 (see Lacan 1993), there is "[a] marked use of the Schreber case and, especially, the *Memoirs,* as a means by which to explore a variety of issues in the arts, sciences and humanities" (7). Schreber's descriptions of his mechanized body is, in this setting, "a means by which" to discuss the relationship between the medium and the human frame, particularly at modernity's onset. Schreber's writings are, after all, contemporaneous with the advances of Marconi and Edison, and his body is receptive and resistant to the new uses of the ether, the airwave, and the wire.

Schreber appeared to be able to discern radio waves traveling and arriving inside him. His body becomes like a radio receiver with access to enunciations that other bodies do not have. He writes of another language that he can discern:

> Apart from normal human language there is also a kind of nerve-language of which, as a rule, the healthy human being is not aware.... The words are repeated silently ... that is to say a human being causes his nerves to vibrate in the way which corresponds to the use of the words concerned, but the real organs of speech ... are not set in motion at all or only coincidentally.... My nerves have been set in motion from without incessantly and without any respite. (1988 [1901]:69)

Schreber vibrates and hums with divine messages from God, repeating the words without involving his mouth or tongue—the words are transmitted privately inside him. His body is privileged to hear the secret "radio" messages.

Mark Roberts, in his essay "Wired: Schreber as Machine, Technophobe, and Virtualist" (1996), writes:

> "Plugged into" madness, rendered into a machine, strapped into restraint, probed by devices, subjected to the psycho- and electromechanical theories of the time, Schreber was naturally intensely aware of the fact that he had become a machine and horrified that he was one. His profound awareness is evident in the many colorful passages in the *Memoirs* that refer to his mechanization, his feeling—or as some would argue, his delusion—that he had become machinelike and was being "run" by someone or something. (37)

Following Niederland's (1974) insight into how Schreber's fantasies reflected his actual experiences with his father, Roberts argues that Schreber lived in a profoundly mechanistic environment. In his childhood home, Schreber lived with devices used and developed by his medical-scientist father; then later, in the confines of the asylum and under the treatment of Dr. Fleichsig, Schreber lived under the pressure of mechanistic ordering. His doctor was influenced by pychomechanics and believed the brain was akin to a machine (Roberts 1996:33; Lothane 1992:211). For Roberts, Schreber's "delusions" are not madness–instead, they are expressive resistances to a regime with an agenda. Furthermore, Roberts argues that Schreber's cosmology prefigures virtual reality.[12] For my purposes here, Schreber's delusions, in extraordinary fashion, serve to reveal much about the more ordinary responses to sweeping technological change and its impact on all sorts of listening bodies, not only on those of the patients.

Later in the *Memoirs,* Schreber's ray communication takes on the ability of "picturing." As his "inner nervous system is illuminated by rays, ... pictures can be voluntarily reproduced" (180). Thus, his interior structure is set up to project images, a kind of interiorized cinema.[13] These images are willful and either remain inside his head or are projected onto a surface outside, where they can be seen by his own nerves and "by the rays" (181). Schreber produces pictures that he wants the rays to view. For example, in bed he sends out the image to the godlike rays that he has female breasts and sexual organs. Schreber is involved then in a reciprocal (but not equal) relationship with the "rays"; each provides images for the other, and Schreber projects a female body image for this viewer.

Freud's discussion of Schreber, limited in scope and criticized by many Schreber scholars (e.g., Lothane 1992), is more compelling in his framing of the psychotic narrative itself. Freud writes in "Psychoanalytic Notes Upon an Autobiographical Account of a Case of Paranoia":

> Since paranoiacs cannot be compelled to overcome their internal resistances, and since in any case they say only what they choose to say, it follows that this is precisely a disorder in which a written report or a printed case history can take the place of personal acquaintance with the patient. (1963:84)

Schreber's memoir is a genre of discursive will that does not surrender to interrogation or lead the reader to distinguish fantasy from reality. What neurotics "keep hidden as secret" (Freud 1963:83), the paranoiac does not need to reveal. The paranoiac places events and their interpretations into an epistemology–and even if he may distort occurrences, he does not evade or repress. Schreber's philosophical text, then, not only reveals a response or a malady related to the Father per se (as Freud maintains) but also is a testimony of a body in (inner and outer) transformation. Schreber's text is a testimony of a body becoming machine becoming woman, a declaration against the confines of the human frame as dictated by turn-of-the-century bourgeoisie (see Guattari 1980). A pained document, it is the narrative of a transgendered body trying to reinvent itself in its "unmanning," both enlisting and struggling against a series of machines in its transformation.

The radiophonic imagination exists in the space created by these divinely transmitted voices. It occurs in Schreber's projections that sever and splice voice and image, redesigning the organs and the outward appearance of the body vis-à-vis a relationship with God.[14] Schreber visualizes a radio wave: "The threads which are pulled into my head—they are also the carriers of the voices—perform a circular movement in it, best compared to my head being hollowed out from inside with a drill" (227). In order to drown out this "radio" he can't turn off, Schreber takes to bellowing himself. Schreber, as a radio receiver, is very attuned and can hear the distress calls from the rays of an anxious "upper God." It is as if Schreber compares his listening to being on the telephone or at a switchboard—hooked up, tuned in, or online. He is part of the medium as he is used and using the medium itself, merging and individuating. Roberts adds: "The voices, Schreber insists, issue from several sources or media, but one of the main sources is the 'talking birds.' The birds are remnants (single nerves) of souls of human beings, which carry with them a particular 'tone message' associated with their respective human souls" (1996:38). Through tones, Schreber learns to discern various "stations" that are being transmitted to his electromagnetized frame.

Schreber's text is also radiophonic in its travels around the world that collect information and report back to its listening audience (himself). With a superhuman ability to transmit and receive, Schreber's text craves a moving home to encase a multitude of living and dead entities. Indeed, he elaborates a haunting of his own corporeality that is transformed into a film projector or a radio receiver, sending out images and registering sounds. Schreber is a reporter, transmitting testimonials about his travels via media.

The Frequency of Disaster

In her essay "Notes on Some Schizoid Mechanisms" (1986 [1945]), Melanie Klein picks up on Freud's reading of

Schreber's perception of the end of the world. For Freud, this sense of the end was the projection of Schreber's inner catastrophe. Although Freud related this inner catastrophe to disturbances of the libido, he also says that "disturbance[s] of the libidinal processes may result from abnormal changes in the ego," according to Klein (1986:199). Klein relates Freud's later theories of life and death instincts, where "disturbances in the distribution of the libido presuppose a delusion between the destructive impulse and the libido" (199). Schreber's catastrophic fantasy thus "implies a preponderance of the destructive impulse over the libido" related to "one part of the ego annihilating other parts" (199).

In Klein's rereading of Freud's Schreber, she de-emphasizes the split of the inner and outer world. This is related to her focus on early childhood. She writes: "If the ego and the internalized objects are felt to be in bits, an internal catastrophe is experienced by the infant which both extends to the external world and is projected onto it" (1986: 200). Since objects are introjected when they are disturbed, it causes a corresponding ruckus in the outer world of objects. As the border between inner and outer is made porous by the introjection of what is also outside, when an interior event creates a disturbance, this disturbance can be seen as an event or an image occurring in the world. When the person is sad, he will see only unhappy images or events or people.

Klein's insight has relevance to radio listening. This listening is an activity that involves an intimate object–the radio–that projects inside like Schreber's rays. The radio becomes both an external and an internal object that corresponds to already-existing mediumistic, uncanny experiences of hearing voices, visitations, and so forth. There is a trepidation in this relationship. When the radio erupts into the narration of actual and dramatized disaster, its words resound with familiarity, and the boundary between the inner and outer, already porous, dissipates completely.

I am suggesting that the radio is also always an internal operation, an introjected transmission. This transmission is clearly enunciated in the confessions of paranoiacs and schizophrenics. Yet this dynamic is always in some way tuned in, or part of the background static for other auditors. As listeners and speakers, we know that the potential for the collapse of inner and outer is there. As Schreber suggests, radio, in its throwing of the voice, was already a function of the psyche years before Marconi met Sarnoff.

3

The Recital of the *Hindenburg* Disaster

THE REPORTING of the explosion of the *Hindenburg* was the first example of a "live" eyewitness broadcast of a major disaster. What was intended to be a triumphant landing in Lakehurst, New Jersey, on 6 May 1937 at 7:25 P.M. reported by Herb Morrison of NBC station WLS in Chicago instead became a horrific affair reported live by a panicked eyewitness and a key moment in radio broadcasting. The immediate irony of the media affair is that this "live" broadcast was in fact a recording played by NBC the day after the actual event. Listeners heard reporter Morrison at 4:30 P.M. on 7 May as if his report were live, but in fact, it was taped. Local stations began breaking news of the explosion eight minutes after the event, but none of the reports had the impact of the real "you are there" testimony of reporter Morrison.

NBC radio was at this time showing off its new ability to transmit reporting from the field to the listening audience through the use of the telephone and shortwave radio. This capability was expanding network radio's ability to be there as the event unfolds instead of reading a report about the event. The *Hindenburg* explosion suggests how the reporting of a disaster contributes to the construction of a national identity fraught with the possibility of real and imagined explosion and invasion, indeed the presence of sabotage and conspiracy.[1]

The flight of the *Hindenburg* was an international one, originating from a militarizing Germany, connecting a so-called isolationist America to a Europe of increasing conflict. Moreover, the promise of a new technology, which in 1937 was used to provide a new, quicker form of seemingly weightless trans-Atlantic travel, was broken, revealing the presence of disaster within the promise of technology. I suggest that the *Hindenburg* disaster is an extraordinary example of a more everyday occurrence.

Distance and Stationary Mobility

Maurice Blanchot suggests that when disaster occurs, it transforms geography: "The distant becomes the close-by, this proximity becomes the obsession that afflicts me" (1995:19). The disaster, like radio, brings the far-away near; it is space travel, a conquering of distance.[2] In her discussion of amateur operators during radio's pre-broadcasting days, Susan Douglas (1987) shows that the urge to close up the space in between propelled radio activities before World War I. These young male hobbyists were not so keen on talking with enthusiasts around the corner. Rather, they searched for connections with voices from distant cities and states.

Both Douglas (1987) and Smulyan (1995) suggest that there is machismo at work in this radiophonic endeavor: "Long-distance reception proved both your radio skills and the strength and quality of your equipment" (Smulyan 1995:14). Along with comradery, there was also competition amongst radio users. The focus of this subculture–in addition to technical mastery and male bonding through the voice (without resorting to the already corporate-controlled telephone lines)–was on stationary movement. They used radio waves to move the voice (a production of the body) beyond the confines of the immediate physical space and, finally, to be heard by another.

Radio use involves at once both travel and staying still. Beginning in the late 1920s, broadcast radio became not only the domain of "escapist" entertainment but also a vehicle for that which is deemed newsworthy by networks, by news wire services, by governments. Indeed, agreements reached by broadcast networks and newspaper chains in 1933 that limited the placement and duration of news were abandoned by 1935. Networks and independent stations began to assemble their own news staffs, whereas previously they had relied on wire services owned by newspaper companies. NBC and CBS opened up news offices in London, Paris, and Berlin. At the start of the decade, radio was relatively news-free; less than 6 percent of airtime was devoted to news. By the decade's end, however, news took up 13 percent of programming, with hourly updates and frequent interruption of broadcasts by live reports from Europe (Sterling 1978:178).

Radio could break news of national import far faster than the print media and began to center on having reporters on the scene transmitting by shortwave or phone to stations. In 1936, CBS was transmitting live from the Spanish Civil War and covering the abdication of the throne by King Edward. Commentator Gabriel Heatter of the Mutual Broadcast System became famous for his reporting from the Lindbergh kidnapping trial, breaking news of the guilty verdict first. Reports of disaster and intrigue increasingly began to move into the home via the radio. Corporate expansion in the radio industry resulted in nationwide audiences that allowed listeners access to events around the world. For the broadcast listener, news of the world traveled to the radio receiver, connecting him to the network but not giving him a chance to respond or to interact with other listeners via the medium.

In *Television* (1992), Raymond Williams argues that by the 1920s technology for the home was establishing "an at once mobile and home-centered way of living: a form of mobile privatization. Broadcasting in its applied form was a social product of this distinct tendency" (26). Radio brought people home. However, it brought them home to a domicile redecorated with a new piece of talking furniture. This piece of furniture provided a sense of mobility as well as privacy.

The rise of broadcasting was accompanied by the rise of audience research.[3] Listeners could feel catered to and provided for; they enjoyed shows that were seemingly created with their tastes in mind. Yet breaking news interrupted the so-called escapist fare that took listeners to places far from economic depression and political crisis. Indeed, by the close of the decade, unscheduled reports from Europe were commonplace. Also speeches by FDR and his allies and enemies, particularly Huey Long and Father Coughlin, became features of the medium, alerting listeners not only to national debates but also to domestic crises.

The ability to redirect two-way shortwave and telephone conversations into radio broadcasts heightened a sense of "being there" via the eyewitness and deepened the reporting of deaths during the "live" broadcast. The studio was no longer necessarily the origin of the transmitted voice, allowing the reporter to send messages directly to the listener via the wattage of the station. Or it allowed the listener to "eavesdrop" on a conversation between a studio and the reporter in the field.

For example, a year before the broadcast of the *Hindenburg* explosion, NBC listeners were treated to shortwave interchanges between a radio announcer and Dr. Max Jordan. The doctor was aboard the *Hindenburg* on a promotional trip from Friedrichschafen, Germany, to Lakehurst, New Jersey. He transmitted using a naval station that the German firm Deutsche Zeppelin-Reederei had received permission to use.

NBC's broadcast begins as the zeppelin is reaching the North American coast. Dr. Jordan is ebullient in this show called "The *Hindenburg* en Route to USA" (1936). He declares that he is aboard the ship the *Hindenburg* on its maiden cross-Atlantic voyage. Sounding drunk with the ecstasy of feather-like travel, he adds enthusiastically: "It is a grand evening at home aboard the *Hindenburg*." His upper-class voice speaks of the night aboard the ship as if he is at an elegant party; his choice of words suggests that home is now a form of air transport and no longer a stationary edifice. Indeed, he is traveling as he speaks to the American public. This thrill is similar to mobile phone users chatting away on the highway (a pleasure much greater than grumbling into a phone at a red light) or to carrying a transistor or portable stereo.[4]

This *Hindenburg* flight was a very heavily touted media affair. The radio event had a corporate sponsor, American Airlines, who advertised its services during breaks from the live broadcast. Atmospheric conditions, at times, often interfered with the clarity of the transmission, but at one point the shortwave transmitter picked up a conversation with the renowned German pianist Van Weigen, who was aboard the ship. As ebullient as Dr. Jordan, he is asked by the NBC announcer to play a song (as part of a preplanned publicity stunt, there is a piano on board). He complies and plays a Schubert melody, which sounds remarkably lucid, clear, and nearby. As these sounds prefigure the next year's explosion at Lakehurst, the lush piano sounds eerie to a contemporary ear. At the time of broadcasting, however, this is a triumphant moment: Dr. Jordan has been given access to the interior of the ship even as it is in transit. He provides his audience with the sounds of a virtuoso. He asks Van Weigen to "play another number later," and Van Weigen eagerly assents. The ability to perform classical music in mid-flight via the airwaves provides a display of the majesty of the linking of broadcast and travel networks. It literalizes the notion that radio conquers space, and it renders the unruliness of distance obedient, gaining entry into realms otherwise impenetrable.

New forms of transport, particularly those that take to the air—the aeroplane and the zeppelin—were readjusting notions of distance and duration, allowing more immediate arrivals between points, travel times that were previously unfathomable. In these endeavors, the radio was there. It was there in mandatory ship-to-shore transmission by an on-board radio officer to a radio station on land. It was also there in its broadcasting form, announcing these events to the potentially mobile public. Such events were news but also served as promotion for the travel industry and showed the listener the increased capacity of the medium.

The Story of the *Hindenburg*

The *Hindenburg* inaugurated its new transatlantic service in 1936. In that first year its service was flawless, avoiding storms and even skirting an approaching hurricane in New

England. The trip was estimated to take two to three days, two days shorter than an ocean liner voyage–and there was no seasickness involved (this was before transatlantic aeroplane flights). As Commander Ernst Lehmann exclaims about an October 1936 flight in his zeppelin-related memoirs: "Not a spoonful of soup was spilled during this flight. Everyone was able to enjoy the beauty of the sea without being obliged to submit to the sea's humours" (1937:343).

An undesignated socialite landing at Lakehurst is quoted in John Toland's book on dirigibles (1957), reinforcing the Commander's pronouncement on the *Hindenburg:* "Traveling this way is a wonderful beauty asset. It is so absolutely calm and effortless. There is no nervous strain. Now any woman knows what that does for your appearance" (11).

The *Hindenburg* was twice the size of the *Graf Zeppelin*–which traveled from Germany to Brazil and had succeeded in making a trip around the world[5]–making it 803 feet, or more than three city blocks long (Brooks 1992:184). Its maximum speed was 83.88 mph. Built for a crew of forty, the ship could transport seventy-two passengers while carrying up to 26,000 pounds of freight. The ship was inflated by hydrogen, seen by many experts in retrospect as causing the fire and explosion. The use of helium could have averted disaster–but the U.S. government, which controlled the distribution of helium gas, did not allow Germany to use any.

Hindenburg flights seemed sure to prove profitable (though the *Graf Zeppelin* had been losing money). Even if the German company charged only $400 to seventy passengers, it would make money (Toland 1957:10). Cargo in the ship's two-year career included antelopes, gorillas, horses, automobiles, and small airplanes; an Indian Maharajah once requested that the *Hindenburg* transport an elephant to the

King of England (Lehmann 1937:336). This request was denied; the elephant was too heavy.

Like the *Titanic*, the *Hindenburg* was opulent and was advertised as such. There were seventy private cabinets, a spacious dining room, a lounge with a grand piano, and two observation lounges. Meals were sumptuous–fresh lobster, newly killed turkeys, French pastry, expensive vegetables, American whiskey, and German beer. On the so-called "Millionaires Flight" of October 1936, meals were served to Nelson Rockefeller, Winthrop Aldrich, and other lesser-known industrialists and aviationists.

The *Hindenburg* flight was poised to be a great success. It could prove that zeppelin travel was safe, cost-efficient, and elegant. It was also, however, a decidedly German affair, and there were four large swastikas drawn on either side of the top and bottom rudders of the ship. Photos of the *Hindenburg* suspended over the Manhattan skyline seem today like a record of a German invasion. Yet they document an accord between the U.S. military and corporations, and a German commercial endeavor that was endorsed by the Führer.[6] Although the *Graf Zeppelin* and the *Hindenburg* were not built as warships (and as a result were highly praised by the non-German press), it is quite clear that they were often viewed as symbols of German technological prowess.

In his memoirs, Captain Lehmann gushes over the (radio) messages sent to him from the Führer. The *Hindenburg*'s maiden voyage over Germany on 26–29 March 1936 was staged as a propaganda event for the new Germany. Political speeches were broadcast on board, and crowds in the city below cheered the *Hindenburg* flight. It was also prearranged that the passengers and crew would be allowed to vote in the national election. The *Hindenburg* was a voting district–

"District LZ 129, *Hindenburg*"–and the 104 Germans aboard who were eligible to vote did so in a voting booth. All voted for Hitler (Lehmann 1937:331).

On the "Millionaires' Flight," Captain Lehmann recounts that as the ship set course, passengers "spontaneously sang the German national anthem" (343). The early triumphs of the ship became tied to German nationalism; the company's newfound success in navigating the air is also the nation's triumph in attaining mastery at crossing borders. Indeed, not only is the German national radio on board transmitting, but so are reporters from the American network NBC. The captain exclaims with pride and exaggerates that these networks "broadcast reports to all the receivers throughout the world" (343). His glee is megalomaniacal. He is convinced that he is the subject and maker of history. Yet in places his memoirs also hint at a humility. He is only the servant for the new technology in the service of his country and, finally, for the progress of the world.

There is a twin achievement celebrated here. His ship masters the air, while simultaneous radio transmittal from on board broadcasts this achievement via the airwaves "throughout the world." At once the ether is mastered by new technological forms that travel seemingly without effort. One is a form of mass transit (the zeppelin), the other is a form of mass communication (the radio). Although the zeppelin has one path to its sole destination and the radio transmission arrives at innumerable locations, they are conjoined. This ecstatic linkage of transportation and communication brings the presentation of the event into both German and American homes, but differently. For the American audience, the glamour and ease of this transportation is portrayed as well as its arrival on American shores. Yet for the German listener, and for the captain, the intensely German backdrop and origin is foregrounded–the technology is mastered by a particular nation-state.

Whereas Captain Lehmann has supreme confidence in his staff, he is less than happy with his passengers on this flight. He writes of his crew that they "radiate calm assurance. They never once doubted that the Atlantic could be conquered" (344). But the passengers did not show up so well in this accounting: "They hovered between nervousness and phobia. Even though they were offered what no transatlantic service ever offered them before–a crossing without seasickness" (344–45).

The captain is decidedly impatient with the passengers' fear. He is assured of the flight's safety. Thus, he reprimands his passenger's reticence and their distrust of the majestic technology that he masters. He even seems to take it personally (as if the passengers have betrayed him) even though zeppelin travel already had a checkered career by this time– there had already been explosions and crashes and disappearances. Yet from his point of view, the *Hindenburg* and the *Graf* had staged demonstration flights in order to erase any lingering fears in the minds of the traveling public. Lehmann is enraged. His point–that zeppelin travel is safe and enjoyable and smooth sailing–has not taken hold despite these efforts and even though the German and American broadcast networks have both worked to celebrate this new route and vehicle. In the NBC broadcasts, however, there are no reports of the anxiousness of the passengers. Instead there is only a melodic sound portrait of a glamorous voyage.

The fatal flight of the *Hindenburg* left the new Rhein-Main World Airport on 3 May 1937, inaugurating a new series of scheduled flights with paying customers. Captain Max Pruss commanded the ship. Captain Lehmann came along as Director of the Deutsche Zeppelin Reederei. The flight was not sold out. There were only thirty-six passengers aboard. Additional crew was aboard for training purposes, and this brought the number of staff to sixty-one.

On 6 May, the ship was almost twelve hours late reaching Lakehurst, due to opposing winds that forced the *Hindenburg* to slow to 45–50 mph. When it approached Lakehurst, dark storm clouds gathered around the station, and Captain Pruss informed Commander Rosendahl that he was going to cruise around the town until the storm passed. By this time, a plethora of reporters, cameramen, and eager onlookers had assembled, eager to witness the landing (Toland 1957:313). The reporters groaned when news that the landing had been delayed reached them and ran for cover when a thunderstorm burst overhead. After the passing of another storm, Commander Rosendahl sent a message via Radio Officer Willy Speck to Captain Pruss that he should come in for a landing (Rosendahl 1938:337). Passengers got ready for the landing, and the huge landing crew of 110 U.S. Navy men and 138 civilians took their positions for securing and landing the ship.

At about 7:15 P.M., Commentator Herbert Morrison of WLS Chicago left the hangar to make a recording of the landing of the ship. The recording was going to be aired for his station's human interest program, "Dinner Bell." He was going to strive to bring as much color as possible to the broadcast because the flight was devoid of celebrities. His reporting technique would have to make up for the lack of name-dropping potential in the passenger list (Toland 1957:316).

Captain Pruss took a sharp, fast turn in his final approach. Some American observers felt that he was traveling too quickly and had made the turn too tight. However, Commander Rosendahl and Captain Lehmann felt Pruss was making a good approach (Toland 1957:317; Rosendahl 1938:356). At 7:19 P.M. hydrogen and water ballast were valved, and the ship descended fifty feet as Pruss gave the orders to the engine men to reverse the engines. At 7:21 the first two landing ropes were dropped; the landing crew tied these to two railroad cars. Radio Officer Willy Speck transmitted to the *Hindenburg*'s sister ship the *Graf Zeppelin,* which was in flight over the South Atlantic, that the *Hindenburg* had landed successfully (Toland 1957:318).

Commentator Morrison was recording his broadcast, announcing that the ship was coming in "like some great feather" although it was being rocked by winds that caused the port rope to go taut and the starboard slack (Rosendahl 1938:356). The ship was now 75 feet above the ground. At 7:25 P.M., as Morrison was in mid-sentence and Rosendahl was standing on the mooring mast evaluating the efficiency of the landing, a burst of flames erupted on the front edge of the upper fin that attached to the hull of the ship. Morrison screamed: "It's broken into flames! It's flashing–flashing! It's flashing terrible!" Rosendahl screamed out: "My God, it's on fire" (Toland 1957:319). Later Rosendahl described the flames in a less exclamatory and a more descriptive style: "It was a brilliant burst of flame resembling a flower opening rapidly into bloom." Even the commander was into the beauty of the destruction of this beloved object, describing it in hindsight as an aesthetic event of the highest order.[7]

A loud explosion followed. WLS engineer Nehlsen, who was inside in the hangar, had to quickly clear his recording disk of debris falling from the ceiling. He gave the okay signal to Morrison to speak. Morrison, convinced that no one would survive, said, "It's bursting into flames and falling on the mooring mast." People were scattering wildly as the stern section, on fire, fell to the ground with a great thud, sending "huge pillars of flames and smoke to great heights" (Rosendahl 1938:357). The bow shot up to a height up 500 feet at an angle of 45 degrees (Toland 1957:321).

"This is terrible," Morrison transmitted. "This is one of the worst catastrophes in the world." Pausing, he turned to his engineer, who pantomimed to him from the window of the hangar to "keep going" (Toland 1957:322). "Oh, the humanity and all the passengers!" Morrison continued, starting to sob. The fumes caused him to choke and the smoke made him unable to see well. Bodies jumped out of the burning zeppelin. Morrison admitted to his audience (who would hear the recording the following day): "I'm going to have to stop for a moment because I've lost my voice. This is the worst thing I've ever witnessed." He then went inside the hangar to resume transmission, but emerged moments later to interview survivors.

Cameramen from Paramount newsreels, initially immobilized by the horror, were ordered to get back to work and film the burning ship. Associated Press photographer Murray Becker, screaming "Oh, my God," kept clicking, later winning a prize for his shot of the stern crashing to the ground (Toland 1957:330). Thirteen of the thirty-six passengers died either immediately or from injuries; twenty-two of the sixty-one crew members died. Casualties were far less than had been initially imagined by witnesses (including Morrison). The spectacle of the tall flames and the sounds of explosions forced them to imagine the worst while being transfixed by the scenario of the disaster.

Captain Lehmann died a day later, still believing in zeppelin passenger travel, but only with the use of helium not hydrogen (Rosendahl 1938:363). Rosendahl, in writing the afterword to Lehmann's memoirs, urged the U.S. government to make its abundant supply of helium available for future zeppelin travel. In this he is implicitly blaming the U.S. government for the explosion, although he does applaud the U.S. investigation into the event. Also he praised the United States for allowing the German government to stage state rites for the twenty-eight German victims on 11 May at the Hudson River–a spectacle watched by 10,000 people.

You Are There

The Inquiry Board ascribed the disaster to an occurrence of St. Elmo's Fire and not to a mishandling of the ship. Conspiracy theories–sabotage and bombs, anti-Nazi plots, and so forth– were also abundant, but nothing was ever proved (Toland 1957:339). At the same time, the official explanation was never believed, and the exact cause for the explosion is still not clear. Regardless, it caused the end of mass transit via the zeppelin.

Moments after survivors began to emerge from the wreckage, Morrison attempted to interview one of them. He spoke first to an industrialist named Mangone, whom sailors tried to steer into an ambulance because his face was covered in smoke and his clothes were partially burned. Mangone refused to leave until he found his daughter in the chaos (Toland 1957:332). Morrison, in his determination, found the German photographer Otto Clemens to interview, and Clemens had a waiting friend who could translate from the German. A report reached Morrison during the interview that "twenty-five to thirty people have been saved." Morrison, who seemed at one point at a breakdown, gasping and sobbing, was still definitely on the job.

Images from the *Hindenburg* disaster arrived quickly to the public through newspapers and movie theater newsreels. Audiences gasped and screamed at the Paramount footage. The next day, May 8, Morrison's 15-minute broadcast was aired at 4:30 P.M. on NBC's blue network. Although it was not live, listeners felt that they had heard "an actual on-the-spot broadcast of the tragedy" (Toland 1957:337). Of course, the word-pictures that Morrison offered to his listeners were prerecorded. It was even by that time a more vital or realistic version of the show *You Are There.*

On the same day that the "live" *Hindenburg* disaster was broadcast, NBC radio ran its show *You Are There.* This show was a simulation of real-life historic events; this particular episode was a dramatization of a suffragette meeting in 1853. An actor played a reporter transmitting information magically through time, as if the "revolutionary meeting" was "live." After advertisements for American Airlines, a booming baritone voice exclaimed, "You are there!" elongating the vowels as if to suggest transport through sound.

The eyewitness has a particular and peculiar relationship with knowledge;[8] however, this knowledge is neither empirical nor learned. It is a knowledge of proximity, a knowledge of history as it is happening, a purported liveness. The listener is in the audible presence of the eyewitness, whose voice surmounts distance. This voice transmits earth-shattering events into language, knowing that he is in the presence of history being made. This voice trusts that words and the medium can succeed and survive any event, even the most disastrous.

The premise of *You Are There* is that radio can enter into historic occasions. It does this, not by creating historical drama, but by recreating the historical event with an emphasis on the fictional eyewitness. The show produces simulations of the past that structure events into newsworthy events of the present. The simulation, which in many ways appears both charming and harmless, has a recklessness in rendering the historic as if were just another chamber with a microphone and a reporter in it. The past goes under the surveillance of the network broadcast and becomes a drama with a makeshift eyewitness as the lead character.

The Proper Place of Disaster

Zeppelins like the *Hindenburg* were described by the media during peacetime as innocent. Reporter Morrison poetically insists that its movement into Lakehurst is "feather-like." Yet there was much tension around the voyage of the zeppelin, related most of all to its place of origin–a militarizing Germany under its enigmatic ruler, a Germany that is sending out its ships over the airwaves, transmitting ship to shore. These inflated objects, taken to the sky, afloat with hydrogen, are already uncanny objects. Perhaps they seem like only mechanized balloons, but there is a sinister element within, in hindsight, an explosive inevitability that presages international conflict. No wonder the passengers trembled as the reporter spoke of being "at home" aboard the *Hindenburg*. As we know, the word *uncanny* is very much related to the home. The explosion was already happening before it actually occurred.

Similarly, Blanchot writes that the disaster "takes place after it has taken place" (1995:40). That is to say, we are always reacting to a disaster's repercussions, not to its percussiveness. In the case of the "War of the Worlds," the broadcast has magnitude and horror, not because it is originary or causative. Rather, it is because the fantasy of invasion as well as the threat of explosion were reasonable fears.

The maintenance of the illusion of an isolated and safe America within the world arena was in jeopardy. Indeed, events in Europe that had direct impact on immigrant American families could be reported almost immediately via the radio. This was a very new phenomenon.

For example, in 1899 when Admiral Dewey defeated the Spanish forces in Manila, news of his victory took days to reach the United States. There were no wires set up for telegraphy, and Marconi's wireless telegraphy had not yet been demonstrated. By the late 1930s, however, news travel was virtually instantaneous, and trans-Atlantic messages no longer needed to be transmitted by Morse code. Disastrous and victorious events of the world traveled to the home via radio. International occurrences reached the domestic sphere. At once this both conquers distance and enables fear. The faraway event comes closer, pervades an interior space. In this way, the *Hindenburg* broadcast is an expression of the disaster that has already happened. It has taken its place in a fractured American setting, unarticulated until panic breaks out.

Disaster, embedded in the landscape, becomes dislodged. An accident waiting to happen is an accident also *before* it happens. Its history is rewritten after its appearance. The eyewitness speaking in the present tense will be subject to a time delay that is due only to his own search for the right descriptive words. The Three Mile Island nuclear power plant leakage, for example, was in preparation for disaster all along. In hindsight, investigations proved that the leakage was inevitable.

A similar story is now being constructed regarding the attack on the World Trade Center: the nation was suffering from lax security systems, particularly in our airports; our intelligence gathering became less than stellar in the post-cold-war period; and our borders were becoming too porous, allowing for enemies of our state to enter too easily. Thus, the potential for such a terrorist attack became accelerated. Such is the case in narratives that explain the syllogistic logic of disaster: all along the event was in preparation, albeit in disguise. With the *Hindenburg,* the disaster was also inevitable–its use of hydrogen rendered it a wafting time bomb, unknown to all until after the explosion.

For Blanchot (1995), the disaster also has spatial implications: it is distance in your face. The telephone, the radio, and the telegram suggest intimacy and nearness, while at the same time circumventing the impossibility of the space in between. The telephone and the radio, in particular, are acousmatic forms where a faraway voice is brought to the listening ear in a magical, unseen way, creating an illusion that distance is itself an easily surmountable detail or is itself but an illusion. The ear bears witness to the unseen. The boundaries between what is near and far collapse, excitedly, hauntedly. The *Hindenburg* disaster (so many events, described as tragedies at the time, are then renamed disasters) becomes a local event. It is local because it is an event narrativized on the ether. However crowded with signals, the ether will enable transmission into so many homes.

Blanchot argues that the disaster "acquires meaning not a body" (1995:39). I take this to suggest that the disaster disseminates. It is amorphous and does not congeal or solidify. Whether it is analyzed, discussed, or ignored, such an event is not without being anthropomorphized or corporealized. For the particularity of American popular culture, both pre-war and postwar, I think there is a movement between body and meaning. In the "War of the Worlds" broadcast, which we will discuss in Chapter 5, the body of one of the aliens is described in great detail; their hideous corporeality is crucial to the horror of their murderous march.

In the American context, the disaster takes on figural aspects. But also for the American, the figure of disaster is silent, or rather wordless, taking on the muted dissonance and velocity of static. The Oklahoma City Bombing, for example, was divided into parts: The first part, the actual bombing, missed news cameras and audiotape; the second part, its deathly effects and its investigations, was a thoroughly mediated affair. The event itself, after the explosion, is silent but spoken for by governmental and media representatives. The accused bombers, potential embodiments of the disaster (also called a "tragedy"), are muted figures, faces drawn and photographed, but wordless to the populace. The viewer/auditor can only study physiognomies to reach underlying pathology. Meanwhile, the camera is poised near the rubble, giddy with aftershock. The reporters are replete with impassioned adjectives, narrating the event after the disaster has taken place, inhabiting the airwaves as our intermediaries between extraordinary disaster/invasion/explosion and everyday panic. What is crucial in these performances is that the disaster is itself always wordless, but then it is narrated by one near to the scene. The narration travels and narrows distance. Later, the corporeality of Timothy McVeigh will become the visible body of disaster.[9] All along, as the story is told via media, he was the disaster waiting to happen, moving from youthful disenfranchisement to murderous alienation to, ultimately, the face of evil itself.

Disaster in America can be divided into two main categories. First, there are natural disasters: floods, earthquakes, tornadoes, hurricanes, droughts, fires. Second, there are so-called man-made disasters. When these are not caused by terrorists, they are often related to human mismanagement of technology (Three Mile Island) or to the inexplicable failure of technology (the recent American airline crash in the Rockaways in Queens, New York). In the case of terrorism, technology is used expertly from a hostile, initially concealed force.[10] Technology is always a factor in this category of disaster.

As discussed in the previous chapter, *technology* is a broad, ambiguous term from the Greek *technē*, meaning systematic treatment of an art. It is used in English to mean "a scientific method of achieving a practical purpose" or "the totality of the means employed to provide objects necessary for human sustenance and comfort." The inference is that technology corrects a lack or inadequacy in nature; nature does not provide all that is necessary. But there is also the suggestion that perhaps technology, however needed, is excessive, a supplement to that which is perceived as part of the natural world.

J. G. Ballard's *Crash* (1973), explores the erotics of human interaction with technological disaster. The protagonist in the novel is excited by his proximity to the character Vaughn. Vaughn is completely invested in the erotic possibilities of car crashes and acts of sex in vehicles while passing by accidents along the highway. For Vaughn–and increasingly for the protagonist–eroticism is tied to the experience of driving and the potential of melding into the machine via destruction. In this possibility, there is an ecstasy. Vaughn's self-destruction, like a truck, moves in on him, but he is forced to rely on chance to crash. The essence of technology related to man also has autonomy. Eroticism is experienced in an attempt to become conjoined into its haphazard essence, in becoming subject to technology's destruction. The car becomes, not a vehicle for transport, but circuitry that can transform the

human body. The danger the car offers is excessive and beck-
oning, not in what it can offer in terms of arriving, but in what
it can do in altering the frame of the body and consciousness.
In this way, what technology (as a commodity form) offers,
beyond its selling points as time-saving and task-accom-
plishing, is an elaborative, eroticized form of danger that
repeats its creators' potential for violence but also exceeds it.
In the crash, the car–a mode of transportation–becomes a
communication medium whereby victims are conjoined with
the technology.

Part of the display of the mastery over technology involves
its destruction, or at least its disassembling. A favorite
vaudeville act in the teens of the last century was a group of
men who would completely take apart and then reassemble
a motor car–within six minutes (see Douglas 1987:140). The
spectacle involved a dismemberment and a reattachment,
showing that the body of the machine was surmountable
and mysterious but also a hobbyist's model. For guitarists
like Jimi Hendrix in the 1960s, part of the theatrics involved
the destruction of an electric guitar by pounding it against
the stage. A gesture of wasteful expenditure in part (see
Bataille 1985), it can also be read to imply that destroying
the instrument grants him expressivity (a perverse musi-
cality) and displays his ambivalence toward the mechanics
of the instrument. The Plasmatics, a rock band in the 1980s,
had a trademark stage act that always involved the female
lead singer's smashing TV sets. They also moved on to
destroying cars and bombing suburban ranch houses in
their videos. I suggest that Americans, who have an enthu-
siasm and a receptivity toward new technology that is documentable both by studies and by sale figures, also have a
relationship to these objects of transmission and transport

that is laced with suspicion and fear–and indeed, with eroticism. The destruction of these objects thus involves an ecstasy. Destruction becomes an aesthetic event.[11]

The Unseen Eyewitness and the Live Broadcast

Commentator Morrison was in Lakehurst, New Jersey, on 6 May to describe the landing of the *Hindenburg,* carrying passengers from Germany for a future broadcast. This event was prearranged to be a great public show of the latest advancement in travel technology–a great tie-in for sponsor American Airlines, which provided passengers with connecting flights to other American locations.

Initially, Morrison is ebullient, describing the approach of the zeppelin in grandiose metaphor: "a floating palace," "a great feather." But when the *Hindenburg* bursts into flames, all metaphors disappear in his speech. In a shaky voice, he says: "I can't talk. This is the worst thing I ever witnessed." He clears his throat and assures his audience that he will try to provide them with "word-pictures" of the tragedy, but for a few moments all that he can recount is the inexpressibility of the flames and gas, repeating, "I can't talk." This repetition itself becomes a word-picture, encouraging the audience to imagine a landscape of destruction that words fail to describe. That is, as the term suggests, Morrison is still able to use his words to project images for his listeners to imagine the event. Transmitted words are at all times–but especially under duress–assumed to include a visual dimension that can be unfurled at the moment of reception. Words heard emanating from eyewitnesses, while purely sonic phenomena, are imbued with the visual. Spoken narration becomes a visual form in its receiving; eyewitnessing involves the ear so as to conjure a sight to behold. Word-pictures become the metalanguage, the camera, and the projector of the eyewitness, presenting that which is "live" to the audience.

The live broadcast becomes an exclamation of the witnessing of death and the failure of language to describe horror as it explodes on the terrain. The listener is left to experience the eyewitness's shock. Yet the eyewitness still struggles to cover up the lurking experience of "dead air"–the dread space on radio when there is no transmittal of human-made sound, only the omnipresent static. Morrison says into the microphone, "I must swallow to keep on"; on the tape his swallow is audible.

In *Noise: The Political Economy of Music* (1985), Jacques Attali suggests that noise itself is a form of sonic disaster; (capitalist) culture tries to transform it into a more manageable sound, for noise means the unfastening of order. Noise is a confessional moment for the culture; sound is an attempt to conceal. The listener, who can only visualize the disaster, hears the noisy shock that is expressed via confessions of inexpressibility.

The eyewitness is posited as the representative of the listening body, for you are there at home imagining the event if he is there speaking of it, using words that conjure up pictures. The eyewitness is an icon of democracy: he relays that which he sees to all who are tuned in to hear; he turns noise into sound. Residing in the public sphere, the eyewitness can enter into the more private spaces of the domestic realm. The eyewitness trusts in the visual, trusts that words can translate the optical terrain, trusts that language can create word-pictures for the listener. The eyewitness's subjective experience translated into linguistic expressivity is taken as fact; his self-interest is in narration. For example, in criminal trials the eyewitness is considered a credible witness because he was there when it happened only by chance. All other parties might lie, but the impartial witness who has observed the crime is always close to truth. In the Western nation-state, in the eyewitness we trust.

The eyewitness enlivens dead air. His audible presence gestures toward satisfying a fetish-like desire for simultaneity. On radio, the eyewitness is, crucially, never seen. The medium produces what we would now call a virtual body. The eyewitness navigates a technological terrain, humanizing it by way of insisting that he is inhabiting the same temporal bracket as the listener. He stresses that he is connecting the listener to the event by repeating that "you are there," but he also only inhabits the airwaves as a radio-body. He reinforces the listening body's passivity vis-à-vis world events of increasing horror and war. The on-the-air eyewitness is the public's representative to events of magnitude, including disasters.

Later in the evening of the *Hindenburg* disaster, the newscaster at NBC studios tried to get in touch with Commentator Herring in New Jersey for an update. A synecdochical logic takes over: the newscaster, a part of the network, is renamed NBC; Herring is renamed as his location, which is Lakehurst, New Jersey. They have trouble getting through the telephone lines, and the newscaster repeats, "Hello, Lakehurst, this is NBC. Can you hear me?" The two individuals, in a panic to provide information, have become a location and a corporation desperate to evade the disturbance of distance so that they may connect. When they do connect, a recovered Herring/Lakehurst says, "I am glad to pass the information along to you." For Herring, information has its own import, and the eyewitness feels a duty to transmit it.[12] To be cut off from the station and unable to coexist simultaneously with the listener in providing information is disastrous for the eyewitness. He is propelled to express his nearness to disaster, reminding the listener that he too may be close to harm's way.

Yet the eyewitness, even as a victim of chance, is also a survivor. Flames jump about him, bricks miss him by inches. Yet the eyewitness speaks of survival regardless. The eyewitness is duty-bound; even when Morrison reports on the failure of language to describe, he is indeed speaking and is successful in describing the inexpressibility of the event around him. Thus, he is able to continue transmitting word-pictures.

The eyewitness speaks in the first person, in the present tense, always enacting upon the listener an interpretation of the experiences of his own senses. A prerecorded show deadens. In the 1930s, radio executives frowned on prerecorded shows, and bands always played live to a studio audience. Even for contemporary TV sitcoms, there will be an announcement to the effect that the show was recorded before a live studio audience—a fact that enlivens the proceedings for the viewer.

Liveness lends authenticity. In television news, the phrase "Now we go live to . . ." is oft-repeated; the suggestion in the "we" is that the audience is included in the seemingly spontaneous shifting of point of view from the calm studio to the chaos of proximity. The fixation here is on a presence enunciating in the present tense. The irony with the Morrison broadcast is, of course, that it was recorded even as it was experienced as a live transmittal from the field. Or, as the French might deem it, the broadcast is *faux direct*.

The repetition of "live" reinforces the sense that the air-waves are thick with that which is deathly. Silence is "dead" air where the humming of transmission and receiving is audible. Like Samuel Beckett's character in *The Unnamable* (1966), language sustains, and even if language perpetuates anguish, it does so heroically. Beckett writes in the concluding passages of the novel as if the word-pictures were the lonely transmittals of a survivalist radiovoice:

> How can I say it, that's all words, they're all I have, and not many of them, the words fail, the voice fails, so be it, I know that it will be the silence, full of murmurs, distant cries, the usual silence, spent listening, spent waiting, waiting for the voice ... it will be I, you must go on, I can't go on, I'll go on, you must say words, as long as there are any. (413–14)[13]

Beckett's protagonist, akin to a disembodied voice on the radio like the *Hindenburg*'s eyewitness, is sustained by the repetition of the failure of words that leads to the inevitability of narrating a story. Beckett writes of words: "Perhaps they have carried me to the threshold of my story, before the door that opens on my story" (414). Eyewitness Morrison, in a moment of crisis, avoids the cries that Beckett refers to by reiterating the impossibility of communicating. Both are using words to create pictures of that which would escape visual depiction. Inexpressiveness succeeds as image. The eyewitness to disaster is a figure that speaks also of the supreme mistrust of language that accompanies and generates the ability and the failure—at once—to witness and transmit, to listen and speak.

From this paradox, the live eyewitness emerges triumphant. He lives and speaks heroic acts in the face of disaster. His voice may narrate death, but even in its panic, it offers survival. In this survival, the auditor hears his own ideal image. The eyewitness exists because of the inevitability of disaster. An event occurs before the speaker; the event changes the speaker forever into an eyewitness connected to the event; the speaker/eyewitness will be interviewed. Disaster's spokesperson, but placing the inexpressible into narration, the eyewitness is an unelected official.

Disconnections

The radio boom in the early 1920s was accompanied by exclamations from both the press and cultural leaders that radio would bring about national unity. For example, journalist Stanley Frost wrote in his *Collier's* article "Radio Dreams That Can Come True" that radio will spread "mutual understanding to all sections of the country, unifying our thoughts, ideals, and purposes, making us a strong and well-knit people" (quoted in Douglas 1987:306). The promise of radio was that national solidarity could be achieved, connecting the Iowa farmer with the New York immigrant, educating all in the proper ways to be American. Radio could provide contact with the outside world while bringing the listener to a safe home.

Indeed, at broadcast radio's inception, the public sphere and popular entertainments were laced with menace. Prohibition (1918–33) brought with it an increase in gangster activity. Public places like nickelodeons, amusement parks, and vaudeville shows were crowded and deemed unsafe by the middle and upper classes, for they brought people in contact with the worlds of prostitution and organized crime.

Radio could prove antidotal to the social ills burgeoning in the public parlors of leisure and could steer people away from the more base pleasures of the popular entertainment at that time. Radio could provide a sense of being an American, hearing proper, educated American voices. It was also viewed as a way to bring people (and especially potentially wayward fathers and husbands) home (to the family), listening.

Thus, radio was perceived as a way to connect disparate Americans into a shared activity. The medium could help to create a new form of exhibiting American-ness: through staying home, or rather by retreating to a private sphere. Both elite educators and corporate executives shared this outlook on radio; this new medium afforded listeners an entry into a national system. By the early 1930s, this system was in place. RCA/NBC quickly emerged as corporate giants, and their nationally produced programs were distributed to local affiliates. Radio had become ubiquitous.

But with the advent of radio usage by the newly elected president with his "Fireside Chats," the realities of the nation's political and cultural life also entered into the home. That is, the nation was joined together not only by listening to *Amos 'n Andy* but also by listening to FDR explain the failure of the banking system and the encroaching war in Europe as well as by listening to news coverage of these events. Whereas FDR may have been quite canny in using the new medium to explain the crisis and his government's ability to generate progressive policy, he also, via a box once reserved for performers fresh from vaudeville and ballroom stages, let a certain kind of public panic into the private sphere.

The corporate and educational propagandists of the 1920s and 30s were right–broadcast radio would serve to connect Americans–but not necessarily to each other. What this meant, however, was that any tremors of anxiousness, distrust, or disaster could also be disseminated through the emerging "You Are There" mentality of transmission. Rather than only establishing a more-educated public learning the pleasures of sounding like an American, this configuration also generated an audience vulnerable to any seismic disturbance that affected the eyewitness with a microphone who was able to transmit "word-pictures."

4

Radio and the Voice and Body of the President

The Fireside Chats

HISTORIANS OF AMERICAN ORATORY agree that radio was crucial to the presidency of Franklin Delano Roosevelt (e.g., Baskerville 1979; Buhite and Levy 1992; Ryan 1988). Indeed, both radio and presidential historians agree that his Fireside Chats served to make him an intimate figure, reassuring to his population, and allowed a patrician, perhaps aloof figure to sound as if he were a man of and for the people.

This attitude is revealed in folklorist Carl Lamson Carmer's poem written after Roosevelt's death:

> ... I never saw him
> But I knew him. Can you have forgotten
> How, with his voice, he came into our house,
> The president of the United States,
> Calling us friends.
> (Quoted in Buhite and Levy 1992:xx)

In his speeches, Roosevelt often asserted that the listeners were known to him and that he identified with the populace.

His speeches are consistently credited with contributing to his popularity and being a key aspect of the success of his presidency. His use of radio, in fact, dates back to his governance of New York (Fine 1977).

As Carmer's poem suggests, listeners felt they knew their president because they heard his speeches. They knew the president by means of his radiovoice. Yet in the poem, radio as a medium is not mentioned; Roosevelt's voice comes into the house seemingly without technology. The radio disappears. It is as if a pure, unaltered voice emerges from its speaker. This voice is present and active, unmediated. The president's voice becomes the radio itself.

Carmer's switching of pronouns in the poem from first person to a more accusative second person, and then to an inclusive first person plural (us), is a technique that Roosevelt uses in his speeches. This pronominal shifting also shows up in letters written to Roosevelt. As discussed by Hayes (1994), who analyzed letters written after the first fireside chat, these documents—even when full of praise—reveal a tension between who is included in the pronouns that signify self, radio-listeners, and the nation.

Roosevelt's speeches were called "chats," emphasizing their colloquial nature, and "fireside," underlining their placement in the home. As such they were intended to seem like natural encounters between president and public ("chat" has the connotation of informal dialog, as opposed to "speech," which implies a passive listener and a skilled orator). They were designed to seem as if the president was responding to the questions and concerns of his people.

Whereas it is common to view the Fireside Chats as reassuring, serving to restore faith in the government, I suggest another facet of listeners' responses and a different reading of these chats. I argue that these chats regulated panic, rather than attempting to calm the listener. In Roosevelt's clear, distinctive, pausing voice is also the determined voice of the politician who is insistent that he is necessary. This voice is necessary not only for its ability to rid the nation of uncertainty and to return it to economic security but also for the production and distribution of this panic as a vocal representation. In this way, Roosevelt's voice is heard as a voice of emergency, and his presidency becomes committed not so much to ending this emergency as to transmitting it, in order to secure a place for Roosevelt's narrating voice. This voice reproduces the panic, even as it suggests that he, and his government, are well on their way to curing the ills of the country. This well-punctuated voice is thus reliant on emergency and transmits it coherently. The listening public is at once hearing the story of the hope for recovery and stability and listening to a confession of emergency via the crisp and amiable voice of the president.[1]

Roosevelt had been struck down with polio in 1921 at the age of thirty-nine. Although he never regained the use of his legs, he was able–through canes and braces and the cooperation of the press–to present an illusion of mobility. Hugh G. Gallagher states in his book *FDR's Splendid Deception* that only two photos (of 35,000) at the presidential library show Roosevelt in a wheelchair (1999:xiii). Via the radio, however, he was freed from the need to conceal his handicapped body. If his head was all that was visible in most photos or newsreels, the listeners could imagine a body, a prosthetic to the president's voice heard on the radio.

Gallagher suggests that Roosevelt used props such as his cigarette holder and fedora hat, and the tilt of his head to make himself distinctive and remarkable (1999:93). In other words, he made himself into–at least in the public perception–a dynamic talking head. Although many people saw the extent of Roosevelt's handicap as he entered and left the podiums from which he spoke, discussion of infantile paralysis was all but nonexistent in the press. "Crippled or not," Gallagher writes, "the nation wanted this man, with all his magnificent qualities, as its leader. So an agreement was struck: the existence of FDR's handicap would simply be denied by all. The people would pretend that their leader was not crippled, and their leader would do all that he could not to let them see that he was" (96). Most Americans believed that their president had recovered from his bout with polio and seemed to focus instead on the face of the leader–indeed, on his voice. This voice emerged seemingly from another body, not his actual one.

As president, Roosevelt governed with two bodies. One body, conjured through his voice, ruled via the airwaves through instantaneous mobility, traveling to all radio receivers, telling a story with the possibility of a happy ending. The other body navigated the corridors of power via the help of aids, hidden behind podiums so as to hide his handicap. His presidency was highly theatricalized–every appearance required extensive backstage preparation.

Kantorowicz's *The King's Two Bodies* (1957)[2] and Marin's *Portrait of the King* (1988) provide insights into the way Roosevelt used a phantasmagoric body to secure his presence. Roosevelt instituted his transmittable voice as a "station" on the radio dial, ever audible, that could always be broadcast. He had instantaneous access to the homes of the population, even though, unlike today's president who does a weekly radio address, Roosevelt gave only thirty-one fireside chats. Nevertheless, the potential and the actuality of these addresses enabled an imagined corporeality.

Roosevelt came on the airwaves at particular moments of crisis. He instituted his voice, not to calm the listener per se, but as a recurring figure of resolve against the constant threat of disaster. Governing via media serves to produce a second body of ideal proportions. To hear the sound of the leader via the radio becomes the way to know the leader; the leader's narration of the nation is also the moment when the leader is presented to the nation. He is heard at, and thus is identified with, moments of imminent danger.

Roosevelt's first address specifically for radio as president was delivered on Sunday evening 12 March 1933. This speech was in response to the banking crisis. His administration did not call it a Fireside Chat. The term "Fireside Chat" was coined by Harry Butcher of CBS, who used it in a press release before the president's second radio address of 7 May 1933, a speech that detailed the New Deal. Butcher's term stuck and began to be used by Roosevelt and his administration. These "chats" were transmitted from the White House sporadically—averaging three a year during the twelve years of his presidency. In other words, they did not follow a set schedule and were not a common occurrence. Yet they were key moments in the nation's history, a time of interaction between the government and its people.

Roosevelt used radio cleverly, but he also used it as way to describe his new policies to Americans without the use of the print media. In the first year of his administration, newspapers were critical of his New Deal and were actively editorializing against his ideas of recovery. Roosevelt's use of the radio allowed him to reach the public without having to rely on newspapers. Furthermore, radio networks were reliant on newspaper-owned wire services for their news, and the print media were very wary of the emerging importance of radio in providing news. The Biltmore Agreement of 1934 between newspaper and radio executives stated that radio news could only be transmitted after 9 A.M. and then again after 9 P.M. so as not to interfere with the morning and evening editions of the papers. Although this agreement fell apart after a year, it is indicative of the conflict between the two media. Roosevelt chose the radio to enable his voice, forsaking the transcription and potentially harsh interpretation of his speeches via print.

In the early 1930s, news coverage was rare on the radio. Music made up the bulk of programming, with comedy and drama also prevalent. Radio was in its "escapist" stage and was one of the few industries that remained profitable during the Depression. Advertising on radio centered on low-cost, perishable–and often ingestible–items (toothpaste, cough drops, cleaners, soft drinks, and so forth); and unemployed and partially employed Americans spent hours in front of the radio. They heard about products that they might well afford, products that promised cures to maladies of the body and uncleanliness in the home. In contrast, the newspaper industry's revenue was falling off, and advertising agencies thus expanded their inroads into broadcasting by creating and producing new radio shows with ready-made sponsors in mind. This, in turn, decreased the operating costs of networks and stations during the Depression. Broadcasting was an industry that seemed–in this aspect–invulnerable to the economic climate.

The interjection of Roosevelt's voice was a startling change to radio. Hard news was covered by newspapers, and even though Roosevelt only presented three Fireside Chats in 1933, it was a momentous shift. A voice that spoke of issues of national and international ramifications in seemingly calm, measured tones presaged a newer state of broadcasting–one where programs were interrupted (or potentially interrupted) by news flashes from eyewitness accounts of disaster and war. Roosevelt became the sole voice during prime time (then 6–10 P.M.) without a private sponsor. Yet some argue that his rhetorical strategies, and indeed the method of presidential address, was influenced by the discourse of advertising. Presidents began to forsake public address techniques. Instead, they used personal testimony—a key technique in advertising—where a narrator in the ad tells a tale in which the product is the hero.[3] So if Roosevelt's voice was a startling change, the ways in which he spoke, in modes that were akin to advertising, were already familiar. Presidents knew that their message needed to be *sold* to the public.

Listening by the Hearth

Roosevelt's first Fireside Chat was broadcast live eight days after his inauguration; in it he explained his administration's response to the banking crisis. This crisis looked like it could cause a collapse of the economy. Banks were closing around the country, and life savings were being lost. The speech is impressive; the banking system of the country is explained clearly.

The speech is also remarkable in the amount of times the president stumbles over his words (five times) and chooses to repeat his phrases as a result of stumbling (twice). He also clears his throat audibly twice. In the speech he expertly constructs a situation whereby Congress is patriotic insofar as the legislative body agrees to extend his executive privilege. But he also sounds perhaps under-rehearsed, and indeed, Roosevelt was known for changing the prepared text as he spoke it in front of the microphone.

The initial Fireside Chat established many of the techniques that Roosevelt would use throughout his radio addresses. The first and most obvious aspect is that he makes no attempt to hide his distinct regional pronunciation that is typical of someone of his social class. The word "again" is pronounced "a-gain" rather than the more standard American "agen"; war is uttered with a broad "a" and a dropped "r"; words like clear and fear (fear is especially repeated in the first chat) are pronounced with two syllables ("cle-a" and "fe-a"). This East Coast, upper-class accent was distinctive and was by no means the most common accent among Americans. Researchers at the time attempted to find out if audiences "liked" this aspect of the voice but could find no apparent opinion for or against his particular dialect (Ryan 1988:23). Of course, audiences had little idea what a president was meant to sound like—Hoover, who had a more standard American accent, sounded "cold and dull"; whereas Coolidge had a nasal New England accent (24). Roosevelt's voice sounded magisterial in comparison—if not particularly American—and powerful in its enunciations that revealed class and education. Moreover, when his voice repeated to its listeners the phrase "my friends," the vocal distinction and the spatial separation between classes was elided—at least during the duration of the broadcast.

Roosevelt's speaking rate in the Fireside Chats was far slower than other political orators on the air in the 1930s (particularly his adversaries Huey Long and Father Coughlin). During the first chat, he spoke at 130 words per minute; his rate dipped to 88 words per minute when he spoke after the bombing at Pearl Harbor in 1941. Normal tempos on the radio at the time ranged from 175 to 200 words per minute. Importantly, his pacing does not vary greatly during the course of his speech. And even though his volume does vary for emphasis, he never even suggests a scream, nor does his pitch rise above a F below middle C. It is this measured tone, steady and unwavering, that suggested the term "reassuring" that was used to describe his speeches. If Presidential historian Kathleen Hall Jameison (1988) is correct in emphasizing that Roosevelt brought a conversational tone to his speeches, the conversation was one where emotional excesses were kept to a minimum and variation was used for decided effect.

Roosevelt used the typical tactic of beginning sentences at a low pitch and then progressively raising his voice during the course of the sentence. Typically, he divided shorter sentences into thirds with two pauses, the final third of the sentence gaining more import through volume and containing the most crucial information for the listener. Longer sentences were also divided into segments of slightly varying pitch and tempo. This can be heard in the following sentence: "The second step, last Thursday, was the legislation promptly and patriotically passed by the Congress confirming my proclamation and broadening my powers so that it became possible in view of the requirement of time to extend the [bank] holiday and lift the ban of that holiday gradually in the days to come" (quoted in Buhite and Levy 1992:13). Roosevelt enunciates this sentence with five pauses; the first three have occurred before the word "promptly" (after "step" and after "Thursday"). Even though he has spoken much of the sentence, he has scarcely introduced the topic; he is creating anticipation for the listener to provide narrative. He then speaks of how Congress has extended his powers (rather than his asking Congress for this extension). As he now has the power to intervene into the banking industry, he has taken deliberate and necessary action. Thus, the sentence also becomes a story in and of itself–in how it is uttered. It diverts and invites its listener to its hinted-at conclusion.

Although Roosevelt spoke slowly, he also avoided "dead air," or silent spaces between words. He did this by elongating vowel and consonant sounds. "L's" are emphasized in his speech, as are the broad "a's" that suggest the diction of an actor. The airwaves were thus full with his sound, even if the pacing was slow. The length of pauses was consistent, and at times the rhythm settled into iambic pentameter. Thus, if each pause was a cause for anxiousness, it also signaled the return of this voice.

These oratorical techniques inspired much aesthetic appraisal from Americans at the time. A speech professor opined that "the cues in Franklin D. Roosevelt's voice–the voice alone–inspired confidence"; while a tailor from Indianapolis treated Roosevelt's 1936 annual message as if were almost purely performance: "It certainly was a masterpiece of rhetoric ... and so distinctly given in ordinary language that even the most illiterate could not help but comprehend every word of it" (quoted in Ryan 1988:23, 24). Many Americans mentioned the rhetorical flourishes at work in his aired speeches in their letters written to the president, and for the most part they seemed to appreciate his devices. As a result, his speeches were praised for their formal, audible qualities as often as they were evaluated for the success of his enunciation of policy decisions.[4]

Although Roosevelt's vocal technique sounded accomplished and indeed quite actorly (as much as it was conversational), he avoided some of the usual oratorical flourishes, using other strategies. For example, he would increase the vocal intensity and volume of succeeding lines, suggesting that in his peroration he was reaching a crescendo. At the end of his banking crisis speech, his volume increases during the anaphoric line "You must have faith; you must not be stampeded by rumors or guesses." His voices rises further in uttering, "Let us unite in banishing fear." Suggesting a climax after the pause, instead he goes down in tone and volume to state: "We have provided the machinery to restore our financial system; and it is up to you to support and make it work." Rather than moving to a more emotive climax, he comes back to transmitting a more matter-of-fact missive to his listeners, indicating their solemn course. He suggests great passion but always instructs patriotic duty instead as the response. This instruction, spoken more sternly, advocates faith so as to follow his policy. The form that this urging takes suggests a passionate, high-volume conclusion that does not come. Instead, he drops to a somber coda that indicates that calm after catastrophe–or the resolution to the narrative he has set up–can only result in the patriotic enactments of duty by the people. As such, he uses strategic pronominal shifting: he moves from the inclusive "we" to the more exclusive "you." This tactic, I argue, creates an anxiousness about who is included in the "we." The embedded logic is that if "you" perform the designated task, "you" become part of this "we."

Roosevelt's speeches are often described as reassuring, yet they bring up questions about inclusion. They also remind the listener of the threat of disorder. The structure and logic of the speech make it clear that the loyal participation of the people is the crucial factor in ensuring recovery. Roosevelt enunciates stern instructions to his "friends" and underlines this follow-up as crucial–he repeats that he is reliant on the loyalty of the people; he alone cannot provide for his people, although he seems to know exactly how they are faring.

Roosevelt speaks of the emotional state of the people, anticipating their concerns and questions in rising voice. Then, in more sotto voice, he provides the course to follow. For example, in his first "chat," after he explains why he has taken over the running and reopening of the banking system, he states: "Another question that you will ask is this: Why are all the banks not to be reopened at the same time?" (14). After giving shape to the people's concern, predicting their doubts, he responds to this imagined question: "The answer is simple, and I know you will understand it. Your government does not intend that the history of the past few years shall be repeated. We do not want and will not have another epidemic of bank failures"(14). Rather than actually revealing the reasoning for his administration's action, his explanation is that this staged reopening of banks is the right thing to do in order to avert disaster. Thus, he defines the populace's concern before it is asked, and answers their question by asserting that this action is best if "we" are to avoid the repetition of "our" recent failures. This technique is powerful; the president knows the listeners' worries before the listener can articulate them, and he answers the unarticulated questions with the answer that as "your government" we must avoid the past.

Furthermore, Roosevelt's use of the plural pronoun "you" and the possessive pronoun "your" was rare in commercial broadcasting in 1933 as a way to address the audience. As radio became commercialized in the 1920s and 30s, commercials and cooking shows (for example, *The Betty Crocker Show*) were the only places where the listening public was addressed in the second person. Dramas and comedies presented their narratives as if the listener were overhearing the programming; there was a "fourth wall" between audience and show.

Roosevelt broke through this wall by using the second person. This tactic strengthened the idea that he entered the home via his transmitted voice; the public was being spoken to directly by a "friendly" voice. This description refers to the sound of his voice and not necessarily to the meanings of its iterations. Indeed, in using "you" he was mimicking advertising, selling a cure via sound and narration.

Roosevelt enunciated his broadcasted speeches almost as if they were "narrowcasted" missives, seemingly particularized for the private home, giving the listener the illusion that he was being spoken to in a point-to-point transmission, rather than overhearing him in a radio address. In this way, the aesthetics of the president's voice become increasing crucial even as he speaks of national disaster, for it is not so important how his administration responds via policy but how his voice can serve to circumvent the audience's responses.

In a satirical essay, "The Radio Voice" (1934), John Dos Passos chastises the transmitted voice of the president for not actually being as omniscient and omnipotent as it suggests itself to be. Dos Passos suggests the visualization of Roosevelt evoked by his speeches:

> Then there is a man leaning across his desk, speaking clearly and cordially to youandme [*sic*], painstakingly explaining how he's sitting at his desk there in Washington, leaning towards youandme across his desk, speaking clearly and cordially so that youandme shall completely understand that he sits at his desk there in Washington with his fingers on all the switchboards of the federal government. (17)

Dos Passos, mocking the president's intense use of repetition, also suggests that he has provided the people with a story with a happy ending:

You have been listening to the President of the United States
in the White House. No wonder they all go to bed happy. But
what about it when they want a wage cut, the bank foreclos-
ing just til next week, the pile up on groceries at the chain
stores, a new bill ... and that it's still raining? (17)

Dos Passos highlights the narcotic-like effect of listening to
the leader's voice, but he also suggests that the leader's
broadcast highlights the discrepancy between the promise
of calm and the experience of panic that exist concurrently
in listening to the chief executive.

The president, if he cannot provide economic recovery or
noninvolvement in European wars, can always provide his
transmitted voice, a voice that insists on a national cohe-
sion. The sounds of the president are distinctive and are
addressed to listeners, but they are not necessarily reassuring. The president offers his voice as a tonic for social ills.

In the Fireside Chat of 3 September 1939, Roosevelt dealt
with the German invasion of Poland and the subsequent declaration of war by England and France. It is a contradictory
speech that on one hand emphasizes the importance of
American neutrality, and on the other, the impossibility of
maintaining such a stance. These contradictions are also
hinted at by the number of times the President stumbles over
his words in his speech.

After encouraging the public to distinguish between
rumor and fact in reporting, he stumbles in the sentence:
"You must master at the outset a simple but unalterable fact
in modern relations between nations" (149).[5] In garbling the
words "at the outset" and being forced to repeat them, he
undercuts the ability of mastering the simplicity, for such a
simplicity is not so easily stated. The following sentence,
"When peace has been broken anywhere, the peace of all

countries everywhere is in danger," underscores the message of impending chaos. He pauses after the word "everywhere," lowers his voice to say the phrase "is in danger." Thus, the pledge of neutrality causes trepidation even in the way it is spoken. It is tentative, and this is indicated through the breakdown of the fluency of words. Neutrality is a contradictory position, formally as well as in content. Even words are taking sides.

Although Roosevelt is trumpeted for the rhetorical mastery of his speeches, they are certainly not without vocal stumbling and mispronunciations that cause him to repeat his words or to veer from his prepared text. In addition to the mistake mentioned above, Roosevelt garbles his words in the contradictory passage: "I myself cannot and do not prophesy the course of events abroad—and the reason is that, because I have of necessity such a complete picture of what is going on in every part of the world, that I do not dare to do so" (151).

He stumbles over the words "and the reason is that" and is forced to repeat them, undermining the message in this complicated sentence. While acknowledging his inability to predict world events, he stresses that this is because "he has a complete picture" of the world. Rather than constructing a "word-picture" for the audience, he alludes to the visualization of a crisis to which he alone has access. Within the radio address, he is referring to a tactical knowledge that he cannot provide here. Furthermore, this knowledge, borne of the necessity of a world leader, provides no template for the future. Yet this proximity to the world scene does provide the ability to see these events in a way that his audience cannot, as an anchoring device amidst the chaos. He is a reporter as well as a president.

Yet in stumbling over words, he lets loose an anxiousness into the airwaves. His words may claim to master uncertainty, but the ways in which the words are spoken undermine this attempt. Acknowledging chaos, he offers his voice, a voice that sees, as order. This offering is double-edged and not entirely reassuring: it becomes a trustworthy, eyewitnessing voice, closest to all arenas of wars (but for now still neutral). The president becomes a radiovoice that resounds like a reporter who narrates and who will survive. As a reporter, he tells stories of himself as hero. As a mediated president, he appears to have an impact on both the media and international arena even as he insists that chaos is everywhere. Thus, this tactic of ruling is not reassuring per se; rather, it disseminates panic at the same moment that it offers the voice of the leader as the person who can reshape the chaos into a semblance of order.

Through his radiovoice, Roosevelt transmits an image of himself without handicap, an image that is omniscient—equipped with a superior knowledge that he can transmit via speech. He confesses this omniscience in the speech on "Democracy, Justice and Freedom" when he utters: "I can hear your unspoken wonder as to where we are headed in this troubled world" (Roosevelt 1995). Roosevelt thus implies that he can intercept the concerns of his people, not only through listening to their utterances, but because he has access to their "hopes and fears" that are not yet stated. If he has a reassuring presence, then he also has access to the interiority of his citizenry.

Some of this access can be discerned in the thousands of letters written to Roosevelt after his addresses. These letters, many included in *Down and Out in the Great Depression* (McElvaine 1983), show that the writers felt close to the president. They also indicate that due to the economic times and Roosevelt's perceived power via his presentations on radio, listeners felt that the president was able to understand and help them. Yet McElvaine suggests that even in the most laudatory letters–some writers wrote verse praising the president as a saint–there "are occasional hints that faith in the president may not have been bottomless" (218). Many letters show a sense of betrayal by someone they trusted. For example, in one letter the writer reluctantly expresses his dismay in not being included in the economic recovery:

> I hope you dont [*sic*] think I am rude in writing you this letter but I just could not my self[.] I just had to do this[.] I want you to know the I wouldent do the slightest thing in the world to hurt your feelings I am one of you greatest admirers but things are so bad everywhere, People dont have the wherewith to procure the necessities of Life we are just slaves and how we hoped and trusted that Mr Roosevelt would be another Lincoln and free us from the slavery that we in today but sorry to say he wants to Build huge Buildings Highways. (quoted in McElvaine 1983:208)

In this letter the writer moves from speaking in the first person ("I") to referring to the "people" and using the first person plural "we." He also uses "you" to address the president at first, but then changes this perspective and refers to Roosevelt as "he." This shifting of pronouns is a major characteristic of letters to the president.

In her study of listeners' letters to the president after the first Fireside Chat, Joy Hayes notes distinct features in their missives (1995). Looking at 803 letters, she was able to divide them into four categories related to their use of pronouns: "I-only," "We-local," "They-national," and "We-national." In the first category, writers referred only to their own particular situation and reactions. Hayes notes that these come from social elites (239) and identified with the president; often these writers comment on his vocal style.

The "We-local" group, making up 18 percent of all letters, presented themselves as part of a distinct social or geographical group. The "They-national" group identified a national group and would use "we" but didn't always include themselves as part of this group. The "We-national" group, however "presented themselves as members of the 'American people' and used 'we' or 'us' to characterize their belonging to or identification with this group" (243). These letters suggest that the American people were unsure how to address themselves as a group in relation to the president. One letter quoted in Hayes's study clearly shows this tendency: "I hope you will continue to come to *us* that way [over the radio], very often. It will do much to restore the confidence of *the American people,* in the future" (243). Another letter included in Hayes's study, which also displays this confusion, reads: "The *people* are behind you. If you need it, go to *them* often for support. Give *us* more radio talks" (243; italics in Hayes's transcriptions).

This shifting of pronouns and use of a variety of ways to describe both the people and the president reveals a confusion about the nation as an abstract and an actual entity. Also it shows that the letter writers, even when approving of their president, are unsure whether to speak to him formally or informally. If the Fireside Chats served to unite the people and to give them hope, in writing to the president, some citizens also reveal their own complicated response to the presidential voice. The listeners' letters are a confession of an ambivalence, even when they are laudatory.

In the logic of his speech of 3 September 1939, Roosevelt can control neither world events nor domestic recovery unless he has the cooperation of the American people–and even then, he is subject to the encroaching conflicts abroad or to the whims of labor or corporate leaders. He does not attempt to hide this; instead, he portrays this scenario as a way to secure power behind him. He asks for trust but alerts listeners to the world stage and insists on his prominence backstage in pushing players on and off the stage. In this performance, another body is generated.

Roosevelt's second and nonhandicapped body is a leaderly corporeality produced by media. This leaderly corporeality serves to conceal his actual body. The second body's voice, and not the actual one, is the one that is heard over the airwaves. The voice is a narrating one. This media body that speaks is unlike the body of the eyewitness; it does not actually exist. It is also unlike he Shadow's body, which loses its corporeality completely and dissipates into voice alone when lurking in the mind of the antagonist. Roosevelt's radiovoice creates an illusion in sound.

The illusion of a second body created by Roosevelt's radiovoice is not a complete, perfect carnality without crease and wrinkle. Some of these flaws become apparent in the instances in which he stumbles over his words, indicating that his fluency is not without impediments. Historians and commentators on his radio speeches do not refer to these flaws in their accounts. Instead, Roosevelt is defined as the consummate oratorical president who is in control of the airwaves and whose fireside chats are warm, persuasive, and reassuring. My argument is that these sporadic and almost rare flaws are also part of the operation of these speeches. Any anxiousness caused by any momentary hiccuping of words is responded to by Roosevelt's continual assertion, not only in content but in form, that he has access to an understanding of the world that, in fact, he can neither transform nor control. Nevertheless, his voice and his words are needed for survival. These words need to be listened to by the citizenry in order to ensure the future.

Furthermore, listening to the president on the radio becomes a crucial, patriotic act where the citizenry learns that the president seems to be listening in to their concerns. This two-way narrowcast may be comforting, but it also resounds with the more grandiose aspects of the ruler as explored by Canetti's paranoiac, who is alert to all plots and thoughts about him (1963:411–64). Roosevelt's intelligence and his more perfect body is augmented by his use of radio. He seems to hear the shortwave transmissions of his people before his people have sent these transmissions to him, or before he has read their letters to him. Through his second body and its radiovoice, he is in virtual touch with his citizenry.

The President's Mediated Body

In *The Portrait of the King* (1988), Louis Marin elaborates the essential role that representations of the king play in giving him the ability to present his power as monarch:

> The king is only truly king, that is, monarch, in images. They are his real presence. A belief in the effectiveness and operativeness of his iconic signs is obligatory, or else the monarch is emptied of all his substance through lack of transubstantiation, and only simulacrum is left; but, inversely, because his signs are the royal reality, the being and substance of the prince, this belief is necessarily demanded by the signs themselves. (8)

Louis XIV rules via images, for it is these images that make him appear within his kingdom as King. These images for

Marin are "a representation of power" within his discussion of the monarch that emphasizes how powerful representational systems are when such systems are coherent and seemingly complete (7). Portraiture of the king does not represent the king, but these images *produce* the king and represent the monarch's power. For Marin, "power and representation share the same nature" (6); and power means "to be capable of force," while representation puts "force in signs" and "signifies force in legal discourse" (6).

Marin considers power as a state of being whose ontology is force.[6] Magisterial power suggests that the leader has access to force even when he does not expend it. Force is transformed by the representational framework into a pose, and force becomes a show of potential. This display enters into a sign system where force does not operate per se but is always held in reserve, discernible in the omnipresence of the monarch. During the reign of Louis XIV, this sign system tends toward the visual. The figure of the monarch is repeated in portraiture. These multiple images are also him; they portray his kingly force.

President Roosevelt used his radiovoice to represent himself as President, an entity different than just elected leader. The President existed, as representation, within the sign systems produced via the radio. Through the medium of radio, Roosevelt elaborates an image of himself, equipped with knowledge, as a representation that elaborates and produces a space on the air. In other words, a radiobody emerges.

This radiobody may not exist as material corporeality, but as a specter it makes an appearance via the medium. It appears as protagonist, as actor with agency, in a narrative that self-generates, making order out of chaos that exists outside and inside the ether. Hearing the voice of the President does not mean attaching this voice to the body of the man Franklin Delano Roosevelt. Once they enter the nexus of the radio, radiovoices have a certain autonomy from the body that has uttered the words. In Marin's terms, radiovoices are representations of power, signifying the force of the Leader to be present through all radio receivers. If, as Marin argues, "the portrait of the king is the king," then the radiovoice of the president is the President.

Gregory Whitehead writes in the article "Radio Art Le Mômo: Gas Leaks, Shock Needles and Death Rattles" (1990/91):

> Radiowaves turn up the juice on the oral vocal body due mostly to the misplaced and Unnameable identity of radio-phonic space. Radiophonic space defines a nobody synapse between (at least) two nervous systems. Jumping the gap requires a high voltage jolt that permits the electronic release of the voice, allowing each utterance to vibrate with all others, parole en liberté. Or, as fully autonomous radiobodies are shocked out of their own skins, they can finally come into their own. (141)

For Whitehead, bodies cease to exist in radiophonic space; the moment of vocal transmission into the microphone severs the voice of the speaker from the speaker's corporeality. Whereas this separation of voice and body occurs with every speech act, when the speaker projects into a microphone, sounds travel into another network completely. Radiobodies reside and travel in, and resound from, this realm.

The listener, then, is hearing voices cut off from source. One is always listening to radio even when one is hearing a particular program, even when one is tuned to the President's frequency. One listens to a radio receiver from which the transmitted voice of the president projects. The radio delimits the appearance of the body of the president; however, it creates a structure whereby the radiobody is made apparent through the voice on the radio, a second body that gives shape to an amorphous medium. The medium becomes the President during the duration of his speech; the president becomes a radiophonic entity.

Dos Passos notes in his parody of the Fireside Chats that Roosevelt always attempts in his narratives to give a sense of place in his utterances. He tells his listeners that he is at the White House, speaking as the President, at his Presidential desk, in proximity to all his advisors, having returned from trips where he has accumulated information to share with his listeners, in control at the switchboards of government, and so forth.[7] (In reality he often remains in his office and rooms, ministered to by his secretary, Miss LeHand–and Eleanor does much of the traveling.) Roosevelt repeats this place of origin almost as a way to safeguard the dissolution of his voice into the media, to emphasize the place of origin of his speaking voice so as to insist that he is not coming from the nonspace of the medium itself.[8] He also repeats his location as a way to ensure that even if he is not apparent to the public as a visual figure, through the medium of radio his projected voice is brought to the multiple homes. This voice is mobile, projects to all corners of the nation, and bears an auditory signature. For Roosevelt, the impulse is to develop a second radiobody, with words attached to speaker, within the medium.

This radiovoice has signature, definition, idiosyncrasy, and imperfection that make it recognizable. This radiovoice, although not omnipotent, is omniscient. Like The Shadow, it is able to listen in to its auditor; through proximity and accumulating intelligence, it has a commanding knowledge of domestic and international crisis (though not the power to end these crises). Indeed, as an everyday epiphenomenon, this radiovoice clues the listener in to the president's second body, a phenomenal media-body: the President.

If in late medieval and baroque ideology the king's second body suggested a divinity affixed to the state, then in American democracy, the leader's second body is an inhabitant of the media. Indeed, the president is the medium: the site of the disembodiment and re-embodiment of the President.

In *The King's Two Bodies,* Kantorowicz bases much of his theory on the commentaries or reports of Edmund Plowden, a jurist during the reign of Elizabeth. Plowden distinguishes between the king's "Body natural" and a "Body politic." The body politic

> is a body that cannot be seen or handled, consisting of Policy and Government, and constituted for the Direction of the People ... and this Body is utterly void of Infancy, and old Age, and other Defects and Imbecilities, which the Body natural is subject to, and for this Cause, what the King does in his Body politic, cannot be invalidated or frustrated by any Disability in his natural body. (quoted in Kantorowicz 1957:7)

Again, I do not attempt to make equivalencies between political theologies of the late Middle Ages, American democracy, and the positioning of the elected president who does not inherit divinity in his title. Yet there are striking correspondences here, relevant to the presidency of Roosevelt and to radio. The body politic is an amorphous body; it does not exist to be observed or felt, since it is not tangible. But as in the portraits of Louis, this body can be represented, powerfully. These representations of the body politic are not simulations of some hidden, obstructed original body. This body is involved in mystical activity, in magisterial movement, and its corporeality is without outline. This second body is capable of force; it is akin to electric energy, a specter with static.

As in the Eucharistic wording "This is my body," it becomes clear that the representations of the political body begin to substitute for the actual body of governance. In this way, a metaphor becomes an equivalence. On air the voice of the president is the President; the listener to the Fireside Chat is hearing the body politic. Relatedly, novelist Eugène Nicole relays how his childhood belief in people living inside his radio was tested when he realized that the characters of a radio drama couldn't be in each radio at the same time. But in the tale, an Old Woman reminds the child: "Like the body of Jesus, while present in each host, is in all the others at the same time" (quoted in Weiss 1996:13). Radio produces the powerful semblance of presence, where each and every radio receiver seems inhabited by traces and remnants of humanity.

Roosevelt's voice on the radio is an instance of the narrating of this body politic, heard but not seen. His radiobody is also a body politic, and in the expression of this body nothing can be "invalidated or frustrated by any Disability in his natural Body." For Roosevelt, his access to a medium to express an invisible political body affords him the ability not to have to hide his handicap. The political body does not compensate for his handicap; rather, it renders the frailties of the natural body unimportant.

Although the king has two bodies, according to Kantorowicz, they form one unit that is indivisible, "each fully contained in the other" (9). The body politic, however, is "more ample and large" and contains more mystical forces that can serve to take away "any Imbecility of [the king's] body natural" (Plowden, quoted in Kantorowicz 1957:10).

The body politic–immortal, mysterious, affixed to divine forces–serves to remove any defects of the natural body, so that the king is always magisterial, at once mortal and divine. The term "Body politic" is used interchangeably with the term "mystical body" in the writings of the medieval jurists (15). Within a monarchy, this suggests that the "fiction of the King's two bodies" serves to align the king's more powerful body with the body of Christ. To emphasize the mysticism within the body politic in the more secular realm of the American presidency serves to return us, not to the body of Christ, but to mediated corporeality.

Radio affords Roosevelt the appearance of mediumistic capabilities. He seems to gain mastery over radio operations through the transmission and receivership of his voice. The President, with a voice that listens in, inhabits radiophonic space with a mystical body that speaks. Whereas this mystical body is annexed to his natural body, this is also the body that rules and has power through its representations. It is a body that is not seen; it is formless but larger than the natural body. Its sounds originate from a presidential office; yet the voice itself resides within the medium.

Consider the phrase "on the radio." When the president is speaking, the technology places his transmitted voice in operation within an amorphous space. He is within a space to which the listener has no access during the duration of his message. The listener is witness to the voice's agency. This voice is not the voice of the president's natural body, not the voice of a radiobody that is "on" the radio but a voice from within radio's operations, a body with mystical abilities. The everyday technology of the radio affords the president power of mystical proportions.

In this aspect, the President is akin to Lamont Cranston's nonvisible body of The Shadow–always able to transmit, always capable of penetrating an interiority, always audible, speaking with the conviction of the state with justice as foundation. Like The Shadow, this voice is already radio: The Shadow can transmit just by producing thoughts; the President's second body already resides within the airwaves, amorphous, but capable of articulation.

This political body, though, articulates conflict and turmoil; it is not merely reassuring and comforting in its argument and its delivery. Its power is almost unfathomable and intangible, and it relies on the ambivalence of the listener to assert its troublesome authority. The political body produces panic and is reliant on this panic to ensure its effectiveness. In listeners' letters to FDR, there are examples of this ambivalence toward relying and trusting a president that is both far away and seemingly near. On one hand, the citizens feel noticed and their needs almost anticipated; on the other, they feel ignored by a president who claims that he is able to listen in.

A Surplus of Listening

In her discussion of the listener's response to early radio, "We May Hear Too Much" (1984), Catherine Covert creates an analogy with grief and assimilation in the popular response to new technology. New communication technologies involve loss: "loss of old behavior, old values, old relationships, old senses of the self" (200). In order to assimilate the new, the uncanniness of radio was given meanings of older practices and objects to compensate for a popular grief. From Marconi to popular reports in the press, radio was experienced and imagined as mediumistic, allied with nineteenth-century practices of spiritualistic endeavors. From its birth, radio was affiliated with the dead. It was enabled not only by technological advancement but also by the more primitive techniques of the deceased, who could use the medium for expression.

Indeed, Gregory Whitehead describes radiophonic space as "a dead nothing" and says that the "life of radio is an after-life" (1989:11). Although Whitehead is writing as a person who has enlisted his voice in service to radio production, there is loss here too–he loses his voice to the microphone.[9] This is never exactly a game of fort-da,[10] because the voice comes back in different form either in headphones or in a recording. Once the voice is cast out, it interacts in another terrain.

Whereas Whitehead is mostly concerned with the event in which his voice enters into this dead terrain, Covert is more concerned with the experience of the listener hearing these dead voices speaking live. Both events of the speaker and auditor, however, involve a sense of loss as part of this generative production process. For Whitehead, the disembodiment is reincarnated as the radiobody; for Covert, "reweaving new patterns of imagination and behavior" was a way for listeners to "encompass radio" in their lives after the medium's disruption of popular consciousness (1984:100). The radio, as new technology, receives meanings and properties from that which it has served to almost replace; analogously, the radiovoice, ripped from a body, receives a new corporeality within its new terrain.

Many media historians argue that there was resistance and ambivalence in the popular response to radio in the 1920s when broadcasting was new. By the late 1920s, the argument goes, radio had become accepted by the populace even as it was hotly debated by governmental, press, educational, and corporate forces. Broadcasting, indeed, had become successfully commercialized, with programming now a flow of shows with designated, scheduled episodes of recognizable, familiar shows and commercials.[11] A reassuring repetition, on one level, had taken place as ownership of facilities and rental of frequencies had become centralized, particularly after the Radio Act of 1927, setting the stage for the Golden Era.

My argument, however, is that the plethora of post-vaudeville, detective, mystery, and adventure programs also always point to the past and often hint at or reveal the more treacherous, deadly cave of radio operations, never entirely escapist because they never completely hide the nature of radio itself. Much of the programming during radio's so-called Golden Era focused on the supernatural, on villainy—and, with *The Shadow*, on the invasive power of the disembodiment itself.[12] The distinctions between popular corporate-sponsored radio and the military's use of radio in surveillance and point-to-point communication are thus not entirely clear.

5

The Case of the "War of the Worlds"

Radio's Double

THE "WAR OF THE WORLDS" BROADCAST, performed by Orson Welles's Mercury Theatre on Halloween Eve 1938, was arguably the most famous broadcast of the twentieth century. Adapted from an H. G. Wells's novel that depicted Martian invaders landing on English soil, this radio version by Howard Koch moved the landing and invasion to New Jersey, where the *Hindenburg* exploded and near the listening area of the New York-based program. Koch's dramatization imitated the form of radio itself by switching from "live band broadcast" to befuddled, yet intrepid reporters in the midst of "conflict," narrating a horrific event. Halfway through the hour-long show, reports of panic reached the Columbia studios as listeners mimicked the frenzied populace in Welles's fictional news bulletins. Psychologist Hadley Cantril writes:

> People all over the United States were praying, crying, fleeing frantically to escape death from the Martians.... Some ran to rescue loved ones. At least six million people heard the

broadcast. At least a million of them were frightened or disturbed. (1966 [1940]:47)

On 31 October and 1 November the *New York Times* reported that hospitals had treated numerous patients for shock and hysteria related to the show. The police reported that in stations in Harlem, Morningside Heights, and Queens, New York, frightened citizens ran in shouting that they had seen enemy planes, had heard the president order evacuations, or had seen poisonous gas coming over the Hudson.[1]

In an apology after the dramatization, Welles explained that the hour-long show was only meant to be the Mercury's way of screaming "Boo" at its audience on Halloween:

> We annihilated the world before your very ears, and utterly destroyed the Columbia Broadcasting System. You will be relieved, I hope, to learn that we didn't mean it, and that both institutions are still open for business. (quoted in Cantril 1966 [1940]:43)

Two days after the show, in a more humbled mood, Welles vowed in a press conference reported by the *New York Times,* never to attempt such a program again ("Radio Listeners in Panic," 31 October 1938, 1, 4). Shortly after the airing of the program, the Federal Communications Commission (FCC) restricted the simulation of news programs within radio dramatizations.[2]

What meanings remain uncovered in this outbreak of mass hysteria? One researcher reports that only 3 percent of the populace believed that the show was an account of a real invasion (Culbert 1976:77), yet many more were panicked into near delusional states by something they considered fake. The broadcast and the responses to it reveal a relationship to radio itself that is related both to radio's intrusiveness and to its intimacy.[3]

During the 1930s, broadcasting structures changed greatly. One of these changes required that listeners believe in the station's ability to move from a report from the field (as in the reporting of the *Hindenburg* disaster), to narratives of recovery and the possibility of peace transmitted from the White House (as in the broadcasting of the Roosevelt's Fireside Chats), to more "escapist" programming that could at any time be interrupted by a reporter from some troubled spot. The site from which the voices emerged varied during this period, with cuts from locale to locale during news broadcasts. This laid the groundwork for the potential to confuse a listening public.

Social scientists and critics have sought to explain the outbreak of panic after the "War of the Worlds."[4] In the social sciences at this time, there was great concern that mass media had a great influence over the citizenry, and theories were developed that implicated media as causing social ills.[5] Also, the effectiveness of propaganda and media witnessed in Europe and the growth of the mass media stateside provoked experts to examine how media influenced behavior, causing conformity as well as rebelliousness.[6]

Rather than focusing on mass hysteria here, I will enlist certain psychiatric writings at the time on delusional misidentification of objects in order to further my discussion of the relationship between radio and listener. In 1923, French psychiatrists Capgras and Reboul-Lachaux treated a 53-year-old woman who believed that the people around her had been replaced by impostors. They diagnosed her as having *"l'illusion des sosies."* The word *sosie* was used by the patient herself and means "the double." It is derived from Greek mythology where in his successful attempt to seduce the married woman Alcmena, Zeus takes the form of her husband Amphitryon, while Mercury impersonates the couple's servant Sosia (the result of this union is Hercules). What Capgras called *"l'illusion des sosies"* was renamed Capgras' syndrome in 1924 by fellow psychiatrists Dupouy and Montassut. Yet their case study did not include an aspect of the syndrome that was an important factor in Capgras's first article. In Capgras's study, the patient also believed that there were doubles of herself working in concert with others to steal her property (Berson 1983).[7]

Discussion of Capgras' syndrome dropped off in the 1940s; however, it has returned to the literature since the late 1970s. Although various authors are not in agreement about whether the syndrome is in fact a symptom of another condition (Berson 1983; Bhatia 1990), they do agree that the syndrome's delusional characteristics are distinct from hallucinations or memory defects or "autoscopic defects" (disorders in self-image) (see Berson 1983). In the last ten years, a new variant of the diagnosis has been discerned: patients report that familiar inanimate objects are replaced by facsimiles (e.g., Abed and Fewtrell 1990; Castillo and Berman 1994; Rastogi 1990). The case report in Abed and Fewtrell (1990), for example, involved a woman who reported that her clothing and most of her crockery and kitchen appliances as well as a road sign outside her door had been replaced by near-identical objects. She reported that once while she was cleaning, the world had become strange to her. She began to study these once-familiar objects. They now had scratches and slight discolorations on them that proved that they were fake. Also her clothing was either tattered or fit differently (915–16).

The dynamics of Capgras' syndrome affords us a new way to look at radio. The "War of the Worlds" broadcast is a simulation of the already-panicked form that radio broadcasting took on in the late 1930s. Radio is akin to a doppelganger in that it replaces actual bodies and voices with radio versions.[8] This conversion is not seamless, and like the women who feels that the familiar world became strange as she cleaned, the listener is not wrong in being deluded by radio.

The *New York Times,* in an editorial on 1 November 1938 titled "Terror by Radio," was quick to pathologize the explosion of panic of "War of the Worlds": "What began as 'entertainment' might readily have ended in disaster. Common sense might have warned the projectors of this broadcast that our people are just recovering from a psychosis brought on by a fear of war" (25). Revealingly, the editorial goes on to blame not only the collective state of the crowd suffering from European news and threats but also the medium of radio itself–and not only Welles's company use of the medium. Radio remains immature and blurs distinctions between fact and fiction, entertainment and advertising:[9]

> Radio is new, but it has adult responsibilities. It has not mastered itself or the material it uses. It does many things which the newspapers learned long ago not to do, such as mixing its news and its advertising. . . . In the broadcast of "The War of the Worlds" blood-curdling fiction was offered in exactly the manner that real news would have been given. . . . Horror for the sake of the thrill has been legitimately exploited on the air. But to disguise it as news, with the deplorable results achieved from coast to coast, underlines the need of careful self-searching in American broadcasting. (25)

The *Times* editorial suggests that the medium can disguise itself by blurring boundaries between just-breaking news and already-existing narrative. Hence, in this view, radio is poised to produce panic. Although the editorialist suggests that radio has "not mastered itself"–the assumption being, of course, that newspapers have mastered their medium–the piece indicates the negative potential of radio that should, in some form, be repressed. This is why the newspaper does not call for reprimanding Welles–for he has only revealed the nature of the beast.

Radio and the Novel:
The Return of the Savage as Alien

In his essay "Wells, Welles and the Martians" (1988), Philip Klass constructs a genealogy of the panic the "War of the Worlds" broadcast produced. His views are in contrast with most social scientists. Instead of blaming the audible warnings of world war and enduring economic instability and the irresponsibility of radio broadcasting for enabling the mass outbreak, Klass argues that the H. G. Wells's novel of 1898, which also enlists a documentary form and is rich with eyewitness accounts, created the kernel of fear that was then transferred to the Welles broadcast: "Wells experimented with innovative ways of attaching reality to fantastic events. . . . He adroitly alternated the names of actual and fictional astronomers and casually referred to early sightings and publications in genuine scientific journals" (48).

Welles did indeed pick up on this strategy from the novel, but Klass does not take into account the differences between reading a physical book of typeset words and listening to a "live" broadcast emanating from unseen bodies. Although Wells's novel is written in the first person, the radio show does not focus on Professor Pierson as a character until after the simulated news program is finished. The radio drama imitates exactly the style of emergency news flashes; it is almost a parody of the eyewitnessing of the *Hindenburg* disaster. As such, the program is spliced and cut up, offering no reassuring opportunity for identification with the voices. It is as much about the terror of radio and the invasion of bodiless voices as about the fear of encroaching world war "anthropomorphized" into Martians.

In the novel, Wells's protagonist acknowledges his own pre-existing alienation after his encounter with the Martians:

> At times I suffer from the strongest sense of detachment from myself and the world about me; I seem to watch it all from the outside, from somewhere inconceivably remote, out of time, out of space, out of the stress and tragedy of it all. (1988 [1898]:26)

No such confessions of fragmentation of self preface the Welles broadcast; this dislocation is performed through the shifting of locale and of voices from ballroom, to newsroom, to airforce airplane, so that the listener no longer "knows" where he is.

Philosophizing on the ontology of the radio, Gregory Whitehead writes in "Out of the Dark":

> Incorporating the promise of universal communication bound together with the more immediate prospect of irreversible decay, the radiobody is a composite of opposites: speaking to everyone abstractly and to no one in particular; ubiquitous but fading without a trace; forever crossing boundaries but with uncertain destination; capable of the most intimate communion and the most sudden destruction. Radio is a medium voiced by multiple personalities. (1992:257)

Broadcast radio is made suspenseful by the potential for danger and by the appearance and disappearance of voices and characters. It allows the private ear a listening device to unvisited terrain–terrain that is experienced only in fragments, in sound bytes. At any moment all during *The Lone Ranger, The Green Hornet, Roy Rogers in the 21st Century, The Shadow,* or any other programs of adventure during the late 1930s, the show could be interrupted for a commentator to narrate a real disaster, war, or explosion. By moving the tale to the radio, Welles is already installing another kind of suspense. On the air, the possibility that the program will be interrupted by the reporting of a declaration of war, an industrial explosion, or the sinking of a passenger ship is a factor that threatens "communion" with "destruction"–to use Whitehead's words.

Broadcast radio inherited this tendency to seek out calamity from its amateur and naval ancestors: the endless quest to locate distress calls and become the first to alert the world to a sinking ship was an endeavor in which many amateurs indulged. Ever since the medium's first point-to-point, Morse-coded transmissions, radio has been caught up in disaster–not only because it transmits news of the event but because the event of radio itself places the user on the precipice of disaster. Welles's program suggests that radio itself is a disaster area.[10]

For H. G. Wells, the Martian attack is, in part, divine retribution for the excesses and cruelty of English imperialism. In the first pages of the novel, his protagonist reminds the reader of the legacy of colonialism:

> The Tasmanians, in spite of their human likeness, were entirely swept out of existence in a war of extermination waged by European immigrants, in the space of fifty years. Are we such apostles of mercy as to complain if the Martians warred in the same spirit? (1988 [1898]:5)

In this way, Wells's narrative, one of the first to be deemed science fiction, is a portrayal of an anxiety of the imperial

Western nation-state. Such a state is both enthralled with and repelled by its own war technology and its advanced industrialization that is fraught with danger and capable of cruelty. In the allegory of this psychic space, the less-advanced and hence defeated Iroquois or Tasmanian returns as a being from outer-space–a Martian perhaps. Such a creature has machines that, unlike our own, do not falter. They kill settlers to these shores as if they were natives of faraway islands, and they kill seemingly without conscience. To a very large extent, science fiction is a genre of this anxiety, and it provokes a fear of the return of the (slaughtered) "primitive," equipped with savage science. This genre is an eschatology of retribution for the guilty Westerner/Christian. Science fiction novels, in this way, are revenge narratives, where the inexplicable hostility of the nonearthly invaders is recognizable in the shadow of the histories of European expansion.

Relatedly, John Broughtman, discussing the communication of missiles in "The Bomb's Eye View" (1996), notes that the "chief" smart bomb used in the Gulf War was named the Tomahawk–"a Freudian slip revealing and reviving primitive fears of alien races" (140). Broughtman also argues, using the name of the weapon as evidence, that "the smart bomb is felt as a threat within the U.S., and especially as a fantasized attack on the white mainstream of the population" (141). The surgical strikes inflicted on the enemy are not, then, so reassuring. The phantasmal massacring primitive returns in the guise of technological warfare. Wells's and Welles's Martians are hostile, mute invaders who speak via the hissing of deathly technology. In other words, they are monsters (or things) of the West, continuing an already-existing narrative.

At the outset of the invasion there is a return of recognizable forces, even though now they are shocking and impossible. An attack of the other-worldly bears the imprint of the worldly. Because of Welles's aliens' relation to Wells's aliens, and because of these creatures' relationship to earlier literary or folk creatures, any entrance of the alien is also a comeback performance. Furthermore, as Wells notes, any haunting refers to the dead and their return. Thus, the appearance of the revenging alien is always a return. In Wells's novel, the aliens are the backwash of imperialist endeavor. In Welles's radio drama, however, the aliens are expunged bodies from the netherworld of radio itself, related more to the expansion of technological networks than to the expansion of empire per se.

These aliens do not speak, but their projectile, fiery missives are reported by the various characters of the radio play. Following Broughtman's lead, I read their use of weaponry as a communicative act. These "utterances" are "a caricature of the way normative communication impinges on the other" and "the trajectories of munitions reinstate–in however abstract, stereotyped, or dangerous a manner–the desire for communicative contact" (1996:146). Welles's aliens are "speaking" via acts of communication that involve destruction but are not only destructive. These speech acts within the frame of the show caricature the invasiveness that radio communications as medium already enacts.

The Radio Broadcast and Ventriloquism

At 8 P.M. Welles began the *Mercury Theatre on the Air* by reading a slightly changed version of the first page of the Wells novel, which speaks of Martian surveillance as if it were a fact. He sets the program a year later, 30 October 1939, a time of economic recovery when the "war scare was over." For listeners who tuned in from the beginning of the show, it is–at least, at first–clear that the program is a dramatization. Welles (or the writer, Howard Koch) sets the narrative frame: "On this particular evening, 30 October, the Crossley service estimate that thirty-two million people were listening in on radios." The drama is thus set as taking place on the radio itself, but in the near future. Welles deems the event "the great disillusionment" and clearly marks it as an event that occurs on radio, not as dramatized by the radio. The radio is the site and subject of the broadcast.

Welles's voice is cut off by the voice of a radio announcer (Announcer One), who comments on the weather, reporting an unrecognizable weather disturbance over Nova Scotia (a hint of the forthcoming Martian landing). This announcer then segues to the Meridian Room in the Park Plaza, where Ramon Raquello's orchestra is introduced. The orchestra plays Spanish music in the style of American big bands. The music, comfortably exotic, is a seamless copy of a live band broadcast at the time; it also plays with the audience's suspense, since reporting of the disturbance over Nova Scotia has now interrupted the program's flow. The two narratives of extraordinary news of import and pleasing dance music are now both set, but one can interrupt the other. Welles has introduced the cut-up transmission of this broadcast, an imitation of radio that is also radio.

The *Mercury Theater on the Air* ran against a program far more popular than itself, *The Charlie McCarthy Show*, which featured the ventriloquist Edgar Bergen and his famous dummy Charlie McCarthy. Ventriloquism may seem like a complicated suspension of disbelief that is more suited to the vaudeville hall than to the radio studio and receiver. The ability to see the ventriloquist disguise the throwing of his voice by not moving his lips is a crucial part of the illusion of the act–as is the talent to hide the activity of the man's hand in manipulating the puppet's body. Yet the "dummy-ness" of the puppet and his straight man are acoustically linked in this vaudevillian show. The audience hears the voices of the dummy and the operator as emerging from the same box. Thus, this depiction of two personalities with matching, distinct voices emerging from one point of origin is, ironically, well-suited to radio.

On radio the speaker into the microphone is always "throwing" his voice; that is, he is giving up his voice to travel via a network so that it appears to derive from another (second) body. The illusion of a sourceless sound is always at play in listening to the radio. The radio receiver, by exten-sion, can be seen as the dummy that speaks. In the home, there is no ventriloquist to be seen.

In his essay "Moving Lips: Cinema as Ventriloquism" (1980), Rick Altman enlists an analogy between sound/image and ventriloquist/dummy. The soundtrack in film is the ventriloquist that "creates the illusion that the words are produced by the dummy/image, whereas in fact the dummy/image is actually created in order to disguise the source of the sound" (67). Sound is thus not secondary in film; rather, it uses "the illusion of subservience to serve its own ends" (67). For radio in the 1930s, with its emphasis on the live broadcast, the source of the sound is always dis-placed from the studio to the antennae, through the ether to the radio receiver. The sound of the show is produced and heard virtually simultaneously; yet its ventriloquist-like jour-ney is unmarked. The show's destination is a multitude of dummys with dials and speakers. Any visualizing done by the listener is provoked by the sound from the dummy-receiver and is done internally, but it will be guided by an unfathomable source of sound: the unseen ventriloquist.

Altman notes that since ancient Greece, the sound of the synchronized dummy is seen as coming from the belly of the ventriloquist. It is not a head-voice; rather, this voice is a body-voice that "reveals hidden truth" (100) less mediated by psychic prohibitions. In Greece, these voices were heard as prophetic;[11] in the United States, they are viewed as comic truth-tellers—and in horror movies, they often become sinister beings who seem to come to life.[12] Nevertheless, the dummy grants license for the ventriloquist to speak what he otherwise might not utter. Indeed, the dummy Charlie McCarthy, speaking in a squeaky voice higher than his ventriloquist, is more cheeky and unguarded than straight man Edgar. And as Altman emphasizes, the dummy voice is a body voice, even as one agrees with the illusion that it comes from that which is not alive. In this way, especially on radio, it can be seen as akin to a doppelganger (a dead copy of a live original) that haunts via electric speech.[13]

The Charlie McCarthy Show (named for the lovable dummy, not the stodgy Edgar Bergen) regularly had ten times as many auditors as did the *Mercury Theater* shows (Cantril 1966:82). Many listeners tuned in to *Mercury Theater* at McCarthy's first break about fifteen minutes into the show, channel-surfing to avoid a train of commercials. As a result, these listeners missed the facts—that the program was a radio adaptation of an H. G. Wells novel, introduced by Orson Welles, since Welles's program was not interrupted by commercials. These interruptions were what listeners used to hearing. In this way, the "dummy" of commercial radio took over–a more sinister Charlie McCarthy, seemingly speaking of his own volition.

The initial musical focus of the "The War of the Worlds" reflects the distribution of programming in 1930s radio: In 1938, 52.5 percent of airtime was devoted to music, and 9.1 percent to drama, 9.8 percent to news and sports (Lazarsfeld 1940:7). It was therefore common to turn on the radio and hear big bands; it was also common in the later 1930s to have this music interrupted by urgent commentator reports from the field. Furthermore, much of the reporting of the *Hindenburg* disaster (not including the "live" eyewitness broadcast, which was a continuous tape) had been fragmented. The space between reports emerging from the field was filled with syrupy orchestrations of popular tunes. These divertissements serve to heighten the horror as the voice of the announcer and commentator is rendered more crucial by its disappearance.

Interrupting Disaster

After the "Ramon Raquello Orchestra" plays a few bars in the broadcast, another voice interrupts the orchestra to bring a special bulletin from a radio entity more global than Columbia Broadcasting, the fictional Intercontinental Radio News. This voice comments on the finding of two professors, Farrell and Pierson, who have observed explosions on the surface of Mars. In an expert imitation of broadcast montage, the announcer returns the auditors to the hotel ballroom where the orchestra strikes up "the ever-popular 'Star Dust.'"[14] This song is quickly stopped as the announcer alerts the listeners to say that the network is going to "take"[15] the audience to the Princeton Observatory but will meanwhile

return to the Raquello orchestra. Announcer Two then introduces Commentator Carl Phillips[16] and Professor Pierson,
who are in a vast observatory. The vastness of the astronomy
building is conveyed to the listener by echo devices. The
voice of Pierson is spoken by Welles, the previous voice of
the dissolving narrator.

Unlike cinema, radio in the 1930s sought to project
sounds as emerging from the same point of origin (Dane
1980). In film "talkies," microphones were placed around
the set and then remixed in order to use effects like voice-
offs and voice-overs, whispers and shouts as opportunities
to elucidate the visual terrain. In radio, voices can't "appear"
from off-stage: they are all center stage. But when reworked
with effects and introduced as originating from a site that is
not the studio, they can resound as if on different planes,
from far away. Distance and locale have to be verbally
announced or devised in the studio in order to be sonically
believed, for the sound is always coming from the speaker
inside the wireless's box. Otherwise, there is no reason to
believe that the broadcast has ever left the Park Plaza ballroom. Reporters have to identify themselves, then identify
their location; listeners make the choice to believe their proximity and names.

In the late summer and fall of 1938, listeners heard about
diplomatic efforts in Munich, with Chamberlain and Dal-
adier buying "peace in our time" from Hitler at the expense
of Czechoslovakian national autonomy. The crisis of imminent war in Europe was brought to the American people
through live broadcasts and simultaneous hookups in four
European cities. These broadcasts had high ratings, and
there was much anxiousness caused by the live broadcast-

ing of world events. As we have recounted, the *Hindenburg* landing, which was meant to be a triumphant show of technology, was recounted live by a horrified reporter who at one point lost his ability to speak. The disaster also revealed international tensions between America and Germany concerning the American monopoly over the use of helium, forcing the German ships to use highly flammable gas. This tension presaged the sense of war erupting in Europe.

Radio researchers Cantril (1966 [1940]) and Lazarsfeld (1940) both cite numerous surveys that indicated that news programs were the most popular programs among the more than 20 million people that made up the listening public–across all examined demographics of gender, education, and age (notably race and ethnicity were not noted in these surveys). Of course, to say that these were the most "popular" programs is misleading: economic recovery was slow, and Europe was nearing war. Keeping up with current events did not necessarily produce enjoyment but ensured a maintenance of fear toward potential enemies within a domestic situation with a still-weak economy.[17]

Walter Benjamin suggests in the essay "Theses on the Philosophy of History" that "the tradition of the oppressed teaches us that the 'state of emergency' is not the exception but the rule" (1969:257). The radio produces a space where this state of emergency can always be tuned into, where the Emergency Broadcast System is ever ready to play its beeping test.[18] The government, in a flash, is able to take over the airwaves to provide instructions for an emergency or an attack.

Following upon Benjamin's insights, an outbreak of panic blamed on contemporaneous emergencies implicates and involves the tensions and repressions of the past. Also, it always implicates the medium that places the event into a news story. Radio, whose transmission runs along chrono-logical time and is legally bound to announce the hour (always already a clock-radio), also repeats itself according to a schedule. Yet this repetition can work to heighten suspense.

The Welles broadcast simulates cuts from the studio and the observatory to the site of the landing in Grover Mills (near Princeton, New Jersey). These cuts are interspersed by visits to the ballroom to allow for travel time for experts Pierson and Commentator Phillips (who explain to the listener that they traveled the ten miles in ten minutes).

The character of Phillips, in strange exhilaration, exclaims to the audience: "I hardly know where to begin, to paint for you a word picture of the strange scene before my eyes, like something out of a modern Arabian Nights!" (WW 11). He confesses to the paradox of witnessing on radio during the age of cinema; auditors denied sight of an event rely on the details of the visual via sound, through speech or "word pictures."

As discussed in Chapter 3, in May 1937, listeners had heard an eyewitness account of the explosion of the *Hindenburg* in New Jersey. The announcer had relayed the bursting of the zeppelin into flames through his own admissions of unspeakable horror, without entirely abandoning discernible words: he kept doing his job. Immediately, he estimated that the explosion caused "400 to 500 foot flames" and recognized that the death of all 97 passengers was "one of the worst catastrophes of humanity": he contextualized the event for the public. In this way, the show brought disaster to listeners' homes via simultaneous narration. Whereas the instantaneous story of the disaster was explained, the focus of the narration was to transmit the visual details of the event.

The entrance of the Martian is preceded by the unscrewing of the top of the cylinder in which the entity is encased.

The listener hears this metallic sound as well as the fearful comments of citizenry assembled in the field. Mixed in are voices of witnesses announcing that the top of the cylinder is unscrewing. Then we hear sounds of the crowd arguing with policemen. A hissing sound occurs fifteen minutes into the program–the moment when many listeners are joining in to avoid the commercials of *The Charlie McCarthy Show.* This audience is tuning in just at the moment of the monster's appearance. They hear the sound of a noisy, fearful crowd in mid-panic as the lid to the Martian spaceship is being unscrewed.

After the top of the cylinder is heard clanking to the ground, the voice of Commentator Phillips describes the appearance of the creature. Reciting his lines with a shortness of breath, he speaks of the difficulty of finding words: "It ... it's indescribable. ... I can't find words .." (WW 17). As much as this is a represented encounter with an extraterrestrial, it is a confrontation with what Kant calls "the sublime."[19] It is also a quotation from the reporting of the *Hindenburg* disaster broadcast when absolute wonder turns to unspeakable, stuttering expressions of horror.

In his discussion of the Kantian sublime in relation to the figure of the alien, Michael Beehler remarks that "language's remarks upon its failure to adequately represent the absolutely alien sublime in fact suggest its presence" (1987:31). The commentator's breakdown of language and his confession that words cannot, at least initially, describe the Martian, serve as proof to the listening public that he is not tricking them: the alien exists. Expressions of disbelief and the inability to speak are tantamount to proof of its existence. Located inside the few seconds of dead air (a cardinal sin for radio) in which Phillips scrambles in silence for words, is the ontological origin of the alien. This alien is born in the aphonic (meaning a loss of voice) scream of the ellipsis. Empirical proof of otherworldly existence is found in the breakdown of language, in a delay of linear narrative in a fearful, silent moment. This aphonia suggests the existence of the otherworldly. The repeated admission of the inability to speak is itself also expressive speech that continues the narrative.

After the threat of a pause, the figure of the commentator does indeed find the breathy, shocking words; for he must, like the reporter witnessing the *Hindenburg* disaster, continue to witness: "The eyes are black and gleam like a serpent. The mouth is V-shaped with saliva dripping from its rimless lips that seem to quiver and pulsate. The monster or whatever it is can hardly move" (WW 16). He compares the creature to earthly and familiar objects: serpent, the letter "V," saliva, lips. He gives a word-picture for the listener to imagine.

When the commentator retreats from the cylinder, the broadcast returns to the studio while he relocates. For about ten seconds, the audience hears the lush sounds of a piano. When the show returns "to the field," Phillips queries whether he is transmitting or is speaking only to himself. He continues to witness for the listeners, but now his voice is calm and determined, filled with duty: "From here I get a sweep of the whole scene. I'll give you every detail as long as I can talk. As long as I can see. More state police have arrived. They're drawing up a cordon in front of the pit, about thirty of them" (WW 17).

He is obligated to provide images, to enable six million "private ears" access to a scene beyond their conception. Dramatically, this is the moment of suspense when it seems as if the threat might be gone. Yet in a minute the Martian arises again, holding a mirror. A weapon fired by the creature, "a jet of flame springing from that mirror" (WW 18), attacks the assembled crowd. The mirror-weapon is not held up to the earthlings; they are denied an actual reflection of themselves or of the monsters in it. Instead, the bystanders/eyewitnesses see an image of a murderous flame. Over screams and shrieks, Phillips announces the trajectory of the flames, even as it moves in on him. When the microphone crashes, there is dead silence, signifying his death.

Gregory Whitehead announces that radio is a "necropolis," filled with voices "articulated by the corpses of advanced telecommunications equipment" (1991:87). This simulated broadcast is swept up in the horrific exhilaration, alive for the listener, laying bare the haunting of the radio by voices thrown into the radio. The moments of silent "dead air" are the seconds of a horror-inducing cacophony in which the narrating voice might disappear, replaced by static. Notions of liveness and the threat of death commingle, causing confusion.

The vocal projections of Commentator Phillips, determined to provide the important details, are prevalent during the initial part of the broadcast as a brave, clear speech against the noise of the audible Martian. The audience was prepped to mourn his departure in a form of tragic identification with the provider of commentary, for he was a hero committed to speaking to his audience, to giving them word-pictures.

After the silence of Commentator Phillips's death, the broadcast continues with the voice of Announcer Two, originating from the studio, saying calmly, "Evidently there's some difficulty in our field transmission" (WW 18). Again the broadcast goes to the piano interlude, then cuts back to Announcer Two, who announces Brigadier General Montgomery Smith.

He speaks matter-of-factly about the institution of martial law in the area around Grovers Mill. Following his announcement, the program returns to the announcer, who learns, while speaking, that communication has been re-established with a survivor of the Grover Mills attack—Professor Pierson. Another dead silence ensues, and then he reintroduces the professor. Pierson offers an explanation of the weapon of the Martians:

> They are able to generate an intense heat in a chamber of practically absolute nonconductivity. This intense heat they project in a parallel beam against any object they choose, by mean of a polished parabolic mirror of unknown composition, much as the mirror of a lighthouse projects a beam of light. (WW 20)

Naming the weapons "heat-rays," he acknowledges that these invaders' weapons indicate that they have scientific knowledge far in advance of "our own."

Announcer Two cuts off Pierson to inform the audience that the burned body of Commentator Phillips has been identified in a hospital and that, even so, reports from Grovers Mill suggest that the situation is now under control. He is then interrupted by Harry McDonald, vice president in charge of operations. McDonald states that the state militia has requested that the entire station be placed at their disposal; he is turning over the station's facilities to the militia. In this sequence, the show's simulation moves rapidly from voice to voice, allowing each speaker only a few words. Pauses are placed between each announcer and commentator, and the show travels rapidly from Phillips's death to the take-over by the military of the station's operations. From this point on, there are no more musical interludes. Instead, the listener only has the opportunity to listen in to the simulation of mil-

itary missives and directives from different points of operation until the broadcast returns again to the station's head-
quarters in New York. Welles's transition at this point from
private station to the military broadcast is crucial. It suggests
that something like the Emergency Broadcast System has
taken over, and the emergency is now upon the listener.

Simulated Military Operations on the Air

Within the narrative of the show, the station is now in the
hands of the military—and for listeners who have tuned into
the show late, there may be no framing of the story. This
begins the second part of the broadcast. Captain Lansing of
the militia announces himself and attempts to calm down the
audience by describing this military operation as less threatening than a routine one. Yet as he surveys the scene, he
erupts into exclamation as he sees "a shield-like affair" rising out of the Martian vessel, supported by a tripod. Excited
and audibly scared, he yells to the audience to "Hold on!"
(WW 22).

At twenty-five minutes into the broadcast, the voice of
Announcer Two returns. He reports that the military has lost
its battle in Grover Mills. Only 120 of 7,000 men have sur-
vived. The Martians have cut down communication lines
from Pennsylvania to the ocean. The announcer speaks in a
grave, slow, matter-of-fact way, yet remains dedicated to conveying the import of the information. He introduces the Secretary of the Interior, speaking from Washington. The secretary sounds very much like President Roosevelt, using a
broad "a" and adding a syllable with the final "r" and "e"
(they-ah for "there"). Reassuring the audience that the
enemy is confined to a small area of the country, he urges

the citizenry to continue the "performance of our duties, each and every one of us, so that we may confront this destructive adversary with a nation united, courageous, and consecrated to the preservation of human supremacy on this earth" (23–24). Not only does this voice sound like the president, but its recommendations are reminiscent of those of Roosevelt. As Roosevelt might say, the cooperation of the people is crucial for the success of governmental policy.

The structure of this segment of the broadcast also imitates radio news as the program switches from commentator or official in the field to announcer in the station. It uses a series of short segments from a variety of locales, and speakers and vocal tones that do not necessarily create a seamless or consistent treatment of the event (a structure characteristic of television news). For example, the announcer in the studio speaks directly after the Secretary of the Interior; he speaks faster, in staccato fashion, and his words undercut the official's plea for calm. The announcer relays that other Martian advances around the country have been witnessed. In a halting voice that picks up pace at the beginning of each sentence and then drops off, in contrast to the measured pace of the secretary, he remains determined to transmit information:

> Although advancing at express-train speed, invaders pick their way carefully. They seem to be making conscious effort to avoid destruction of cities and countryside. However, they stop to uproot power lines, bridges, and railroad tracks. Their apparent objective is to crush resistance, paralyze communication, and disorganize human society. (WW 24)

The Martians have focused in on the communication and transportation networks of the country; thus, they have jeopardized the working of the radio system and put at risk the flow of information in the invaded nation. The announcer transfers the broadcast over again to the military after an unbearable silence of 10 seconds; this time to the Office of the 22nd Field Artillery preparing for attack. With this, the audience begins to listen in to the tactical operations of the Air Force and will be subject to information and orders it can not quite understand.

At thirty-two minutes into the broadcast, the action moves to an air force plane where an officer and his gunner are about to attack the Martians. They speak in military short-hand and are successful in wounding one of the Martian tripods, but Martian gas moves in on them. They explode into coughs, and the sound of an engine failing fills the sound-scape. The broadcast switches to the commander of an army bombing plane, self-named as "V-8-43." With halting excitement, he describes the march of the Martians toward New York City and the squadron's approach to the enemy tripods. As the Martians attack his ship with flame, he continues his narrative (like Commentator Phillips). He relays his final attempt to attack the enemy. His voice falls off into silence, continuing to be audible until his demise.

Apart from its broadcasting use, radio was most actively used by the military for communication purposes in both wartime and peacetime. During World War I the U.S. Navy in fact recruited many of the same amateur radio users that they had previously tried to chase off the airwaves. By 1936 the number of radiomen in the U.S. Navy reached 4,000; 2,500 had been amateur radio broadcasters (Woods 1974: 231). The military, like the emerging broadcasting corporations, provided job opportunities for radio technicians.

After the sinking of the *Titanic*, Congress mandated that all vessels, including naval vessels have their radios sets tuned on at all times. They became part of a system that required a central command to help navigate the air and sea. This entire system ran independently of the broadcasting system on wave lengths unknown to most listeners except those intrepid enough to penetrate military and shortwave frequencies. By the mid-1930s this communication system became quite complex, for it had to link up and coordinate the movement of amphibious operations–the advance of land, sea, and air forces.

The role played by radio in being able to arrange the movements of diverse troops, fleets, and squadrons allowed for the possibility of imagining such military campaigns. These transmissions–and the tactics of these transmissions–were kept very separate from other uses of radio. Before World War I, the radio was used by both military and nonmilitary primarily for point-to-point transmission; postwar uses became more similar to what one describes as broadcasting. In the military, radio functioned as a way to communicate between battalions and squadrons but also as a way to keep those communications separate from the public and unknown to the enemy. Welles, in representing the banter between airforce flyers, is playing with these secretive codes, having his air force men use encoded speech as communiqué but then, when the scene develops, as a request for contact with anyone. The broadcast layer of radio has been peeled back to reveal military communication under the surface.

A new voice now emerges in the broadcast, called "Operator One" in the script. It repeats its declarations of location: "This is Bayonne, New Jersey, calling Langham Field...." Then it asks, "Come in, please.... Come, in please...." (29). Another operator responds, his voice equally shortwave-like:

sounding as if it emerges from far away from the microphone, nasal, speaking in abbreviations. It urges Operator
One to speak. Operator One begins his report of the destruction of the eight bombers and states that the enemy is now
discharging smoke "in the direction of . . ." (WW 29). Like
Commentator Phillips, the commander, the officer, and the
gunner, he dies in mid-sentence from the weapon of the
Martians, and the listening audience hears his death.

Operator Three's voice now comes in, proclaiming, "This
is Newark, New Jersey . . ."(WW 29). In the logic of radio
transmission inherited from both amateur and early military
use, the place one speaks from is the name one calls oneself. While stationary, one renames oneself in this shorthand
through one's location on the map; whereas in transit (in an
airplane, for example), one becomes the name of the vehicle (V-8-43). Since the voice is thrown away from the location, the naming of the voice bears a direct relationship to
this original location in an attempt to link it to this specific
place-name rather than to lose it completely to the more
nefarious regions of radiospace. It is the ventriloquist's
attempt at reclaiming the thrown voice.

Operator Three warns the population to evacuate, and
again he relays that the smoke is spreading and moving in.
In this repetition, he too dies on air. Operator Four's voice is
heard, speaking in code: "2X2L . . . calling CQ." After no
response, he sends out a message to another: "2X2L . . . calling 8X3R . . ." (WW 30). His voice sounds like it is affected by
helium, high in register and nasal, but still occupied with the
business of military communication.

Operator Five (8X3R) announces himself to 2X2L, and
2X2L reveals his panic in response to his found companion
on the air: "How's reception? K, please. Where are you 8X3R

... What's the matter? Where are you?" (WW 30). Operator Four's (2X2L) voice trails off to bells ringing, and the announcer at the radio station says that he is "speaking from the roof of Broadcasting Building" (WW 30), once again performing his duty by identifying himself via his locale. The announcer's voice alternates between halting with the horror at the Martian invasion of New York and excitement at the spectacle: "Now the first machine reaches the shore. He stands watching, looking over the city. His steel, cowlish head is even with the skyscrapers. He waits for the others. They rise like a line of new towers on the city's west side" (WW 31).

The Martian machine is given an organic identity: called "he," the machine "waits" and "watches." Its movements have the personality of an animated object like a huge puppet or robot come to life. Whereas the creatures that inhabit this machine are virtually indescribable and unfathomably grotesque, the machine that transports them is recognizable: it has arms and a head. It is a medium—a medium of communication via its weaponry as well as a medium of transportation via its ability to navigate the landscape of country and city. Humans forced to observe and then to fall in its path can understand the media-ontology of this being; the announcer is forced to marvel at its mastery.

The announcer's voice slows, then moves down in pitch to utter, "This is the end now" (WW 31). He sees the smoke move in on him, people jumping into the East River, and after he announces that the smoke is fifty feet away, the audience hears his body drop with a clunk, leaving the body count to five who have "died" on air.

Again, after a long pause of dead air (a decided motif that marks the death of each character), Operator Four (2X2L) announces his presence: "2X2L calling CQ" (WW 31). He repeats this call three times and then asks, "Isn't there anyone on the air? Isn't there anyone on the air? Isn't there anyone ..." (WW 31). He announces his moniker again, and then his voice trails off. At this point in the simulation, there are no bodies on the air. 2X2L becomes a radio-dummy left with no ventriloquist: there are no human hands at the controls to manipulate the broadcast and to provide voices with which to interact.

Tactical communications by 1938 had been completely transformed by telephone, telegraph, and radio—and, of course, by the invention of the airplane. As David Woods indicates in *A History of Tactical Communication Techniques* (1974), in the twentieth century the "battlefield is growing" (257). Emerging communication equipment should become streamlined so as not to interrupt troop movement. Woods refers to the airplane itself as a new communication medium (similar to the way Broughtman refers to the missile's trajectory as a projected speech act). Airplanes signal to those on the ground and to others in the air in certain specific codes. The military tactical communication simulated in this broadcast depicts the loss of mediumnistic mooring from ground-controlled operator voices; 2X2L is lost without the operator—his own missives return to him on air. There is no masterful voice choreographing his flight into formation and the performance of mission. The program serves to peel away the layers of broadcasting. What is revealed is the military encampment that patrols the borders of mass media. This patrol is verbal; it speaks here in its most desperate, battered voice, repeating its strange name of numbers and letters. Then even this voice is gone. In a little more than thirty minutes, Welles has depicted the forced evacuation of the radio networks. He has told the story via sound bytes and a variety of voices that fade, cough, and expire into dead air. With the plaintive cries of 2X2L, Welles has made the system seem unmanned.

After the disappearance of 2X2L, an announcer of the program itself relates: "You are listening to a CBS presentation of Orson Welles and the *Mercury Theater on the Air* in an original dramatization of *War of the Worlds* by H. G. Wells" (WW 32). There is a station identification break, and the musical theme of the show returns. The dramatization returns in another form, with the survivor, Professor Pierson, but the damage has been done. In the twenty minutes since the late audience tuned in to the simulated news broadcast, Welles has exposed the removing of voices from bodies that radio always performs and alerted his audience to the fear of invasion from which it was already suffering.

The Return of the Survivor

The survivor—like the ghostly alien—begins by returning to the narrative. Following the break, the program continues with the voice of Welles. Now he is playing the astronomer, Professor Pierson, who believes he is the sole survivor of the Martian attack. The program no longer imitates the structure of news flashes and interrupted music programs and military operations but returns to the more reasoned form of radio drama. Pierson is similar in tone to the protagonist in the Wells novel: articulate, estranged, questioning. He describes traveling through the devastated and unpeopled landscape toward the city. As one of the few to survive the invasion, his character represents the resilient male valorized by radio adventure series. He encounters another survivor, solemnly, in northern New Jersey. This survivor, who is filled with grandiose schemes to attack the Martians, strikes the more self-possessed Pierson as foolhardy.

Pierson moves on and reaches the city where he sees the decaying bodies of the Martians. In the epilog-like last passage of his interrupted monolog, he relays that the Martians were destroyed, not by human-made weapons, but by airborne bacteria. Back at his observatory in Princeton, New Jersey, with the return of normal society, all has become "strange" to him. The last lines begin anaphorically with the word "strange." He observes the town around him through a window (in the Wells novel, the protagonist views the stars via a telescope) and all is strange: the campus, children playing, people entering the museum where remains of the Martian machine are kept. None of it seems real and verifiable to him. The event of invasion has brought out the estrangement inherent in everyday objects, rendering them as if they have been replaced.

This confession of estrangement occurs in the end of Wells's novel, but it also occurs throughout the book. The novel's Pierson, witnessing the Martians' first attack, does not feel the strangeness until after the heat-rays have subsided—then he realizes that it "left the night about me suddenly dark and unfamiliar" (WW 21). It is not the Martian artillery that is strange, but the everyday, familiar surroundings that seem as if they have now been replaced.

At the close of the novel, Wells writes:

> I go to London and see the busy multitudes in Fleet Street and the Strand, and it comes across my mind that they are but the ghosts of the past, haunting the streets that I have seen silent and wretched, going to and fro, phantasms in a dead city, the mockery of life in a galvanised body. (164)

The life he sees is specter-like. The multitudes are replaced. The originals are gone. Flawed doubles whose bodies are energized by electricity walk the street. Like the patient whose familiar objects were tainted and became strange in a moment while cleaning, Pierson (in both the novel and the radio adaptation) sees humanity taken over by a strange ghostliness of familiar figures. In this way the two treatments of the tale of the "War of the Worlds" are also enactments of the *"l'illusion de sosies,"* where the appearance of estranging impostors is enabled by the fantasy of other-worldly invasion. The heroic survivor of each rendition is left with the vision of uncanny doubles seen through the frame of the window.

The Uncanny Double, the Alien Next Door

Michael Beehler argues in his essay on American alien-ology that in "The 'Uncanny,'" Freud invokes the alien object (as the uncanny, the inexplicable, the foreign, the unfathomable, etc.) but always returns and refers back to the subject man. "In Freud's story of the uncanny," Beehler writes, "all aliens are ideally documentable as the signs and symbols that disclose man to himself. There is no room in the economy of psychoanalysis for aliens who do not repeat the story of anthropos" (29). The concept of the alien for Freud does not exist autonomously but in relation to the human who witnesses it, and the uncanny is but the self in disguise; the uncanny is doomed to the ontology of the double.

As discussed in Chapter 2, Freud's *unheimlich* takes on a before and after story. Early in his essay Freud states: "The 'uncanny' is that class of the terrifying which leads back to something long known to us, once very familiar" (123–24). The shock of the unfamiliar involves repression; it assumes an estrangement from something once known as non-threatening and everyday.

Freud relates this "return" of the once-familiar to the repetition-compulsion in the unconscious that he has just identified in a contemporaneous work, *Beyond the Pleasure Principle* (1961 [1922]). Referring to the fort-da game in Freud's essay, Beehler writes: "Man comes to know and protect his identity by throwing his voice, by projecting and repeating himself in alien form" (29). The child's game is also a series of speech acts. It involves the repetition of the child's voice, which also returns to him like the wooden reel that he throws out over the edge of the cot, out of sight, but still attached to his hand through the medium of string.

Moreover, taking a cue from Beehler's word choice, the child is involved in a radio-like act of ventriloquism by "throwing" his voice. On one hand, the repetition of the accompanying words "fort" and "da" are the child's simultaneous narration of the action. This narration is that which allows Freud to discern the event's inner logic–the action does not exactly speak for itself but requires words. The child is at once reciting and enacting a story through voice and manipulated object. Whereas this event is a compensatory achievement of "an instinct for mastery" (Freud 1961 [1922]:10) over the departure of the mother, the narration of the event can also be seen as a repeated encounter with the strangeness of the child's voice. This strangeness is how the child comes to know himself, how he comes to narrate his attempt at mastery. He throws his voice into the trajectory of a wooden reel that disappears over the precipice of a cot and then returns via his manipulation. His narration is an attempt to transmit his voice into the object, a ventriloquist-like endeavor to animate the toy via voice. His narration is a way to speak in a "body-voice" by redirecting his utterances through the dummy.

The sound of one's own voice, as an assertion of individuation is also a sign (or symptom) of estrangement. Slavoj Žižek writes:

> The moment a living being starts to speak, the medium of its speech (say, voice) is minimally disembodied, in the sense that it seems to originate, not in the material reality of the body that we see, but in some invisible "interiority"–a spoken word is always minimally the voice of a ventriloquist. (2001:440)

It is as if inside the body there is also a radio (or a dummy) that projects voices.

The radio, in this schema, is the housing of the paradox of a demarcated self encountering and producing strange voices. In the "War of the Worlds," the pilot "2X2L" repeatedly sends his voice to seek out the voice of another to acknowledge him. Repeating his name as a way to gain mastery over the situation, he can only hear his own voice come back, revealing its strangeness. Even though no one responds, he keeps on enunciating his moniker to maintain his identity even as he sounds increasingly odd and alone. He is throwing his voice out for no one to hear but himself. This is the nightmare of the radio announcer: to speak though abandoned by the imagined listener, heightening the alien-ness of the transmitted voice.

In the Welles broadcast, the familiar structure of radio returns. But this simulation is an estranging double. However fictional, it is doomed to haunt as fact. In "The 'Uncanny,'" Freud pays particular attention to representational fields where there "are many more means of creating uncanny effects . . . than there are in real life" (1958:158). A storyteller has the benefit of choice: "He can select his world of representation so that it either coincides with the realities we are familiar with or departs from them in what particulars he pleases" (158). In the uncanny narrative of Martians, there is the troublesome commingling of "fact" and geographical actuality. Freud also identifies another mise-en-scène of the uncanny, one that is "produced by effacing the distinction between imagination and reality, such as when something that we have hitherto regarded as imaginary appears before us in reality, or when a symbol takes over the full functions and significance of the thing it symbolizes" (152).

The alien is an example of the menacing double, a doppelganger par excellence, because it does not reflect the human form but anticipates and precedes it (while mimicking earthlings' warring capabilities). In the broadcast, the Martians are treated as unfathomable, virtually indescribable organisms that do not speak. They are believable only through the depictions of their military might, which speaks as if it were a communication medium. For the protagonist, humanity becomes ghostly and robot-like, and the earth itself becomes strange, while the remains of the Martian machines are familiar. The radio, at once ventriloquist and dummy, wooden and electric, commodity and companion-piece, is an ideal place to enact this estrangement.

In explaining the origin of the (double) *unheimlich* in its opposite, *heimlich,* Freud unravels their various meanings in German as well as the words' translations into other languages. One of the meanings of *heimlich* is "homely," meaning related to the home, "also in the sense of a place free from ghostly indulgences" (130). A connotation of *unheimlich* is of a haunting, referring also to a house, but as "unhomely." Freud also realizes that one of the meanings of *heimlich* is laced with anxiousness, a precarious embeddedness: "that which is concealed and kept out of sight" (129). This secretive aspect of the familiar undermines the originality of the unfamiliar; like the ghostly, the alien, its emergence is reemergence. The unfamiliar is a fragment, once unheeded, now blown up to monstrous proportions. Through these definitions, it can be suggested that *unheimlich* might not "originate" from its forerunner, but that both words' connotations are expressed simultaneously even when only one has been enunciated, and that the words' meanings burst from their boundaries.The *unheimlich* is always involved in the origin of its opposite.

Furthermore, framed within the contradictions of this opposition, the radio as an object/commodity of the home, a piece of furniture that can be dusted as if it were a table, resonates with the meanings of unfamiliarity. Possessed by voices, radio is convivial, alive, realistic, illusionary, morbid, generative. At once both unhomely and homely, the radio is an uncanny object without a history of familiarity attached to it.[20] Its unpredictable, secretive "everydayness" coexists with its reassuring strangeness.

6

Echo's Broadcast

Desire and Disembodiment

Introduction

THEORIES ABOUT the experience of sound have a
tendency to perceive sound as gaining a body. Via synesthetic impulses, sound itself moves toward a visible presence.[1] Sound wants to be seen and is often deemed as having materiality. As Mary Louise Hill notes in her discussion
of the female disembodiment in radio, "The voice itself is
the metonymy for the absent body, the object for which the
displaced female voices express a desire" (1996:118). The
corporeality of the voice is the surrogate for the physical
human body.

Roland Barthes (1985) emphasizes the "grain" of sound–
a physicalization suggestive of a material or a texture (e.g.,
the grain in wood). This stress may be a poststructural preoccupation with the "text," a text being a physical entity
denser than sound waves, animated by reading or energized
by "hearing" the voice (of the text, that is, and not necessarily of the writer). Literary critics of very different emphases
and outlooks speak of the text as having a voice, or a writer

developing his voice; likewise, they speak of the "body" of the text. On one hand, written text is ascribed a sound; and on the other, like speech, it is described as having a body.

Importantly, in remarking upon sound as a corpus, one is not referring to a body that is invisible, nor are these sounds images. Rather, they make appearances via sound– a conjuring. That is to say, they are at once phenomena and phantasmagoria. Sound stretches into the visual. Also, sound frames the visual and produces a lens for viewing the framed event. This is perhaps most evident in the use of the voice-over in film.

Kaja Silverman notes in *The Acoustic Mirror* (1988) that in Hollywood cinema, the voice-over–or *acousmêtre,* as Chion calls it–is virtually always male. She describes this disembodiment as maintaining its source in a place apart from the camera, inaccessible to the gaze of either the cinematic apparatus or the viewing subject. It violates the rule of synchronization so absolutely that the voice is left without an identifiable bodily origin. In other words, the voice-over is privileged to the degree that it transcends the body (49). This voice-over presents itself as an "enunciator" or a "metafictional voice" that is the "point of discursive origin" (51). Yet for Silverman, this voice-over can also occupy a space that is extradiegetical or outside the narrative, even as it is the "enunciator" or the "origin." The male voice-over can hold a place that seems outside the story even as it appears to be the engine that drives the narrative.

The female voice in this storytelling technique, however, is not permitted the mobility that invisibility provides. It is always attached to a visible body. When a female voice-over is used, this voice is folded into "an inner textual space, such as a painting, a song-and-dance performance, or a film-within-a-film," says Silverman (1988:56). Female voices are placed inside the story, never attaining a narrativizing distance or able to comment on the visual terrain of the image. Even as such voices may seem to soar above the bodies and landscape of the image, it is always pinned to a particular place in the image.

Amy Lawrence, in *Echo and Narcissus: Women's Voices in Classical Cinema* (1991),[2] argues that in classical film "sound is conflated with the feminine" (111). She writes:

> Sound itself, as a cinematic register, is "feminized," assigned the role of the perpetually supportive "acoustic mirror" [Silverman's term] that reenforces the primacy of the image and of the male gaze. Sound is made to point away from itself and back to the image and the narrative, while woman is made spectacle for the former and recuperated by the later. Both sound and woman, in effect, have been made Echo to a vain and self-absorbed Narcissus. (111)

For Lawrence, sound within cinema is subjugated, as is the placement of women within the narrative. This differs greatly from Altman's theories, which suggest that cinema may in fact be guided by voices in ventriloquial fashion. For Altman (1980), the image is patina-like. One scratches the surface of cinema and hears a radio-like drama ruled by dialog and music with accompanying moving images. In this view, sound is not feminized but given primacy over the image.

Theories of the voice in cinema provide insight into understanding the differing importance of "voice" to all narrative endeavors. For example, finding one's "writerly" voice does not refer to speech; it means one has developed an audible signature. Finding one's voice is to claim a discernible, singular identity, as if the voice were there all along, waiting for the artist to end his search and make a set of metaphorical vocal cords something that can be owned and displayed. Finding one's voice, then, is akin to claiming authority–as if one were speaking in a filmic (male) voice-over, able to narrate–and hence navigate–the visual terrain.

In Hollywood cinema, the preoccupation with attaching filmed body to recorded sound enforces a regime where the female face must speak while being seen. The female character can never enunciate without her body being visible. Silverman points to the bias of the voice-over and its implications for the viewer cinematically: the male voice-over retains expressivity as long as it is freed from a specific visible body; the female voice-over is always tied to an observable body. This configuration disallows female voices a place outside the story. Instead, in Hollywood film this separation and reunification of sound and image forces the female to remain a character and not a narrating entity influencing the story. In her discussions of the disembodied voice-over, Silverman does not call such a cinematic entity a body. For her, the voice-over is more a textual agent than a virtually visible spectacle in and of itself.

Importantly, Silverman resists depicting the maternal voice as a "sonorific envelope,"[3] a depiction that film theorist Michel Chion nuances in his work. In this view, the voice of the female is a potential return for the listener, returning him to the wondrous haze of sound where the infant is not differentiated from that which he hears (for Chion this maternal voice is confining and is that which must be escaped). Silverman deems such a reading of the mother's voice a fantasy that emerges both from psychoanalysis and from film. She sees this fantasy, not as fictive, but as a retroactive trope, "a reading of a situation that is fundamentally irrecoverable" (1988:73). That is to say, the fantasy of the sonorific envelope is applied to experiences of the past only in hindsight, and the original experience of such a child in maternal surround-sound is impossible to recount. It is, however, available for fantasy.

Silverman's distinction is important for approaching the character Echo in the story of Echo and Narcissus. Echo's disembodied voice is not retroactively heard as maternal by its auditor. Her repetitions fill up space but provide no envelope for Narcissus. Rather, Narcissus rejects her sound-body. Echo is held inside the story even as she also maintains a place outside as a narrator by parroting his speech. Yet ultimately, the telling of the tale is in the hands of the writer Ovid and those who use Echo as a symbolic force in their own work, who pin her to the body she no longer has.

Echo's Narcissus

In Ovid's *Metamorphoses*, the myth of Narcissus is actually the story of Narcissus and Echo. A fragment of this tale of asymmetric and unrequited loves has become paradigmatic for modern psychoanalysis. The name Narcissus has become an adjective, a noun, and indeed a key word for popular pathologizing of an entire era or genre (e.g., texts as diverse as *The Culture of Narcissism* by C. Lasch [1979] and *The Pastoral Narcissus* by C. Zimmerman [1994]).

Unlike Narcissus, Echo has come to signify an acoustical phenomenon and not a psychological stage. Oddly enough, she transcends the tale and is conceptual, whereas Narcissus remains a character and a possible pathology. Echo, in contrast, has served as inspiration for poets and is deemed a literary device that refers back to the work of a predecessor or to another time (see Hollander 1981). Yet if Echo is reinstated into the narrative, the story may be read as an articulation of the polylogue or drama between voice, body, and image. This articulation has important ramifications for the reception of radio and serves as a model for the involvement of the witnessing narrator with the event. In this way, the tale of Echo is also contemporary.[4]

Before Echo stumbles upon Narcissus in the forest, the nymph has raised the ire of Juno (Hera), wife of Jove (Zeus or Jupiter) by engaging Juno in endless conversations while she was attempting to catch Jove during his indiscretions with mountain girls. Echo's interruptions lent the girls time to flee Jove and take cover from Juno. Realizing Echo's game, Juno becomes furious. She deprives Echo of the ability to initiate conversation. Instead, as Ovid writes, Echo "retains the last sounds that she hears and says them back again to those around her" (96). Thus, she can only repeat the tail end of another's speech.

Yet this punishment for wordiness also serves to give the speaker/listener a sound bite. It encapsulates what has just been said and witnesses the original speech act itself. It is proof of the projections of utterance. Echo is a reporter or a gossip columnist. But her repetition of heard words also renders them uncanny. For example, she turns Narcissus's expressions of disgust into declarations of love. When he pronounces to Echo, "May I die before I give you power o'er me," she confesses her situation in repeating his words, "I give you power o'er me." Repetition affords her expressivity as well as the ability to confess her desire and also her vulnerability.

Echo is still in corporeal form when she encounters Narcissus. Following him in the forest, she longs to entice him with her poetry. However, her attempts at seduction can only take the form of parroting his own words and then only after he has spoken. Both know nothing of the curse on Narcissus. A young man who was also rejected by Narcissus had once uttered these words: "O may he love himself alone . . . and yet fail in that great love." These vengeful words, heard by Nemesis, become Narcissus's fate. Echo can not steer Narcissus away from his destiny through her declarations of desire.

Narcissus senses Echo following him and calls out; Echo mimics his short sentences. Significantly, even before Narcissus fails to recognize the image in the pool as at once an image and an image of himself, he fails to hear her words as also a rendition of his own speech, or a reflection in sound. He does not recognize himself in her words; his speech is made other by hearing it again in another vocal register. That is to say, Narcissus's interaction with self-hearing in the story precedes his attempt at self-seeing, although it is Narcissus's gaze that has come to fascinate psychoanalysts. Echo's voice is the voice of the other even as it is a voice that reverberates in a space of narcissistic interiority.

Narcissus is at first intrigued by this voice, although he fails to recognize the words. The voice repeats "here let us meet." Yet the word that Echo repeats, *coeamus,* has a double meaning: it also means "let us copulate" (Loewenstein 1984:54). An expectant Echo catches up with him and starts to embrace him. Instead of responding to her amorous overtures, he flees, shouting, "May he die, before . . ." Echo turns her face away, and in a cave her body becomes a "shade," then "a sheet of air," then "bones"; and finally her body is metamorphosed into rock. Without corporeal form, though, Echo remains a voice–a voice with a noisy body.

Ovid's story suggests a relationship between radio listener and radio voice, a relationship that is reliant on the severance of the actual speaking body and the voice. This is what happens to Echo; her body wears away. This transformation is a physical manifestation of the psychic effect of erotic rejection. Her voice, a transmittal of ur-radio waves, remains. This transmittal produces a virtual body of identification and nonidentification. The reader/listener is placed into her position: we too are rejected by Narcissus; yet we think we might be the one to seduce him and thus save him, so we can avoid the painful narration of his demise. Through Echo's placement as spectator–no longer as an actor (her voice continues to see, even though she lacks both face and body)–we watch Narcissus's disastrous transformation into a plant by pummeling his body. Echo's positioning in the tale, as one punished for desire but still articulate, is still a strong alternative to a complete Narcissistic identification, which would be–all tales told–madness.

Theories of Narcissism

In "On Narcissism: An Introduction" (1963[1914]), Freud argues that all humans emerge from a narcissistic position: "We say that the human being has originally two sexual objects: himself and the woman who tends him, and thereby we postulate a primary narcissism in everyone, which may in the long run manifest itself as dominating his object-choice" (69). Some move on to narcissism itself (or secondary narcissism) with its focus on self-love; others move on to object choice (which can be of the narcissistic type). For Freud, the story of love per se is tied intimately with his interpretation of the tale of Narcissus, for choices are always related to these two original sexual objects: the self and the mother. Even in graduating to object-choice, narcissistic impulses affect both of the two types of object-choice.

Homosexuals–who, as the story goes, are more prone to revert to narcissism–take up the subject position of their mother and seek out their former selves in their object-choice. Or, in repelling a homosexual desire, the homosexual reverts to the narcissistic stage as protection against this desired other. Thus, the figure of Narcissus as well as the condition of narcissism remains affiliated with homosexuality. An indulgence in the self and/or an over-identification with the mother serves to mark one as having homosexual tendencies. In this way, Narcissus is always aberrant and yet ordinary. His affliction, however commonplace, is nonetheless worthy of pathology. As we will see, so is Echo's affliction. Each personifies, I argue, a perversion of the senses. These everyday perversions influence twentieth-century media.

Narcissus, who in the tale is desired by many of both genders, may identify with these various desires for him, but he must thwart their seductions because they are threatening to his particular form of self-maintenance. The Freudian theory of narcissism, as Laplanche (1993) defines it, contains three propositions,

> a libidinal investment of the self, a love of the self–a thesis which is anything but surprising; but the libidinal cathexis of self occurs in man necessarily through a libidinal cathexis of the ego, and–the third thesis–this libidinal cathexis of the ego is inseparable from the very constitution of the human ego. (67)

This love of self, while surrounded and sustained by threat, sets up a libidinal involvement in the self that occurs through a libidinal investment in the ego. The love of self operates in a contained manner but is produced via the ego investment. This is a circuitous schema that involves a complicated interiority, requiring fortitude to maintain. The narcissist requires training; he is an athlete of the psyche.

In the essay "Narcissism and the Double" (1971), Otto Rank argues that the double is not only a personification of self-love; it is a way to thwart the inevitability of death (as in Wilde's *The Picture of Dorian Gray* [1890]) and to preserve the integrity of the self against the invasiveness of the other. Allen Weiss argues similarly that (secondary) narcissism "often reveals a search for immortality and the desire for the artist to be his or her own cause, *causa sui*" (1994:76). Narcissus wards off the advances of Echo (heard as other) so as to sustain himself by the seeming permanence of the visual image, an artwork he has that is also a depiction of his double.

In a rendition by Conon that is slightly older than Ovid's, Narcissus is looking for his dead twin sister (see Zimmerman 1994:1–22). It is her image, identical to his, that appears in the reflection. This "alter ego," for which he has renounced all others' desires and which might grant him eternity, is also that which enables his death, even though he searches for this image in order to survive. As Rank states, the double "reappears ... as the messenger of death" (1971:86). Echo reports this trajectory–Narcissus's unconscious movement to his own death via the majestic illusion of the visual image–but is unable to influence his death drive. This drive masquerades as a search for love, or as a desire for reuniting with his double, or twin. The double, which appears as protection against death and neutralizes the power of the nondoubled other (via offering the personification of self-love), is in fact carrying the announcement of an obituary. Echo is unable to intervene in this deathly system of representation and can only report Narcissus's death. Echo's reporting expresses her grief.

In an earlier myth about Echo (and one more popular in antiquity), she rejects the advances of the god of nature Pan (from whence comes the word *panic*). In the poem "A Lesson to Lovers" by Moschus (in Theocritus 1928:459–61), Pan is in ardent pursuit of Echo (see also Loewenstein 1984:23, 24), yet she loves another (who loves another, who in turn loves another). Each persona repeats the words of love to his beloved who then repeats it to one who uses these words for another; love and rejection are expressed via repetition at the same time. Acoustic reflections bounce off the surface of another in unintended directions in this tale about the transmittals of infatuation.

Yet Freud relies heavily on a visual vocabulary in his descriptions of love and narcissism, whereas Ovid juxtaposes sound and visual image in the interplay between Echo and Narcissus. For example, in discussing "narcissistic identification" in the melancholic in "The Libido Theory and Narcissism," Freud writes that the "object has been, as it were, projected onto the ego" (1966:427). Identification is placed as it were within a cinematic apparatus, with the object projected onto the private screening room of the ego. Thus, in the withdrawal of the libido from the object in melancholia, an interior cinema is unreeled, with the beloved object replacing the ego, which is then treated, like the now-hated object, outside the frame. In Freud's "pictorial description," the cinema played out is silent; words convert to picture.

After Echo's loss of body, Narcissus makes an appeal by the pool when the image remains silent to his pleas:

> O may I fall
> Away from my own body—and this is odd
> From any lover's lips—I would my love
> Would go away from me. And now love drains
> My life, look!
>
> (*Metamorphoses*, Book III)

Narcissus, not knowing the precariousness of the "I" when disembodied, pleads for his self to be severed from his body. The love that has at first fascinated him turns quickly tortuous. Unlike Echo, it cannot respond to him in words that repeat the intent of his own sounds. His image takes on more sinister proportions, draining his life, seemingly reprimanding him.

In "Libido Theory and Narcissism" Freud discusses the role of the conscience, or what he calls here the "ego-censor," for the extraordinary disorder of narcissism allows insight into the more ordinary workings of the ego. This ego-censor, able to discern the distance between the actual ego and the ideal ego, also seems to operate as an exterior force, judging and disparaging:

> We believe, therefore, that the patient is betraying a truth to us which is not yet sufficiently appreciated when he complains that he is spied upon and observed at every step he takes and that every one of his thoughts is reported and criticized. His only mistake is in regarding this uncomfortable power as something alien to him and placing it outside himself. (1966:428–29)

Freud emphasizes that this surveillance is akin to a scrutinizing eye, not as an all-hearing ear. This "spy," a double agent for–as well as against–the self, seems to rely on visual equipment even as it seems to "hear" thoughts and criticize them.

Freud's retelling of the narcissistic adventure is based on the banishment of Echo from the tale. With her premature exeunt, the narrative and analysis loses the emphasis on notions of libidinal investment in both sound and visual images. Instead, Freud's retelling and reading focuses more on interior surveillance and the mechanical in the dramaturgy of the (disturbed) psyche.

In "Narcissus: The New Insanity" in *Tales of Love* (1987), Julia Kristeva, in contradistinction to Freud's stress on the image in primary narcissism, writes:

> The ideal identification with the Symbolic upheld by the Other thus activates speech more than image. Doesn't the signifying voice, in the final analysis, shape the visible, hence fantasy? ... Poets have known from time immemorial that music is the language of love, and it has led them to suggest that the yearning captured by the loved beauty is nevertheless transcended–preceded and guided–by the ideal signifier: a sound on the fringe of my being, which transfers me to the place of the Other, astray, beyond meaning, out of sight. (1987:37)

Narcissus's image is silent; he cannot throw his voice ventriloquist-like into the reflection to make it speak, even as he sees its lips move. In addressing his narcissism, there is no voice to "transfer him to the place of the Other"; he has renounced Echo. By this act, he has also renounced the role of auditory identification or, as Kaja Silverman might posit, he does not submit to "the fantasy of the maternal voice" (1988). Narcissus's return to narcissism has expunged the maternal ideal and its voice from his primary narcissism. Narcissus then subtitles his silent movie at the pool in words drenched in disinvestment.

For Kristeva, Narcissus has set up a psychic space in his adventure to find love, and by means of renouncing Echo, he gazes on an image that he does not know he is producing–he projects upon a screen of emptiness. Kristeva writes:

> Narcissus is not located in the objectal or sexual dimension. He does not love youths of either sex, he loves neither man nor women. He Loves, he loves Himself–active and passive, subject and object. Actually Narcissus is not completely without

> object. *The object of Narcissus is psychic space; it is represen-*
> *tation itself, fantasy.* But he does not know it, and he dies. If
> he knew it he would be an intellectual, a creator of specula-
> tive fictions, an artist, writer, psychologist, psychoanalyst. (116;
> italics in the original).

Narcissus, then, is not without object, for the sought-after
object is dispersed into a psychic space of representation.
Narcissus's perversity or "madness" is one of not recogniz-
ing representation and not giving this representation speech.
Discerning the outline of the imaginary double, a madness
of intoxicating spectacle runs amok, not the tragedy of self-
love per se, but the desirability of representation that drains
him of his self-love. For as Rank suggests, self-love always
cloaks the menace of the other in a disguised image of the
self as another. Narcissus's portraiture haunts because it is
neither he nor his twin; visual representation betrays his
adventure in the woods. Though never a chatterbox like
Echo, he is left virtually silent, sighing in grief. His words of
farewell to the image at the pool have little impact save for
Echo's repetition that reverberates around the forest.

Echo's reporting to the forest inhabitants of the death of
Narcissus can help to advance an understanding of the imagination of disaster and its transmission through media. Ever
since the *Hindenburg* disaster and the reporter's emphasis
on being at the scene and speaking from the place of catastrophe to an audience, twentieth-century media and its talking heads have become increasingly involved in the pursuit
of simultaneity and what has come to be called the "live"
broadcast. There is a logic at work here. Since one hears
oneself live without time delay or having to wait for rewind-
ing, the listener should be able to hear the voice of another
simultaneously at the scene, even if it is far away, even if it

is via radio waves, even if it is transported by an echo. The messenger must use the medium in order to transmit at the very moment of the tragic incident. The *Titanic* disaster is in part blamed on the fact that nearby ships did not have their radios turned on to hear the distress calls. Disasters as media events are fixated on the nearness to the deathly and the ability to still transmit from ship to shore to an audience that listens as the narrated event unfolds.[5]

This simultaneity enables a narcissistic-like identification between voice and listener. The radio listener hears an image of himself as he would like to be (or used to be, or believes himself to be). The immediacy of the live broadcast, in all its excitement, spurs the ability of the "signifying voice" (in Kristeva's terminology) to transport the listener. We hear our ideal selves, reporting and surviving the event.

Echo's choice of Narcissus both as subject for "live" narration and as object of desire is far from uncommon (he was sought after by many, and he rejected all suitors, both male and female). Yet it smacks of her desire for desirability, a return to a time (before Juno's curse) when she was sought after by Pan and others and was not the go-between for Zeus and his admirers, when her seductive powers of speech were matched only by Narcissus's physical beauty. Thus, in desiring Narcissus, Echo is attempting a return to what she considers her previous self—attractive and equipped with verbal mastery far beyond the powers of repetition. But in repeating Narcissus's words, she is hearing herself speak the words of another. She has internalized and externalized the voice of the other simultaneously. Her object-choice, like that of Narcissus (as per Kristeva), is also a space of representation: Narcissus is the surface against which she also bounces her own voice; she desires the agency of Narcissus's vocality to gain her expressivity.

In the specificity of the eyewitness broadcast, whether live or simulated as in the "War of the Worlds," the relationship between speaking (radio)bodies and listening (physical) bodies becomes frenzied. The involvement of the psyche and the senses in the audience is fragmented, enrolling fantasy to elaborate imaginary bodies. The survival of Echo's voice and the self-destruction of Narcissus's body are at stake in the identifications of the listener.

For the listener to the "War of the Worlds" broadcast (or the *Hindenburg* disaster), such identifications are traumatic. In the command "You are there," there is a narcissistic identification that has an enclosure (*"You are there with me live, confusing me with you. One of us may not survive"*). These are the stakes involved in the enunciation of word-pictures. Chatty Echo, ace nymph reporter, produces a narrated cinema of horror by means of her word-pictures. Narcissus is a disaster waiting to happen, and this, in part, is what makes him so erotically fascinating and his story so crucial to witness.[6]

After Narcissus and Echo meet, Narcissus rebuffs Echo's amorous hands. She leaves him, and her body begins to melt away and become rock. Narcissus's lack of desire for her has served to destroy her body, going beyond Juno's curse. She is not what he is looking for; her body is not a companion to his voice; it is not within his space of representation but falls outside the frame. After her body's disappearance, however, Echo does not die (significantly Echo outlives Narcissus, for the triumphant eyewitnessing voice is also the survivor of embodied catastrophe). Ovid writes: "Vanished in forest / Far from her usual walks on hills and valleys / She's heard by all who call; *her voice has life*" (97; italics mine).

Thus, in the myth the disembodied voice is alive without physical body. For the listener, this is the case with the radio broadcast as well. The voice with life enables a narcissistic-like identification, not because there is a living body behind it, but because there is a virtual, morphing body inherent in the voice. This body is never rebuffed by narcissistic standards of visuality. A sexy-sounding voice never disappoints, except when one meets the "real" physical body from which it issues.

In the essay "Economimesis" (1981), Derrida uses the term "hear-oneself-speak" in order to discuss the privileging of speech; he posits that the spoken voice is perceived as primary in Western thought. In his schema, the voice is a boomerang that returns sound to the self. But indeed, one feels one's voice through the body and not because sound leaves the corpus and returns. That is to say, the body transmits live from the vocal cords to the inner ear. We feel our own sound as vibration as we hear its possible integrity as words. Furthermore, one gets to hear oneself as if the other were speaking, and this voice becomes an "object-choice." The medium of the body does not disappear in transmission; it is transmuted.

As Kristeva notes in her discussion of narcissism (1987:37), the voice sparks fantasy, frames the visual image, and suggests psychic transportation into another realm. The echo also transfers one's voice into another's, rendering it strange. The self is split into the visual and the acoustic. In Ovid's tale, the split self is composed of nonidentical doubles as surrogates for seeing and hearing. Narcissus's absorption into, and separation from, the visual image is a tragic unknowingness enabling the death drive. Echo, as Rank describes her, is an "acoustic personification of a reflection of a self" (quoted in Laplanche 1976:68), a reflection that resounds with disidentification. The tale allegorizes one's disidentification with one's words, for Narcissus can not identify with his own words–they return to him strange and unsightly. This complicates Derrida's notion of self-hearing; words spoken that may start out sounding sweet can return sounding bitter and seeming to originate from another source altogether. Self-hearing is illusionary and creates a makeshift object to desire.

In cinematic terms, Echo's voice is the voice-over–narrating, framing the visual with text disconnected from a body. Significantly, however, as Ovid writes, this spoken word has "life." This voice is also independent from a living body. In Ovid's tale, not only does Echo's voice have life, but her voice is also virtually live; it is concurrent to the event, fragmentary, a mimetic commentary. It grants a spatial dimension to bracketed, narrative time. Echo's voice exposes and surmounts distance while revealing no origin–hence, it is akin to a radiovoice. Echo's radiovoice is familiar, reassuring, and identifiable, but it bristles with the uncanny. For Narcissus, it as if he has heard that voice before, and this is why it sounds so alien to him.

Even as Narcissus pummels himself into a flower, Echo is there to narrate the event, forgetting her resentment and feeling "a pity at the sight." She repeats his last words, which have a special significance for her: "O darling boy whose love was my undoing . . . goodbye." Echo's grieving voice alerts the forest and the river residents to Narcissus's demise. His body is replaced on the funeral pyre by a flower. Echo survives as missing image of the voice; Narcissus is replaced by a symbol.

The Body of Echo

In invocations since Ovid, echoes are frequently referred to not only for their acoustical qualities but also for their supernatural qualities. Specifically, echoes become a way to hear the past or the dead, and they foreshadow the vocal disembodiment that inhabits the twentieth century. Echoes are repetitions with repercussions; they refer to or give voice to the dead. They transmit directly to the auditor. For example, Wordsworth writes in "Yes, It Was the Mountain Echo" (1814):

> ... Yes, we have
> Answers and we know not whence;
> Echoes from beyond the grave,
> Recognized intelligence!
>
> Such rebounds our inward ear
> Catches sometimes from afar–
> (1994:241)

An echo is an explicable acoustical phenomenon. Yet in this verse, it carries with it a message from the other side in its abbreviated response to the call of the living human. For Wordsworth, this response reverberates in a space of interiority–"the inner ear"–although its origin is "from afar." This is the inner ear that is akin to insight as well as the ear that feels one's speech before it returns via the ears. Wordsworth's sense of the echo hints at a radio-like construction. He receives transmission from an unfathomable yet coherent place.

For Geoffrey Hartman (1979), "Wordsworth's words are antiphonal to the phoné of a prior experience" (193). *Phoné*, meaning sounds or voice before the form and origin are known, are echoed in the words of the poet. The form of the poem itself echoes song in Wordsworth's self-appraisal. For Wordsworth, the echo is more majestic than its origin. It can fill up the mountain and the valley with sound, and it can also resound in a space of interiority. The echoes grant the dead the ear of the living as inspiration and not just as haunting.

Wordsworth acknowledges that he receives inspiration from listening:

> ... I would stand
> Beneath some rock, listening to sounds that are
> the ghostly language of the ancient earth,
> Or make their dim abode in distant winds.
> Thence did I drink the visionary power.
>   (Prelude II.306–9 [1805])

Wordsworth's listening is synesthetic: sound is converted to a vision that he can taste. Importantly, though, it is a privileging of sound as that which not only reverberates via repetition but also can be transferred into objects for other senses to behold. We hear Echo in this work before we can see the gaze of Narcissus. The torment of Echo's echolalia provokes the working of other senses. Echo always marks the past, however recent, by repeating words just said. Echoic reflections refer to the sound events that have occurred, but they inspire a vision that lies ahead.

As a result, these echoic reflections are not quite concurrent: They begin with a sound, but they return after the original sound has finished—in other words, there is a time delay. Mirrored images, however, change instantly with movements in front of the mirror. Narcissus's image in the pool moves in sync with his changing pose, whereas Echo's voice begins only where his leaves off. In a scenario involving contemporary media, the "live" image can simultaneously capture the event, but the live narration of the event is always slightly behind the event that is unfolding. For example, the reporter at the *Hindenburg* disaster can only announce the explosion after it has begun to happen. The search for words, or the reflection of their sound, causes him to lag behind the event.

Echoes, as acoustic phenomena, are reflections of sound against solid surfaces. The result of this reflection is not instantaneous; the sound returns "at least one-fifteenth of a second after the originating sound" (Hollander 1981:1). Echoes can thus appear, not as repetitions of speech, but as continuations of them. In longer utterances, the first words will not be heard in the echo. Only the last words of a phrase will be audible in the silence. Hence, Echo's ability to repeat only the end of another's speech; she relies on silence or a space between sound to appear.

Thus, echoes appear as repetitions with a difference. Although they never alter the tempo or elongate or shorten any part of an enunciation, they seem to cut up speech and to vary its timbre: convex surfaces will make the echo louder; planar surfaces will render the echo softer. Caves (as hollowed-out spaces) and low lands with distant mountains (as reflecting surfaces) emerge not only in mythology but also in science as the breeding ground for the organic disembodied voice. Indeed, serial echo effects can be found–analogous to a hall of mirrors–in areas where sound is bounced from surface to surface, endlessly seeming to abbreviate speech even as it repeats the utterance.

Seventeenth-century musicologists and encyclopedists Marin Mersenne and Anthanasius Kircher began to develop a science called echometry. They played with the innate distortion and shortening of the echo so as to change a word from its initial form into a series of other words by bouncing the sound against a succession of surfaces. For example, in *Phonurgia Nova* (1966 [1673]), Kircher discusses experiments in which he directs his voice against five walls, each surface further away and each slightly longer than the previous. In speaking the Italian word *clamore* (outcry), the first echo returns as *amore;* the last syllable's echo becomes the Italian word for king. The echo's repetition with difference becomes a way to enunciate words–or possibly phrases–not spoken. The echo's distorted mirror grants unintentional expressivity to the voice; its reproductions have an autonomy independent of its source. To repeat Ovid: "Her voice has life." With the echo, the voice has no body other than its own; furthermore, it can appear to announce the words of the dead from its own body.

In musicology, as stated earlier, the term "sonorous body" was deployed by Rameau and the Encyclopedists (see Rameau 1971 [1722]). It referred to a collection of sounds sung or played together that constellated into a collectivity or a body. Sound, then, an invisible wave, is given a visuality, a physical presence, a figure of corporeality. In this way, a sound that is recognized as human (and/or human produced via striking or strumming an instrument or a surface) is affiliated with a body that is imagined, contingently placed within a visual frame.

In segments of the American popular imagination, the radio has become a peculiar mediumistic space for receiving the ululations of mysterious sonorous bodies. For example, as mentioned in Chapter 2, Carola Morales of the American Association of Broadcast Phenomena reports receiving tapes from listeners who, in the static between stations, hear the voices of Carl Jung, Friedrich Nietzsche, Adolf Hitler, and Mel Blanc as well as dead loved ones (1993:330–31). The airwaves thus become a chatty graveyard where the dead speak through a radiobody.[7] In this way, the dynamics of pure presence have changed; a human voice negotiates an economy affiliated but severed from an originating corpus. Echo's sonorous body is then analogous to a radiobody:

seemingly sourceless, reflective yet autonomous. Echo retains these qualities in other renditions of her story.

In the essay "Aliena Verba" (1984), Joseph Loewenstein discusses the troubling presence of the nymph in classical verse, asserting that Echo appears almost like an analyst, revealing "another scene" of narration. When Greek scholar Callimachus announces that his beloved Lysanias is *kalos* (fair), Echo repeats his words, but returning only with the word *allos*–which means "another" or "an other." As in the experiments of echoic iterations of Kircher, Callimachus is playing with the acoustic fact that however accurate the echo may be, it is sequential, an event in linear time. It occurs after the original speech act, making audible repetitions of only the ends of speech acts.

Loewenstein insists that the aspect of the echo that is *allos* sums up the conventional function of this echoic device: denying the integrity of the bond between lovers, Echo also denies the integrity of the speech. A speaker can no more control his words than a lover can control the beloved. Both utterance and beloved are not limited by the speaker's or the lover's intention (18). Thus, in Callimachus's poem, the beloved is revealed by Echo's "slip of the tongue" as estranged or as belonging to another; the speech act is not performative in ways that J. L. Austin used the word (see Chapter 1), for the words do not match a deed or issue forth a contract. Instead, echoed words disenfranchise the speaker from his speech. Loewenstein continues:

> In Callimachus's poem, Echo acts as an analyst, and her rep-
> etition, by demonstrating the semantic indeterminacy of an
> utterance, extends and reorganizes the public context, the
> narrative situation of speaking.... As analyst, Echo reveals
> the speaker's imperfect knowledge of his world, renders the

primary utterance ironic, and so destroys that proximity of
word to meaning so dear to intimate discourse. (18)

In another instance, Loewenstein finds Echo's analyst-like
function in the words of the lyricist Ausonius, who enlists the
"Aristotelian identification of hearing with echoing" (25).
Ausonius's Epigram XXXII, translated by George Turberville
into the poem "To one that painted Eccho" (1567) depicts the
workings, announces the ancestry, and identifies the home-
lands of Echo:

> Daughter to talking Tongue, and Ayre am I,
> My Mother is nothing when things are waide:
> I am a voyce without the bodies aide.
> When all the tale is tolde and sentence saide.
> Then I recite the latter worde afreshe
> In mocking sort and counterfayting wies:
> Within your eares my chiefest harbour lies,
> There doe I woonne, not seene with mortall eies.
> And more to tell and farther to proceede,
> I Eccho height of men below in grounde:
> If thou wilt draw my Counterfeit in deede,
> Then must thou paint (O Painter) but a sound.

Echo, who is a sound without body, external to the lis-
tener/speaker, also resides within the ears of this person.
He hears his own words as *verba aliena.* Loewenstein writes:
"Echo no longer haunts the landscape; instead she teaches
the painter that the speaking self is as haunting as any external presence, even if that external presence be invisible, for
the internal locutor is ... equally unimaginable" (25–26).

Echo, then, in her repetition, provokes a self-haunting. She
distances the speaker from an immediate and lingering connection with his own words, rendering them uncanny. The
enunciatory act is a strange event producing otherness; Cala-

machus's intimate beloved, represented in words, returns to him as foreign or as the beloved of another. The figure of Echo, as well as the acoustic phenomenon, also enables the sense of doubling as the self encounters the almost familiar–speech, sound enunciated by self–as also belonging to another.

In Turberville's word-picture of Echo, the daughter of "Ayre [air]" and "tongue" has a menace; her words have a "mocking" and "counterfeiting" way. The speaker no longer hears himself speak but listens to his words return from outside, distancing sound from intended meaning and sending them back to an unintended auditor. In much of the mythography of Echo (I cite only a selective fragment), Echo emerges as an ur-radiovoice with a sonorous body. Her wisdom and her proximity to events reveal the distance between word and speaker, an uncanniness that is based in the doubling of self in sound, so that hearing oneself speak is unfamiliar, a missive from transmitter to receiver and not a return to a knowable self. Echo, herself a familiar unknown, returns with repetitious speech in an ironic rendition. She fills up silence but estranges speech.

The story of radio operations, exemplified in the American 1930s, is also the story of Narcissus and Echo. Strange speech, once seemingly familiar, dislodges panic in the promise of stability and growth. In broadcasts that were initially assumed to be reflective of the broadcaster, the transmissions begin to sound autonomous and menacing, operating from their own sonorous radiobody. In the case of Welles's "War of the Worlds," the broadcast echoes radio programming with such fidelity that it produces more than a familiar alarm. This alarm is related to the menacing double that the echo unleashes through mimesis. Welles's program removes the *k* from *kallos,* provoking the panic of *allos* to transmit.

Echo's Image, Narcissus's Voice

Although the audience for the "War of the Worlds" broadcast was both male and female, the cast for the performance of news programs was entirely male. This reflects the placement of women on radio: they were employed in dramas and comedy shows and in musical shows, but not as newscasters. According to radio researchers Cantril and Allport (1971 [1935]), surveys on radio listeners showed that

> 95 percent of our subjects [40 women, 40 men] indicated their preference for male voices.... [It] turned out that the chief basis for this preference lay in the rather constant impression of affectation and unnaturalness created by women's voices on the air. Along with this impression, goes the judgment that men as a rule are more persuasive and more interested in the material they read. (137)

In their surveys, women were preferred to men only in a few categories of broadcast: poetry, fictitious advertising, and abstract material (135). Cantril and Allport viewed this "data" as perhaps more indicative of cultural attitudes toward women than a comment on female performances on the air. Amy Lawrence (1991:18) argues that since a speaking voice tends to command authority, women on radio were not usually allowed to speak. However, they could sing–as long as they remained within certain vocal ranges. The division of labor in radio repeated and reinforced the sexual division of labor in the larger prewar economy. Popular radio was a male domain, as was the military and amateur radio. Women's voices were forced to the borders of the radio.

In the 1935 study by Cantril and Allport, men were considered to be more trustworthy, especially when it came to concrete facts. Women were deemed as unsuitable for reciting facts. Used more for ethereal purposes than for hard news, the female voice was considered almost troubling, undercutting the believability of facts; that is, like Echo, these voices were believed to be laced with counterfeit and irony.

One area where male announcers fared markedly better than women was Cantril and Allport's category of "How well personality known from voice" (131). That is, both female and male auditors were able to reconnect with male commentators more easily, discerning between each voice. Female voices became a sonic blur, lacking signature, perhaps always the generic voice of a woman, an echo rather than a radio personality.

Lazarsfeld (1940) notes that one reason radio listeners preferred news on the air rather than print journalism was that the radio is intimate. He quotes some of his subjects without indicating gender:

> It is more interesting when a person talks to you.
>
> I like the voice. It is nearer to you.
>
> A voice to me has always been more real than words to be read.
>
> I like to hear a voice better than reading. It's more exciting.
> (181)

This research suggests that in the 1930s radio was energized very much by male homosociality and mandates about female heterosexuality. The radio voice was experienced as urgent and close and actual; it was also decidedly male (one thinks of the plethora of masculinist adventure programs as well). This male voice was isolated, recognizable and repeated, eroticized, identified with, or desired. This voice commanded that "You are there" and was paid to narrate disaster, petitioning for psychic travel to events far beyond the domestic sphere. It was a reprimanding voice, always near to catastrophe, unable to protect the listener–a male voice of panic. The listener cathects to his survival. This survival is played out again and again in *Flash Gordon, The Shadow,* the *Hindenburg* disaster, "War of the Worlds": the leading man not only narrates and echoes disaster in panicked form, but he gets to recite the epilog as well.

This male voice on radio is different than a baritonal Narcissus who has turned away from the pool. He not only survives the narrative, but he also survives the disembodiment of radio operations that severs glottal functions from corporeality. His voice becomes that of a radiobody, and however strong this estrangement might be, it bears the marks of a signature voice. The paradox is this: *I recognize myself sounding like another.*

In the model of disembodiment that I use, the voice of Echo is female. Yet in Ovid's narrative, Narcissus refuses to hear his repeated words as his own when reverberating outside his tessitura, or vocal range, when they are uttered by Echo. These words, like Echo, are foreign to him, even though he has just said them. When Echo says "Why run from me?" she is parroting him; but for Narcissus, the voice's origin is from outside his body. Its desirous tones are strange to him even as it rebounds with his desire.

The Glück opera *Echo et Narcisse* also plays with the notion of the mirror and the double. In Glück's version of the myth, Narcissus realizes his blunder at the pool, rejects death, and comes to return Echo's life-affirming love. In order to subvert this revision, in the production directed by Herbert Wernicke and performed at the Schweitzinger Festival in 1987, the stage was covered by mirrors. During his aria, Narcissus picks up reflection after reflection, gazing lovingly, singing his desire. After he furiously rebuffs the obtrusive Echo, and she stumbles from the stage to become a disembodiment, the stage is cleared of mirrors. Narcissus is unable to actualize his infatuation for his image without her; Echo is the device–as much as the reflected visual image–that enables his self-infatuation. Realizing his folly, he sings for the return of Echo. She returns vocally, repeating his words from offstage. But her image is also seen via a mirror that the character "Love" holds up downstage. Her singing image is projected onto the mirror, unseen by Narcissus, who laments upstage, but seen by the audience. Narcissus declares his love for the disembodiment that repeats his melody, while Love gives Echo's body back to her. The "couple" are reunited as is intended by the libretto; but in this production, their reunion is that of an estranged couple who cannot be rid of each other. They take up opposite ends of the stage. Echo throws down the Narcissan flowers he offers her. Echo and Narcissus are inextricably linked, but they are not happy in this linkage; the conflict between representations in sound and sight still continues. At the production's end, the chorus stands between the disagreeing couple, singing of the glories of love, trying to keep the curtain from closing the scene, and attempting to insist on a happy ending in which images of self in sight and reflections in sound can be reconciled.

This production, by subverting Glück's retelling of the myth of Echo and Narcissus, shows how this "coupling" is mutually reliant upon each for expression. Echo needs Narcissus's words in order to speak for herself, otherwise there is nothing to report and no possibility for sexual longing. Narcissus needs her spoken desire for his body in order to find delight in his own image. This production highlights the schism between the spectacles of sight and the composition of sound. Endlessly mimicking and renouncing each other, Echo and Narcissus personify this divide. For Narcissus, hearing himself as female is an unbearable haunting. This haunting propels him to the sanctuary of the visual image, but the image before him remains unbearably silent, tormenting him. Unlike the male radio personality who sounds so reassuring to the audience, in the myth he is unable to survive his story, for it is a story that, through the proxy of Ovid, is narrated by Echo.

The Gendered Disembodiment

Radio is the exemplary playground for the disembodied voice. But this in no way means that this voice is without gender. Inasmuch as there is a desire in the audience to connect the voice to an imagined body, there is also a search for an origin: from what sort of gendered body does this voice project? With the actual visual field denied to the listener, the confession of gender becomes paramount, even if it is not discussed. On radio, as the cited research indicates, women's voices were heard as less trustworthy (like a chatty Echo). Yet the Welles broadcast shows that male voices can perform a disastrous tomfoolery through sounding typical and imitating existing broadcast forms with fictional content. Indeed, the 1930s male radiovoice sounds almost like a parody of refined masculinity that perhaps one should hold in suspicion and not consider cohesive. But since women's high voices were avoided, deeper male voices were used to avoid the dangers of the border between the gendered vocal ranges.

In Ovid's tale, Echo's body slips away. She is a symbol of mimesis whose femininity has lost its original body. Her fate is object-choice, deprived of both Narcissus and narcissism. The monster in the "War of the Worlds" broadcast, however, is of unspecified gender–an "it," a thing, as is the object of the radio receiver–and this is a key element in its monstrosity. For on the radio, gender does not disappear; without the visible body, the confession and expression of gender becomes more crucial. Echo is still female even without a body–since the imperative for voices to have a gender is omnipresent. The Martians, seemingly genderless, can therefore not be humanoid, and they fall on the side of primordial, pre-gendered technology.

In her essay "Developing a Blind Understanding: A Feminist Revision of Radio Semiotics" (1996), Mary Louise Hill suggests that listening to radio is similar to translation, a movement from source text to target language:

> A radio listener encounters the words and sounds on the imaginative terrain of the mind. That listener, too, compares and tries out meanings, images, physical and emotional responses within the imagination, in order to produce an image or response.... [T]hese images or responses are not fixed: they develop and change as the experience continues. (117)

The potential for a radical repositioning of gender is imminent, for the impact of the listener in finishing the text is greater than in traditional theatre or cinema, where sight is operative from the start. Yet despite Hill's views on the potential for listening, during the 1930s male voices patrolled the airwaves, serving to isolate and identify female voices and hence a certain radiophonic femininity. Within a medium that ensures the disembodied voice, women were virtually affixed to a particular body. The female voice, unlike Echo's, is disallowed from traveling free from an assumed body; this is why a female character's looks are often described in popular radio dramas and programs, whereas a male's appearance is assumed.

In Hollywood cinema, as Kaja Silverman (1988) notes, the disembodied male voice-over is a very common narrative device, especially in postwar films. For instance, in *Double Indemnity* (1944) and *It's a Wonderful Life* (1946), the character of Walter and the angel Joseph are without bodies on screen, yet they have overarching significance to the structure of the storytelling. The female voice-over is prevalent in Hollywood cinema, but this voice is virtually always attached to a specific body on screen. This attachment allows the words to have an interiority of being inside the story, as opposed to having an impact on the narrative from outside. In this way, the viewer/auditor has access to the secrets of the female character.

For instance, Silverman notes that in *Darling* (1963), during the opening credits, we hear a female voice musing over her troubled life as the camera pans a model's face on a city billboard advertising a magazine issue. The viewer connects this image to the voice; the model's voice and face are severed yet linked. Predictably, the film serves to diagnose how this woman's image of modish vitality becomes so distanced from her actual experience of loneliness and disinvolvement. Immediately, the audience has been provided with a clue to the vast distance between appearance and reality. The voice is truthful, and the attachment of the voice to the body will lock the audience's attachment to Darling's "real feelings," feelings she never shows to the men and women in her social world.

There are notable exceptions to this drive to gain female interiority via the play of severing and reattaching of body and voice in classic Hollywood cinema (and indeed many more examples in the history of avant-garde, experimental, and feminist film). One noteworthy break is Joseph Manckiewicz's *Letter to Three Wives* (1949), which Kaja Silverman suggests may be the only Hollywood film to use a disembodied female voice-over (1988:49).[8] Because I am positing Echo as the first instance of the disembodied voice and locating it as a female voice stripped of body, this film has great importance. Additionally, *Letter* is a retelling of the myth of Echo: it is a cautionary tale of the repercussions and the threat of husbandly waywardness and female disloyalty. The story is filled with the repercussions of Echo.

The disembodiment, Addie Ross, lurks in the suburban town where she has always lived, wreaking havoc in the lives of three wives. Addie is single (she was left by her husband) and is a close friend of all three husbands, who cannot help but gush with superlatives when Addie's name is mentioned (to the chagrin of the three wives). In the opening sequence, the voice (not yet identified as Addie's) hovers above the image track. It comments on the suburban town and its inhabitants in almost cruel tones, disparaging its insular, status-conscious ways. When the camera reaches the home of the first couple, Debra and Brad, Addie commences with an analysis of their marriage, and the audience is forced to view their union through the eyes of the absent Addie. Her soft voice is dispassionate, ironic, and always more biting than the dialog of the embodied characters.

Addie, like Echo before her, is disembodied in the logic of the patriarchal narrative because she has interfered in the sanctity of a marriage (Echo served as a chatty distraction to Juno's pursuit of the adulterous Jove). When two of the wives, Debra (the young housewife married to a wealthy erudite businessman) and Rita (significantly, a radio writer married to an earnest schoolteacher), drive in the car, they discuss Addie. On the soundtrack, Addie talks back to them and answers the audience's implicit question–"Yes, they're talking about me, I'm Addie Ross"–in a self-congratulatory manner. Addie agrees when Debra admits that if it weren't for Addie, "they wouldn't have much to talk about," and in Echo-like fashion repeats her sentence ironically.

The audience doesn't know that the two women are en route to meet Addie and another housewife (Laura May, married to an uneducated but successful merchant) in order to chaperone a school trip up the Hudson in a boat. Addie isn't there, and Laura May informs the two women that she has heard that Addie has left town. As they board the boat, a messenger delivers a letter to the three women. Addie has informed her friends that "she will always remember her dear friends." But at the last line she adds (and the audience hears her voice for added emphasis): "I have left town with one of your husbands."

This updated suburban and vengeful version of Echo moves in out and out of the story, having a cruel impact on the women and creating intrigue for the men. Her female voice is that which was avoided by radio listeners in the 1930s: she is deceitful, untrustworthy, ethereal. She is cast like a female radiovoice in the midst of a film; her beauty is continually described, yet left to the imagination of the viewers. She is a narrator whose attractiveness is narrated by the characters she describes.

Each wife has reason to believe that it is her husband who has left her, and when each descends into an explanatory flashback, the voice of Addie returns, haunting them. Addie inhabits the same temporal plane even as she hovers above it spatially. She is an entity in the present tense, not only narrating events in the past, as other female voice-overs usually perform. It is as if she is an omnipresent psychic force, set upon a suburban community to cause chaos, a force that is also inside each of the women. In each of the three flashbacks, the woman comes to realize how she has acted against stability within her marriage. They have defied their husbands in order to claim a sense of self, but this has risk involved. Their husbands might leave with Addie.

Like Echo before she meets Narcissus, Addie is the masterful image of woman as charmer and manipulator even though she is never seen but always sees. The camera teases the audience with the strict divide between Addie's vocal and vocalized presence (she is often the subject of other characters' dialog) and her absent physicality. Addie becomes a lurking presence who haunts the other characters' memory. She tantalizes by her absence; she whispers to the audience, reminding us by repeating other characters' phrases, that she is at the center of every frame and the subject of all dialog. She is a radiophonic entity within the cinematic enterprise, reminding all viewers of the important flirtation and desire inside the soundtrack itself. She serves to prove that cinema, as Rick Altman (1980) argued, is ruled by soundtrack; this film suggests that cinema is akin to a radio drama with pictures.

The radio is a force in the film. Rita (Ann Southern), the career wife married to the underpaid but earnest schoolteacher George (Kirk Douglas), is a radio writer. The radio is an omnipresent feature in their home, with a radio in the living room and one in the kitchen, listened to all day long by the wisecracking maid. When a visiting station executive (a masculine woman named Mrs. Manly) asks the maid what she listens to, the maid replies, "The police transmission."

The executive is confused by this answer, and the maid explains that she likes listening to the voices even though she has no idea what they are talking about.

The film plays with this pleasure of hearing throughout. The disembodied Addie propels the story and is situated so as to sound ideal. The maid likes the manly voices on the police broadcast, avoiding Mrs. Manly's station and its commercials. She and the audience like to hear a voice that seems to emerge from beyond the visual frame. This is erotically fascinating, especially as we learn of each man's desire for this disembodiment. At the same time, the maid is energized by the male voices coming from the kitchen's radio. She is perfectly happy not to see them but to overhear their transmissions to each other—that is to say, her eavesdropping is erotically charged.

Following Sue-Ellen Case (1989), Hill suggests that representing women's split subjectivity on stage would entail the use of "voice-over, monolog, and disembodiment" (1996:118) and that as such, the radio is a theatrical medium conducive for this endeavor: radio is always already fragmenting, partial, demanding completion by listeners even as it shifts broadcasting locales. If, as Case suggests, women can not fit into "a single, whole, continuous subject," the radio is an arena that offers such representational opportunity. In *Letter to Three Wives,* the woman who listens to radio (the maid) and the woman who becomes symbolically like the medium (Addie) wreak havoc within the suburban locale of the film, serving to curtail the orderliness of the film even as they stoke the narrative's engines. Indeed, although they are curtailed and brought to some sort of regulatory, cinematic justice, they also remain fragmented, disembodied, and partial portraits.

This may explain, in part, why women are still less likely than men to be disc jockeys, and why mainstream films don't feature female voice-overs more often—this disembodiment still creates much confusion. The voice that is heard as female and is not matched to a body is dissembling, estranging—or it is heard as fantasy, and hence potentially enveloping.

The Renouncing of Echo

The untrustworthy, uncanny voice of Echo turns *kalos* to *allos* ("you're fair" to "you are an other"); this voice also serves as inspiration to poets like Wordsworth, haunted by the past and with an ear to the ground. The mythography of Echo is disparate: ironic and playful, analytic and wise, deceitful and needlessly truth-speaking. Crucially, and in each instance, her voice remains female even as it is depicted as speaking from no apparent body.

During the 1930s, popular radio was increasingly filled with the serious business of panic. On all sorts of frequencies, male voices that listened to the resonant tones of their own voices also awaited potential attack from an unknown source. In their narcissistic identifications (for this time the image in the pool speaks but is not seen), they delimit the reappearance of Echo. Their dramatic vocalities are always in response to Echo's haunting, that is, to hearing themselves as "*allos*." Even as they renounce Echo through their proclivities, she enables their radiovoices and serves to define their radiobodies. Their radiobodies are male in response to her; they flee her in narcissistic fashion, no doubt headed to disaster.

In the Ovidian tale of Narcissus and Echo, Echo's amorous defeat also spurs her return, in voice. She broadcasts her distress and Narcissus's demise at once. That is, she reports the disaster. This is a disaster she survives, but at the cost of her body. Indeed, "her voice has life," but what is also apparent and crucial is that her voice remains female. The broadcast disembodiment in the 1930s was decidedly a deeply and almost caricatured male voice–in part, perhaps, to protect against the perceived havoc-wreaking potential of the female voice. Ironically, it was these male voices, baritonal and seemingly sturdy, that expressed and produced so much panic.

These voices pushed the fragmented, split-subjected Echo from the center, even as the reporting radiobody was reliant upon her model of disembodiment and witnessing. Echo remains close to disaster, surviving it and narrating it in as close to real time as possible. This is the imperative of the eyewitness, whose proximity to the scene of catastrophe enlivens the broadcasting industry. Echo is pushed to the margin of the narrative or myth, yet she is the one whose words ensure survival. In this way, she is the forerunner of the reporter/commentator. Also, she is the paradigm for the play between proximity and distance to disaster that is so crucial to post-*Titanic* communications.

7

Body and Space in the Radio and Internet

Like the radio before it, the introduction and commercialization of the Internet has provoked great cultural change. Both media have been seen as a threat to standard modes of communication as well as a way to ensure stability in communication systems. The Internet was much discussed by the president of the country in the 1990s, and the governance of cyberspace has become a key part of the purview of the FCC.

In the late 1990s, mail-order companies reliant on new technology (dotcoms), once very promising to the growth of the economy, became the junk bonds of the '90s. All the commotion caused by this techno–Gold Rush is within the tradition of introducing new media to the American public. There are legal problems about monopolistic practices such as the court case between Microsoft and the Justice Department and there are publicity outlets which repeat that new technology wrests the user free from the doldrums of the everyday life. Using and investing in the Internet became akin to a patriotic act even as its governance remained controversial. The medium became the center and the manifest reason for a quasi-national debate, particularly as so-called cyber-terrorists attacked the most popular Web sites and warnings about viruses circulated via e-mail.

The debate about the role of the government in administering the Internet and the privatization of cyberspace is lacking in historical insight. On the surface, the purpose of the debate is to create safety and order where once there was danger and chaos, with children and the innocent at risk. They are at risk because perverts, pornographers, and carpetbagger-like merchants exist on the Internet as well as legitimate businesses and interacting citizens. As we can learn from radio broadcasting, and as we can now clearly discern with the history of the Internet, government will intervene in order to create guidelines about appropriate content and access, but it will also ensure that private interests prevail over an articulation of public need.

The introduction of both the Internet and the radio were surrounded by much utopian rhetoric. Each medium was seen by certain groups of educators, social critics, and policy experts as having the opportunity to produce a more united America, with shared experience and reference points.[1] The hope is that with the growth of each medium, citizens living in remote areas or isolated from others become connected. Indeed, the nation becomes more inclusive, sharing a common culture.[2]

With the potential of each medium in mind, maverick community-minded users in the beginning and at the end of the century imagined a more interacting, communitarian America. In this America, the citizenry reappears as interacting disembodiments, sharing information and participating in the development of new environments. With the radio, users interacted via code at first and then with voices; with the

Internet, typed words and imagined bodies became transmitted conversations and Webcammed images. In the early 1990s, for example, Howard Rheingold, an active member of the pioneering Internet community the WELL, and often cited for his work on computer-mediated communication (CMC), warned against even his own tendency toward idealizing new technology. In his book *The Virtual Community: Homesteading on the Electronic Frontier* (1993), he writes:

> The wise revolutionary keeps an eye on the dark side of the changes he or she would initiate. Enthusiasts who believe in the humanitarian potential of virtual communities, especially those of us who speak of electronic democracy as a potential of the medium are well advised to consider the shadow potential of the same media. . . . Because of its potential to change us as humans, as communities, as democracies, we need to try to understand the nature of CMC, cyberspace, and virtual communities in every important context–politically, economically, socially, cognitively. (15)

Even as Rheingold urges his readers to adopt a more measured response toward the new forms of mediated communication, he can not help himself. He adds that CMC is also poised to transform not only sociality but also the human frame–cognitive workings can also change in unforeseen ways due to the new technology. New technology disallows predictability.

Even a writer as nuanced and insightful as Donna Haraway in her landmark "A Manifesto for Cyborgs" (1985) is influenced by the notion of the radical, almost unknowable changes that technology can bring upon sociality. She constructs her own tale of unpredictability due in part to heretofore unforeseen developments. Her notion of the cyborg signals the advent of the posthuman;[3] cyborgs become their own programmers and move beyond the restriction of binarist structure and thought. For her, the cyborg, when it comes into consciousness as such, celebrates the technological prosthetic to the human frame and endorses the integration of systems in ways that cannot be fathomed. For Haraway, the cyborg creates an unwritten future.

Mark Poster, in his recent book *What's the Matter with the Internet* (2001), tempers much of the utopian impulse in discussing the Internet. Yet he too suggests that the future of democracy is unpredictable due to the impact of new communications technology:

> The wrapping of language on the Internet, its digitized, machine-mediated signifiers in a space without bodies, introduces an unprecedented novelty for political theory. How will electronic beings be governed? ... Assuming that the U.S. government and the corporations do not shape the Internet entirely in their own image and that places of cyberdemocracy remain and spread to larger and larger segments of the population, what will emerge as a postmodern politics? (187–78)

Of course, hoping that the U.S. government and the corporations will not succeed in shaping the Internet may not be so realistic. Still, he posits an answer to his questions: "One possibility is that authority as we have known it will change drastically. ... The Internet seems to discourage the endowment of individuals with inflated status" (188). Using scholarship as an example, Poster argues that existing authorities and textualities are challenged by the Internet and hypertextuality, and he suggests that traditional political authorities may follow suit.

This narrative of unpredictability due to technology and new media is picked up by those whose interest in the Internet is more profit motivated. For example, Bill Gates, president of Microsoft, uses the term "punctuated chaos" to describe business's "constant upheaval" that is "marked by brief respites" (1999:412). Even Gates, who undeniably exerts a great influence on how Americans use their computers and access the Internet, enunciates this tale of disorder due to unforeseen factors. For Gates, businesses get a bit of reprieve where they can catch up, but the velocity of change is ever-accelerating in a digital economy. This offers possibilities for the entrepreneur and for the consumer in Gates's worldview (and of course Microsoft products enable a preparedness to change!) Microsoft provides order in a sea of generative but potentially dangerous chaos.

Slavoj Žižek takes a more cynical attitude toward proclamations of the newness of cyberspatiality, virtuality, and the promise of the Internet. In an interview in 1996, he states:

> The so-called "virtual communities" are not such a great revolution as it might appear. What impresses me is the extent to which these virtual phenomena retroactively enable us to discover to what extent our self has always been virtual. Even the most physical self experience has a symbolic, virtual element in it. (Lovink 1996)

Žižek insists then that the self is virtual from the get-go, an illusionary construction. New communication allows us to see these symbolic connections rather than changing sociality itself.

More recently, Žižek has taken on some of the assumptions of disembodiment and cyberspatiality. In the essay "Against the Digital Heresy" (2001), he writes: "The ultimate lesson of cyberspace is an even more radical one: not only do we lose our immediate material body, but we learn that there *never was* such a body–our bodily self-experience was always already that of an imagined constituted entity" (55). For Žižek, cyberspace clues us in to the actuality that the narrative of the organic, coherent body was a fiction from the outset. The disembodiment that the Internet seems to provoke reveals, not a new state of existing in and out of corporealities, but an existing way of being. The Internet, for Žižek, is not a new zone of unpredictability that enables new constructions of multiple selves; rather, it is a way to expose myths of embodiment and the self.

What is being stressed in many of these tales of marvelous unpredictability and newness is that communication technology is the girder for emerging forms of cultural organization that will require human adaptation and popular customization. The future is caused by technology, a technology that can promote improved forms of human interaction and bring a disparate nature (or world) together. What is being elided here is that part of the reason the future is undecided is that research is being done in relative secrecy and the user is not made aware of it until it is about to reach the marketplace. That is to say, we as consumers rely on researchers rather becoming expert ourselves when it comes to new developments. Increasingly, even as it may become easier to navigate computer desktops and use browsers, it is becoming more difficult to comprehend the workings of systems. Systems are magical when they work right, but antagonistic–or just a pain in the ass–when they do not (when one's computer crashes and one has forgotten to "save" one's document!).

A similar type of quasi-utopian rhetoric was also prevalent in the days when radio was becoming popularized and commercialized. The roots of the word *utopia*–from the Greek "no place"–suggest why it might be particularly useful in describing an ideal mediated society. The radio and computer-mediated communications as media also suggest a negative space that exists beyond a precipice. The space is enlivened by the activity of the user, but it escapes standard cartography. Cyberspatial regions resist spatial designation; interactions seem to appear on the user's computer screen, but this is only a representation of an interaction that occurs in an unfathomable, unmarked space, a "no place." As a circumvention of actual geography, this may explain the Internet's allure; it is an illusion of transcending that which confines the body to a particular space.

Even as users either applaud the speed of their connections (or, in the case of radio, the clarity of the voice) or grumble over the slowness of downloads (or the crackle of static), it is the relative control of the unseen administration of broadcasting and computing systems that creates user distrust. The circulation of a computer virus, the expansion of an inbox due to unwanted e-mail from seemingly anonymous sources, the moments when the Emergency Alert System tests its ability to take over the operation of a station—these bring the user to the potential for disaster. This sense implicates both the medium and the object that transmits and receives the medium.

The crashing of a computer or the contagion of a computer virus takes on sinister proportions; it can seem to be part of a "plot." Edward Tenner, in *Why Things Bite Back* (1996) uses the term "revenge effects" to explain how mechanical objects seem to impart damage on the human frame and psyche. With computers, part of the virtual revenge targets the body. From carpal tunnel syndrome, to eye strain, to the notion of viral contagion in interactive systems, the victim is an actual or virtual body. As we begin to use terminology of the computer to describe our own bodies and activities, we begin to attribute human-like or organic qualities to the machine and to the networks that link computers. This commingling may serve to naturalize the computer, but I would argue that the strangeness of the Internet and its expanse does not entirely dissipate.

Pleasure of the Medium

In its early stages the Internet, like the radio, did not transfer the human image in its transmittal. Of course, this has changed—the Internet transmits writing[4] and the radio transmits speech (after the Audion tube). The two media are linked in this aspect—they privilege the isolation of either written or spoken language as forms of human communication. Television, in this way, relies much more on the image. Even the Internet, with its focus on the World Wide Web and the ability of "the Web" to fold already-existing media into its operations, is still a written form of media: it relies on the "1"'s and "0"'s of binary code.

The pleasure of the medium is not so much related to its ability to transmit the entirety of the human form but in fragmenting it (or as Žižek might say, in realizing that we are always already fragmented). The Internet began by isolating and transmitting. It will lose its intense involvement of the user, I believe, when its "band width" becomes so wide that it simulates the complete human frame and involves all the senses in its transmission.[5]

"The pleasure of the interface," according to Stone (1995), is reliant on the partial nature of the transmission. Transmissions that privilege a particular sense—hearing (the radio), seeing (the Internet) provoke imagination, invite the fantasy of a total form.

Through its isolation of the senses, radio encourages completion by the listener; it requires listener involvement. Yet the medium as an industry becomes less democratic as it becomes popularized. It establishes itself as a one-to-many broadcasting institution, and the user is unable to send responses or have an impact on the structure of the broadcasting system. Kate Lacey in *Feminine Frequencies* (1996) argues that the development and popularization of radio in Germany in the 1920s and 1930s was profoundly undemocratic even as it brought information to large groups of listeners. The democratic development of the medium would have meant "general access to the reception and production of information" (5). A similar critique is put forth by Horkheimer and Adorno (1996:121–22), who argue that the radio developed along authoritarian lines as a mass form because it involved the activity of one "active" source of speakers and the untransmitted "passive" responses of listeners.[6] The telephone, however, involved person-to-person communication, ensuring that listeners are also speakers; and it involved interactivity from its structural inception, continuing through its popularization. Currently, with mobile phones, users are re-experiencing the pleasures of connection and accessibility in partial transmission. This is related to other uses of radio, "walkie-talkies" and CBs and ship-to-shore radios, where users on a mission can keep lines of communication open even as they are in movement.

This feature of interactivity and reciprocity was part of radio's pre-broadcasting appeal with the radio adventurers–and indeed, with military users–but when the medium became administered by corporations with governmental cooperation, this aspect–one of the medium's "selling points"–decreased. Radio became, on the manifest level, virtually a unidirectional, one-to-many broadcasting medium (at least before radio call-in shows, which arguably allow listeners a voice).

Even after radio became virtually synonymous with broadcasting, there were disparate attempts by groups and individuals to emphasize a more decentralized and interactive use of radio. For example, American Radio Relay League, a group organized to protect and promote amateurs, urged users in trade magazines to "Come In With Us and Enjoy Real Radio" (quoted in Czitrom 1982:72). The amateurs looked down upon these new corporate-sponsored ventures and saw broadcasting as only one of the many functions of radio (Gernsback 1922). They viewed the ability to speak to one another, to monitor government transmissions, and to disseminate information through networks of users as equally important uses of radio. Radio could be a watchdog for the people, monitoring government activities.

Czitrom (1982) suggests that amateurs also indulged in a pleasure of communication itself—they enjoyed both the form of transmission and assembling the needed technology for "ether talk." Content was not solely crucial for them; contact was the thing. It enlivened dead air; it proved the circumvention of distance. This use of radio, which was gaining in popularity, was a threat to the telephone companies, however. Steering radio toward broadcasting and away from user-to-user interaction was advantageous to the Bell company.

As radio become commercialized, the utopian rhetoric initiated by the early "pioneers" was also usurped. In the 1920s, talk of radio tearing down barriers, uniting the nation, educating the uneducated, and assimilating newcomers helped to extend the new medium's reach. Michele Hilmes (1997) argues that creating a nationwide corporate-controlled system also led to a belief that a country of divisive people was also being united through hearing these "American" voices. Hilmes cites Benedict Anderson (1991) when she writes that "the nation found a voice through the radio, the 'imagined community' of the twentieth-century United States began to take shape" (13).[7] As America's expansion continues into cyberspace in the twenty-first century, with new immigrants settling on the country's physical edges, the Internet works to create a new American online.

Although Internet service providers and browsers as well as content providers allow for textual and graphical interchange between users, as corporations increasingly gain control, proclaiming that they now provide information to the consumer rather than a service to the user, Internet users become increasingly engrossed in reception and less involved in production. Simply put, the user becomes more of a pure consumer unable to influence structures, a hunter and gatherer of Web sites, collecting experiences. Former producers of knowledge become involved in the search for, and consumption of, information. At times the speed by which a consumer can reach information is unprecedented and unfathomable. Alternatively, sometimes the system seems too clogged and the provider is at fault. The metaphor of the freedom of the highway—and the containment of the traffic jam—becomes inevitable.

Mark Poster discusses how the need for consumption in capitalism created a need for industry to teach humans to consume more: "The consumer had to be produced, so to speak" (2001:41). In the 1990s, a new kind of consumer was produced: one that is Internet savvy, full of shortcuts and bookmarks, committed to gadgetry and online hours. Involved with various cyber-personae, such a consumer is

poised halfway between nerd and suave global citizen, reading *Wired* magazine.[8]

Military Upbringings

The development of the Internet by military-sponsored
research and then its subsequent commercialization via the
World Wide Web also echoes the story of radio in important
ways. The Internet began from ARPANET (from the Department of Defense's Advanced Research Project Agency or
ARPA) and was devised as a structure to defuse and decentralize and store information in case of military attack,
specifically nuclear attack. The Department of Defense saw
this as a central pursuit for postwar research and spent mil-
lions of research dollars funding scientists at various insti-
tutions (see Stone 1995; Rheingold 1994). Although by 1968
it was clear within the military that ARPANET had other
uses (see Rheingold 1994:24), the Internet is partially the
result of American cold-war culture. The expanding notion
of defense as defining the nation in a cold-war scenario (i.e.,
the need for preparedness) and the extension of the military
into the university via research dollars and areas of endeavor
are key factors in development of the Internet.

Indeed, a vital aspect of the defense industry is its role as
a nationalized communications corporation, serving to structure systems of information in America. The military strategies of using new technology greatly affect corporate and
consumer usage. The radio too, at a crucial time during its
development, was under the governance of the military. Radio
became controlled by the Navy with the American entry into
World War I. After the war, this state monopoly became the
state-sanctioned monopoly RCA. Directly after this virtual

takeover of a medium by a sole corporation, the radio became less interactive and soon began operating under the one-to-many broadcasting paradigm. Radio was brought under military control as way to protect the citizenry and to delimit amateur activity. This centralization served to structure the broadcasting industry that soon followed upon the end of the war; it also made less possible other uses of the ether.

Similarly, the Internet's introduction to the public intensified after the end of the Cold War. This intensification was concurrent with the establishment of the United States as the sole superpower in a global environment. Thus, the radio and the Internet were trained during periods of war; they were enlisted. Later, when peace arrived, they became popularized and were brought to civilians.

Thus, although deemed "global," the Internet is also American, and its lingua franca is an American English. Although the Internet has attained a certain level of autonomy from the environment in which it was produced through its usage by amateur users and renegade individuals, as a communication medium it still bears the marks of its site of development. If the Internet can be imagined as a "decentered" environment where notions of center and margin do not mark identifiable places, it is not especially the result of academic planning or theorizing. Rather this "decenteredness" is a result of military strategizing with the enemy in mind.

Privacy and security are key concerns for all users. Users fear that through the expert use of decoding and encoding, identifying numbers (social security numbers, credit cards, PINs, passwords, and so forth) are in jeopardy and that these sequences can be revealed and private spaces can be breached. This is not only an issue of loss of privacy but also of a bordered identity. With each unauthorized invasive maneuver, mainstream media reminds the consumer that hackers are still able to wreak havoc. Such villains can gain access to protected realms, take on inappropriate personae, and crash online gated communities. Recently in New York, for example, a hacker used the computers at the Brooklyn Public library to get credit card numbers of the wealthy and famous, causing front page headlines.

The computer and the Internet have deep roots in military espionage, defense, and security. Encoding and decoding, by necessity, are the preoccupation of computing systems–computers convert all messages to binary codes. In fact, techniques of decoding German encoded radio transmission developed by mathematician Alan Turing during World War II led, in part, to the construction of the computer.[9]

For Internet users, the threat of electronic surveillance and the use of "secret" passwords that enable entrance into protected spaces mimic a military-like endeavor into the civilian quotidian. One is constantly showing identification at the crossroads of the Internet; in order to gain access into spaces, one presents a series of numbers and characters that are "proof" and represent the presence of the individual for whom they are assigned. Once "inside," one is within a space that is seemingly protected. A user's foray into the Internet is energized by these notions and by the experience of proving identity, using numbers as codes for names and deploying aliases in interactions. The consumer revels in cold-war gadgetry and techniques of evasiveness; he becomes James Bond online.

Frontiers and the Sheriff

The Internet's military upbringing is reflected in the forms of its current use: users "salute" each other with assumed names, identifying themselves with a secret "serial number" that has been assigned by a Web "master." Clearly, the space has its hierarchies or ranks. Early Internet/software designers/users, called "techies"–or in the more outlaw form, hackers–were proficient in navigating within the structures and viewed themselves as trailblazers into new terrain or as exploring a new frontier. Some amateur radio operators were also seen as reckless and obtrusive (especially by the U.S. Navy, which, in the teens of the past century, was increasingly involved in monitoring and managing emerging communication systems). Yet the popular press often depicted these boys and men as adventurers and heroes involved in travel that placed their bodies in a stationary position behind a receiver and transmitter–Jack Londons and Lewis and Clarks of the airwaves. They were romanticized heroes–discovers and inventors.

The interlinking of the military and the communications industry is complicated; it relies on renegades to further capabilities and to address the particular needs of both industries even as it professes the need for "team players." Hence, radio adventurers, castigated at the time of the sinking of the *Titanic* in 1912, were recruited by the Navy in 1917 to become part of an elite force against enemy powers. Bad boy hackers of the 1980s, once a menace to corporate computer systems and hence to national security, now develop software at Microsoft and advise presidential committees on cyberspace policies.

The utopian rhetoric that accompanied the Internet and the radio served to put forward the notion of a pure expanse that needed to be cultivated and settled. Those perceived as mavericks who ventured forth first were used to settle these nether regions. In the essay "Woman and Children First"

(1995), Laura Miller discusses the deploying of the metaphor of the frontier in discussing the Internet. For Miller, the Internet has been seen as a space that has to be tamed and settled (by men, and then by governmental intervention). In this process, the Internet moves from a lawless and adventuresome landscape that requires steel-minded virtuosity in those who settle it, to a more staid, domesticated space–a virtual suburbia. Once settled, the more dreary and law-abiding aspects of the larger culture move in. America continues this process of growth–from explorer to inventor to technician. The imagined frontier has become settled and now is suitable for the entire family, with restricted use for the children.

The term most used for what is traded via the Internet is information. Certain postmodernist theorists have focused on this aspect of the "net" and have put forward comparisons or parallels between the notions of information capital and virtual capitalism, discerning a revised economy that centers on the "flow" of information. Again, what is emphasized is "newness." Corporate leaders and alarmist commentators (for example, Baudrillard's disdain reserved for simulated realms in *Simulations* [1981] versus Gates's embrace of chaos as good for business) repeat similar phrases. This sleekest, fastest communications media will prove to be entirely transformative of every aspect of contemporary life, replacing key aspects of social existence, and perhaps endangering face-to-face interaction while enabling instantaneous communication.[10]

At one level, this is empirically accurate–the newness and popularization of the Internet is fact–but it misses the mark by failing to structure an enduring discussion on the politics of the medium. What is ignored in these discussions is the need for America to repeatedly rejuvenate mediated communication systems (without modifying production processes) and then to reinitiate a framed national debate. Experts admit that systems are not yet secure and that the safeguards are not entirely in place. This confession serves specific goals–certainly not those of the "masses" of cyberspace visitors, but neither those intended by Bill Gates. This confession allows for a call to bring in "the sheriff" in the guise of new legislation.

Building a Bridge to No-Space

In 1984 cyberpunk novelist William Gibson in *Neuromancer* coined the term "cyberspace" to describe and name the space that exists between users and the technological apparatus, that is, the space between two users of a phone conversation or the space that an e-mail missive navigates. As such, for Gibson, cyberspace is "a consensual hallucination" (1984)–not the actual space that lies between individuals involved in mediated communication, but the imagined space that users share. For Gibson, cyberspace exists as a "graphical representation of data abstracted from the banks of every computer in the human system. Unthinkable complexity. Lines of light ranged in the nonspace of the mind, clusters and constellations of data. Like city lights, receding" (51). In this prophetic description, cyberspace is not, in fact, a space. It is a willful shared abstraction, reliant on representation and the concerted effort of the user–a space that is completed by the activity and not the passivity of the user. Moreover, Gibson is foregrounding the visuality of this nonspace: It is a site of lights and graphic representation, not another arena for words, either spoken or written.

Since the time of Gibson's imagining of cyberspace, the Internet has vastly changed from its original configuration to convey more of this experience of visuality. At first, the Internet was rich with words; now its interactions are heavy with the transfer of words and image (and sound), especially with the privileging of the World Wide Web. Cyberspace now names a seemingly more ordered, shared plane that is bordered by the frames of the online service provider and browser rather than providing vistas onto endless space. Elaborate graphics serve as accessory to a simulated environment that is entered via the keyboard, mouse, modem, and monitor. At the user's will, computers connect into a net of circuitry. Users identify with the object that provides them with some agency in these environments–the mouse and cursor. These interfaces allow the user to know where he is located in or on the screen or site.

This interface or actor within the cyberspace is akin to the ventriloquist's dummy. The user has a proxy within the virtualized environment who is the user's representative, whose movements are controlled by the user. This dummy or interface is subject to change. Stone (1995) writes that the interface is a metaphor and never exactly or concretely a mouse or an elaborate cursor. The interface's task is tangible: it mediates between (and within) "bodies and selves that may or may not be within physical proximity" (89). The visible instrument that enables interactions stands in "for absent structures. . . . They're not where you could see them. It doesn't even mean that they are inside the machine; they are in an elsewhere." This "elsewhere" that Stone writes of could be called "symbolic exchange," a nonspatial term. More often, this "elsewhere" is deemed cyberspace. The interface changes, and the representation of the elsewhere is transformable. The visible dummy navigates this moving terrain. It gives the physical user a sense of place and location and the pleasurable sense of a splintered self. Yet this visible interface is a surrogate for the interface within cyberspace that is only represented on the screen. This visible interface is appealing, pleasurable. The avatar appears to navigate space with virtuosity, but cyberspace lurks beyond its representation and remains unfathomable. That is, for most users the actual interactions that occur, the dialog in codes, are not visible. They remain beyond the user's reach. What users do see is how these interactions appear. Users do not access the commingling of codes in these nether regions that create the visible interactions between two or more typists at their keyboards.

Gibson's vision of the imaginary space in between machines and people and circuitry and hardware has been achieved, but only virtually. There is no total immersion in this environment, and it remains distressingly two-dimensional; the relationship between user and dummy is fraught with distrust and is not yet fluid or seamless. Actually existing cyberspace is not yet an entire alternative to that which is deemed "reality"; it does not place the body beyond the screen inoperative or dormant. Cyberspace is not akin to the "holodeck" that simulates total environments on *Star Trek* episodes. Nor is cyberspace a theme park placed at the potential mastery of one's fingertips that involves all the senses.

As indicated earlier, the fact that cyberspace is still only a partial and fragmented experience of the body may also explain its popularity. The virtual dummy remains two-dimensional, only occasionally hearing sounds, and has squinting eyes adjusting to the variegated typefaces. This is its success: like the radio, the (early) Internet isolates and foregrounds words (here written) but still allows the user to assert his particularities.

The Internet is the privileged setting for cyberspace. It is not the only "space" envisioned by Gibson–he imagined all intersections between man and technology as potentially cyber. Yet with the information superhighway, this circuitry seemingly became an official part of the American future, a new Alaska or Hawaii, more accessible to the contiguous forty-eight states. Our leaders invoke this information-rich future repeatedly in vague terms. In this view, the Internet is both a medium of communication and a mode of transportation for information. As such, it propelled the nation into linking with the next century, ahead of the rest of the world. ("Global" in this context means only that America controls worldwide networks).

Spatialization of Disaster

With the Internet, the notion of creating national unity via a communication medium, a notion that was enunciated with the growth of the radio broadcasting industry, returns. This unity is achieved, not through participatory democracy, but through consumer usage and, with the tech stocks of the late 1990s, the collective excitement of a gold rush. Yet as so many computer images and words with complicated and competing ideologies are mounted onto the small screen of the terminal, the potential for estrangement is also accelerated (or for investors, the potential for losing money is increased).

Computer-mediated communication is overwhelming in its provocation of wonder; yet it never seems to be fast enough, and it always seems to include extraneous information. That is how the computer and the modem are poised: they are placed against a frontier that appears unbounded. Its unfathomability serves as proof of its existence for the user. Since the Internet is overwhelming to understand, it serves as proof of how it extends beyond the finite. As Pascal wrote: "We know that there is an infinite, and are ignorant of its nature" (1967:451). Numbers extend beyond the countable, and this, in part, is the proof that such numbers are possible. The Internet, approached by the computer that is finite, is an encounter with the infinite. It is pure expanse. We are told that we are only beginning to understand its capabilities and its everyday uses, as if it were part of the brain that we have not yet utilized.[11]

The ubiquity of sound now on the Internet has distinctive ramifications on the cloaking of information and the packaging of entertainment. Sound moves around corners, whereas an image must be directly gazed upon by eyes. The human ear does not need to be trained on the sound; the sound travels to it, and it enters the orifice of the ear. Sound lends a sense of depth to an environment perceived as flat. The body of the computer is becoming affixed with a prosthetic of radio voices (indeed, increasingly, radio stations are online), which will serve to give dimensionality to the screen. Also, the proliferation of sites equipped with sound on the Web can serve to render the space a voice all its own, no longer only a medium for communication, but a medium that communicates itself.

One thinks of the plethora of science fiction that dwells on the dilemma and devilry of the talking and nearly autonomous computer network. When the technological network begins to talk, then we are all in trouble. Remember Hal of *2001: A Space Odyssey* (1968), or the clipped tones of the sentient beings in *The Matrix* (1999). Once the system speaks, it begins to speak for itself. It can begin to speak against the humans who have programmed it. Give the machine the ability to say words, and you threaten to give it autonomy.

The Space of Cyberspace and the Body of the Radiobody

Even as the Internet is often thought of as a space, it is, more accurately, a series of circuits that intersect, sending electric requests back and forth to each other. These requests do not create an unseen architecture that is in any way actually girded. Rather, they create an imagined structure with unending complexity.

In contrast, the pneumatic tubes that were installed and used in Paris beginning in 1866 were actual physical spaces. These tubes were used to send messages around the city in an elaborate partially underground array that enabled the sending and receiving of notes between *arrondissements* (Hayhurst 1997). A precursor to e-mail, pneumatic tubes interlinked and relied on suction to send messages. As such, these tubes were dimensional. That is to say, whereas the movement of the cylinder through the pneumatic tube was traceable and knowable, the location of the e-mail missive between sender and receiver can only be imagined; it cannot be mapped onto negative or positive space.

In the film *The Matrix* (1999), the human's disembodiments live in a setting that does not exist but is supplied to them collectively by the evil artificial intelligence. They are complicit in the maintenance of a virtual construction of a city. Likewise, the Internet is understood via a series of spatial metaphors that do not accurately describe the transactions but instead give the user a sense or an illusion of location. That is why, in part, when multiple-user domains or dungeons (MUDS) became popularized, their name changed to chat rooms.[12] This name change suggests a domesticated place within a home, not so much dedicated to role-playing per se (MUDS began with the role-playing game "Dungeons and Dragons") but geared for the less formalized chat.

In the more ubiquitous chat rooms, the user is made to feel as if he has entered a space, rather than with a MUD, where he has entered into a series of interactions. The chat room is a room defined architecturally before one has entered; the multi-user domain is defined by the interactions that produce it and is hence less reliant on spatial notions. The dungeon as a space, too, is underground, sinister, a place of imprisonment; it also figures in the games as a location. But it is not simulated; rather, it is imagined.

Web pages are given addresses, as are e-mail mailboxes, to suggest that they are actually stable locations that a user goes to or emerges from within an administered postal system. Again, this metaphor is perhaps useful in conceptualization, but it is entirely misleading if one is attempting to understand the binary digits and the transitions achieved through a computer sending data via a modem. In fact, one could say that the Internet and its house-like conception is all wrong. Rather than being conceived of as a series of connections, it is visually represented as if the user negotiates pre-existing structures that have places on a map just beyond the user's grasp. The user's agency of self-governing interaction via circuitry is lost. One moves one's mouse over a textual plain upon which one can have no impact.

The American Internet has moved from its conception as a storehouse for military information that could survive a nuclear attack, to becoming the domain of college-educated users prone to role-playing and compelled to compile data, to a place for consumers searching for bargains in discount cyber-malls. The Internet has moved into the suburban home with software's iconic use of mailboxes, addresses, and rooms. In its spatial configurations, the Internet seems to mimic postwar history in abbreviated form. With the information superhighway, the Internet moves from metaphors of domesticity to those of movement; if previous metaphors suggested travel between fixed places from a stable originary location, the superhighway suggests endless travel. This travel is "super" in that the drivers stop by at all the shopping malls along the way. Then the driver can come home to his very own address, as if private property can be found online.

Theorist Lebbeus Woods notes that in nonarchitectural settings, "space is usually discussed in terms of human presence within it" and that the space is shaped to serve human function (1995:298). Architects, however, design rectilinear space in "pure abstracted form" whereby an office and a bedroom are virtually undifferentiated and design follows mathematical principles—human function requires adaptability to the preconfiguration of work and living spaces. Space is abstracted. It is its own presence. That is to say, a building is replete with presence even if it is uninhabited—or rather, even it if only exists as a computer document that suggests dimensionality. It is an authored document; the author has a voice; the document has presence.

Unlike space, cyberspace is not girded by Cartesian notions, yet it requires the presence of disembodiment to energize the notion of space. In fact, as a spatialized non-space, it is reliant upon the interactions of "disembodies" and the repeated use of descriptive metaphors that naturalize the notion of space. Interaction, or communication between circuitry, creates "space," as does word choice enlisted in narrating the experience retroactively.

Radiovoices, which to the listener seem to take on their own embodiment in the corporeality of the radiobody, do not rely on notions of space. These are voices with bodies that seem to emerge from the nonspace of the void of the ether, a void that Gregory Whitehead has called a "graveyard" which "nobodies" inhabit. Hence, radiovoices arrive to the listener with ambivalent results; these voices travel through unfathomable terrain that is, for the listener, never quite familiar. As Whitehead depicts in much of his work, for the speaker in front of the microphone, the voice is wrested away as the microphone allows for the transmittance of the resulting sounds. For the listener, radiovoices emerge from this uncharted terrain, a nonspace without metaphors to domesticate it. It is heard in uncanny circumstances.

The radio disembodiment in the 1930s is both reflective and descriptive of its era, an era when voice and communication systems became paramount as a way of ruling and a mode of conducting warfare, a way of institutionalizing the transmittal of information into the home. Like the Internet in recent years, the radio in the 1920s and '30s made its entrance into popular acceptance and commercial viability in part by generating excitement and unpredictability, in part by offering unity and community. Once advertising proved to be the way to make money, the medium was swiftly commercialized and made mundane as a household fixture (both as part of the furniture and as an appliance or tool for information and entertainment). However, at its inception, the perils of being connected were part of the experience of listening to shows. As Raymond Williams suggests in his discussion of broadcasting, the interruptibility of the programming flow, from soap operas to news flashes, is part of the flow itself (1992:85–90). Radio, then, as the primary form of media in the home during the 1930s, not only reports disaster and transmits governmental response to disaster, but is itself disastrous: the dream of a nation unified by media is a populace living with the companion piece of catastrophic connection.

In the 1930s there was a plethora of programs featuring ghosts and disincarnates as heroes and villains, dummies and ventriloquists, mimes and monsters. Live and simulated programs such as the *Hindenburg* disaster and "The War of the Worlds" addressed the failure of technology via technology itself. They portrayed the defense systems as malleable, and national borders as porous. Today's Internet is partially the result of the defense industries' need to defend and disseminate information. Yet it is also a vehicle for simulated travel and a space for storage. In the 1930s, the voice of President Roosevelt, especially via airwaves, led certainly to a dramatic expression of governance by mediated vocality. But this transmitted display, like today's dissemination of information, was never entirely reassuring and led to the attempt to manage panic while remaining near enough to danger to narrate the event.

Media, then, are not harmful in their portrayal and endorsement of violence or sexuality. Rather, twentieth-century media, like the spiritual medium, channel the inexplicable, permitting the user to invite sonorous or textual voices into the home in ways that never become entirely familiar or comforting. The story of the Internet and the domestic spaces it seems to produce and inhabit–a tale of uniting the nation in an imagined but shared space produced by communications technology–is reminiscent of the radio finding its central place in the American home. The potential for estrangement inherent and intrinsic to media becomes aggravated to the point of hostility at moments of crisis and catastrophe. And it is at such moments that the unseen and invisible hand of corporate control exercises the power of the uncanny to work with antagonistic force. With democratization, the media might lose these harsh sounds. Under further corporate control, conspiracies and viruses will continue to proliferate even as consumer needs appear to be met.

Notes

Chapter One

1. I derive the term *radiovoice* from contemporary radio artist and theorist Gregory Whitehead's words *radiobody* and *voicebody*. I use the term to emphasize the severance of this voice from the original speaker. My usage of *radiovoices* is meant to suggest that one is listening to voices that are disembodied and that operate with a relative independence. These voices appear to originate from within the radio, and not from live speakers in a faraway locale, as if there were Lilliputians living inside.

2. See Pierre Schaeffer's *Traité des Objets Musicaux* (1966) for his use of the term *acousmâtique*. Michel Chion adopts this term for use in his theories of sound and voice in film. The word was found in the French dictionary by Jerome Peignot; an adjective, of Greek origin, describing a sound one hears without seeing the source of it (see Chion 1993).

3. Cantril and Allport in their 1935 study found that "most people [both men and women] would rather hear a man than a woman speak over the radio" (127). Indeed, most (63% of men, 60% of women) preferred baritone voices over tenors and basses in both singing and speaking; and alto voices were preferred two to one over soprano voices (101–2). These statistics are misleading because men were more prevalent on the radio not only as newscasters but also in dramas, comedies, advertisements and as vocalists. Indeed, deeper male voices were more often heard than higher voices. In radio's earlier history female voices, especially those with higher pitches, transmitted less well, but Cantril and Allport

acknowledged that mechanical factors were negligible by 1935. The female voice was highly debated within the radio industry and its publications in the 1920s. Historians and theorists are still attempting to explain the seclusion of woman's voices to singing and to speaking only about certain topics in certain ranges.

Amy Lawrence, in her discussion of the female voice in media, suggests that having a singing woman was more socially acceptable than a speaking woman. Lawrence writes that: "a speaking woman puts herself in a position of authority–a definite breach of propriety" (1991:18). In this view, speech commands respect and this was a respect that was not to be given to women on air. Women can sing or be funny, but they cannot read the news with tonal dignity–this is the male domain.

Similarly, Michele Hilmes, in her essay "The Disembodied Woman" (1997), argues that the debate focused not on the technical aspects of transmitting higher voices but on the appropriateness of women announcers. For example, W. W. Rogers of station WWJ stated in *Radio Broadcast* magazine, "I do not believe that women are fitted for radio announcers. They need a body to their voices" (quoted in Hilmes 1997:142). To disembody a woman is, in this view, improper. Hilmes notes that women's voices on air were at first found too monotonous and then heard as having too much personality (143). Women's voices had best stay at home–and radio allowed a voice to travel.

Thus, in many ways, audiences were being trained to want to hear gender and vocality as they had been hearing them already– and radio could challenge gender norms. Cantril and Allport (1935) found that women's voices were preferred only in the reading of poetry and abstract passages, the areas where female broadcasters were used. The researchers reported that prejudice played a major part in their finding that listeners judged female voices as affected and unnatural, and male voices as more trustworthy and persuasive (127–32). Radio in the 1930s became a realm dominated by baritonal voices. Female voices, particularly soprano voices, were heard as less authentic and the male voice was real and convincing, especially when it was "harsher and deeper" (135). It is particularly compelling that the researchers used the word "harsher" to describe this voice. The word suggests that there was an element of hostility in this voice as well as comfort, recognizability, and trustworthiness.

Two harsh voices of the 1930s were the anti-Roosevelt sounds of Huey Long and Father Coughlin. They varied pitches, spoke quickly, and conveyed their anger and mistrust of the government by utilizing the top and bottom of their voices. In Father Coughlin's thinly disguised anti-Semitic speech on the radio, "Persecution: Jews and Christians" (1938), he varies his tempo from 100 words per minute to 275 words per minute (the normal speed of radiovoices at the time was 175 to 220 wpm). He often moved his baritonal range into tenor regions. He also increased his volume as he explained, incredibly simplistically (not to mention historically misinformed) how fascism arose out of communism, and how (secular) Jews were behind communism and thus that Jews were to blame for the rise of fascism (see Warren 1996). In a speech later that year on "The Impending International War," Coughlin spoke extremely quickly, averaging around 205 words per minute. He also pushed his range from a low mournful B to an alarming F sharp, using far more tones than the four or five notes that FDR relied on for expressivity.

In Huey Long's anti-FDR speech of 1936, "St. Vitus' Dance Government," the words emerge vitriolically. He ranges from 185 to 265 wpm. This speed renders words almost unintelligible; they begin to blur together. In his diatribe against big business, and in speaking of his compassion for blacks (while using the word "nigger" unabashedly on network NBC), his voices rises far higher than Father Coughlin's to a B below middle C, especially as he speaks of the horror of government policy and its dictator-like endeavors. In comparison to the measured tones of Roosevelt, these orators sound frenzied, impassioned, hysterical.

In popular Western notions of pitch, high notes signify passion, while low notes convey melancholy. As a result, words of contentedness sung slowly by a bass at the bottom of his range will inevitably sound sad to an ear trained by traditional interpretations of tone; whereas the same words sung with a quick tempo at the top of a soprano's range will sound fiery, perhaps crazed. Similarly, increased volume of the voice signifies increased emotion, particularly anger. These notions of pitch, tempo, and volume are used to effect in oratory techniques. On the radio, gesture cannot, of course, be a factor in technique, and thus inflections of the voice become more crucial. Senator Long and Father Coughlin used these vocal attributes in their broadcasts in order to unsettle listeners.

Since they sounded fired up, speaking with immediacy, they also could not in any way be heard as reassuring. They wished to alarm listeners to the disaster of government and big business, and they used their voices as panic itself.

4. Slavoj Žižek, in the essay "Against the Digital Heresy" (2001) takes on some of the recent theorizing on disembodiment and cyberspace, particularly Katherine Hayles's *How We Became Posthuman* (1999). Žižek uses an analogy with ventriloquism (which I also use in Chapter 6) when he suggests that the speech act itself is a disembodying act: "The moment a living being starts to speak, the medium of its speech (say, voice) is minimally disembodied, in the sense that it seems to originate not in the material reality of the body that we see, but in some invisible 'interiority'–a spoken word is always minimally the voice of a ventriloquist, a spectral dimension always reverberates in it" (2001:44).

Žižek argues that speech seems to occur from an outside since it comes from a mysterious place inside the speaker. I would argue also that since the speaker inherits the language system from the culture (or more immediately, from one's parents) and does not invent utterances, words themselves can seem to come from another source. Speech is always already ventriloquy.

5. Lori Seggio first used the term "Oz Effect" in my History of Broadcasting class on 15 October 1997, referring to the "War of the Worlds" broadcast.

6. In using the word *representation,* I am thinking of the ways in which Stuart Hall nuances its usage. He designates "three approaches to explaining how representation of meaning through language works" (1997:24). The first two are the reflective approach (meaning lies in the object, and the representation reflects it); and the intentional approach (the representation means what the author/speaker/artist intends it to mean). The third approach is the one valorized by Hall: the constructionist approach. This usage implies that "things don't *mean:* we *construct* meaning, using representational systems–concepts and signs" (25). Hall acknowledges that representations do have a "material dimension": they have "sounds" or "images" or "marks." Yet "representation is a practice" that conveys meanings (25).

In Roosevelt's radio addresses, his words not only carry his intentions or reflect a specific social reality but also construct a meaning for listeners. In using the word "representation," I am also playing with the notion of the president as a representative of the people. In what is called a representational democracy, he stands in for the citizenry as their surrogate in matters of the state both nationally and internationally.

7. For a very interesting discussion on séances, spiritual mediums, and their relationship to new technologies, see Steven Connor's "The Machine in the Ghost: Spiritualism, Technology, and the 'Direct Voice'" (1999). Also see "A Gramophone in Every Grave" in his book *Dumbstruck: A Cultural History of Ventriloquism* (2000).

8. See the work of Susan Douglas (1987) for more discussion of the impact of the radio boys.

9. Tales of surviving the disaster–as well as heroic rescues– became common media fare after "9/11." Of course, these are important stories to tell, but such experiences began to fall into for-mulaic structures, sentimentalizing experiences.

Chapter Two

1. Edison was, in fact, concerned with being able to record the last words of the dying via his invention of the tin foil phonograph. See a recent biography by Neil Baldwin, *Edison: Inventing the Century* (1995:85).

2. The direct voice is a voice that "speaks independently of the medium's vocal organs" (Connor 2000:364). For Connor, the medium acts "as a telephonist rather than as a telegraphist" (365), connecting herself and the séance with voices that come from the beyond.

3. Relatedly Carolyn Marvin, like McLuhan, asserts that technology such as the electric light bulb is also an information medium (1988). She shows how the light bulb became the focus of public spectacle and entertainment and argues that "for late-nineteenth-century observers, the electric light was a far more likely mass medium than any point-to-point invention such as the telephone or even wireless" (190).

4. Heidegger works with another notion of the danger of technology. In his essay on technology, "The Turning," in *The Question Concerning Technology* (1977), he refers to turning danger into saving power "where Being suddenly clears itself and lights up" (44). In this flash of truth that emerges from danger, technology reveals its own essence, which can allow for Being's revealing of itself through the disentwining of the two. But clearly, the approach to this turn is fraught with "danger." For Heidegger, in this essay, it is not

a question of whether technology has become almost autonomous and has gained control over man as if it were a foreign agent keen on conquering. Nor is it a question of developing a strategy for gaining mastery over technology as if it were an uncontrollable feral child. Rather, the essence of modern technology has served to place man and things within the dominion of "Enframing," where objects lose their significance as objects and are placed in an order that is seemingly manicured safely but remains a space where truth is concealed. This danger, for Heidegger, is embedded and lurking: "But the danger, namely, Being itself endangering itself in the truth of its coming to presence, remains veiled and disguised. This disguising is what is most dangerous in the danger. In keeping with this disguising of the danger through the ordinary belonging to Enframing, it seems time and time again as though technology were a means in the hands of man" (37).

Thus, man's relationship with himself and with technology becomes disguised and hence dangerous, even as it appears orderly. For Heidegger, it is not so much a danger due to a perceived autonomy of the technological object; instead, the object is sewn into a process of Enframing with its user, an entrapment that serves to blind the user to the "objectness" of the object. To put it another way, the computer user has commingled too much with his machine, and yet hopes to place it within a hierarchy of objects; the radio user has committed to hearing himself enunciated by an object that the user still thinks he can turn on and off, an object that allows himself a voice.

These philosophical processes of revealing, of denying an openness to Being, transposed (without making equivalencies) into more psychoanalytical terms of projection, introjection, and identification, suggest that Enframing disguises the object through a relationship of false intimacy that serves to disguise the user to his Self. For Heidegger, this disguise is dangerous, lurking, placed within a frame of unknowingness.

Of course, this frame can turn into an insightedness, in an inflashing. Revealingly, Heidegger's use of the word *flash* seems to owe more to photography than to lightning. As a philosopher in the modern age of technology, Heidegger views Enframing within a certain historical frame, one whose vocabulary is imbued with embedded relationships to technological objects that often do not come to (electric) light. The flash is enabled as much by technological instruments of the post–Menlo Park era as it is by an electrical storm due to meteorological factors. Heidegger's language is infused with embedded analogies with the operations of media.

5. For a popular attempt at explaining the vengeful aspect of technology, see Edward Tenner's *Why Things Bite Back: Technology and the Revenge of Unintended Consequences* (1996).

6. Although Orson Welles has one of the most recognizable and distinctive voices in radio (and film) history, there are qualities in his voice that make it quite representative of the radiovoice of the time. It was baritonal, booming; moreover, in its very tones it suggested a personality. This aspect of the radiovoice, the importance of its expressiveness, was not lost on American social scientists of the 1930s, although their concerns were far less aesthetically concerned. For example, in their experiments on voice and personality, Hadley Cantril and Gordon Allport, who conducted much research on radiovoice reception, also distinguished between voice and speech. They were concerned "with the psychodiagnostic significance of voice considered as an expressive agent" (1971 [1935]:110). Cantril and Allport's experiments used 24 untrained (nonactor) male speakers reading passages from Dickens or Lewis Carroll, to a total of 655 listeners. In a radio studio, listeners heard brief speeches from different speakers either from behind a curtain or broadcasted to them and were then asked to make judgments about the speaker: age, height, complexion, vocation, political preference, ascendance-submission, and so forth.

Results in this experiment were contradictory. Listeners were 7 percent more accurate in discerning personality when the voice was hidden behind a curtain and not heard on radio. Blind listeners were decidedly less accurate than sighted listeners. The researchers concluded that voice conveys accurate information "concerning outer and inner characteristic of personality" (122). Hadley and Cantril further noted that listeners fared far better in discerning speakers' interests and traits than their features of physique and appearance (123–24). They concluded that the voice indicates the interior aspects of the speaker; the speaker can be "known" to the listener.

In addition, the fact that this complicated study was done in the 1930s shows the fascination the voice had not only for the lay listener but also for the social scientist. Disembodied voices were commonplace. This raises important questions for both the listener and the expert: Could these voices reflect realities of personality, and did the sound of the voice reveal secrets about the actual body of the speaker? Can the listener gain an understanding of the speaker and know him just by listening to him? The undertaking of these experiments reveals the societal anxiety around the ascendance of the radiovoice. If the relationship between listener and speaker is intimate, is this intimacy trustworthy, enduring, reliable? And what other forms of intimacy has it supplanted?

7. Laurie Anderson played with these perceptions of the audience when she transformed her alto voice to baritone by use of technological equipment in her performances and recording of *Home of the Brave* (1986). The audience was invited to search for a male body that did not actually exist but that emerged from the workings of equipment of vocal decoders. She put on an acoustic mask, making no attempt to hide the technology that enabled this feat. The "male" voice that came from her sounded uncanny, severed but still connected to her body.

This notion of the voice guiding the visual scene and manipulating the ways images are seen also reverberates in the work of Rick Altman, who argues that the relationship of the soundtrack to the image in film is akin to that of the ventriloquist and the dummy (1980). I use his arguments further in Chapter 5 in my discussion of Welles's "War of the Worlds."

8. This fantasy is restated by males abducted by aliens of contemporary America, who also report involuntary emissions while abducted. See, for example, *Secret Life* (Jacobs 1992).

9. Avital Ronell in *The Telephone Book* suggests that the schizophrenic "has placed telephone receivers all along her body" in order to ensure her "stationary mobility" (1989).

10. Deleuze and Guattari, in *Anti-Oedipus: Schizophrenia and Capitalism* (1983), describe the machine as "a system of interruptions or breaks" (36). A desiring-machine, then, is a name for how desire moves through breaks in culture: "Desiring-machines are binary machines.... Desire causes the current to flow, itself flows in turn, and breaks the flow" (5).

11. Freud's reading (1963 [1911]) of Schreber's amazingly detailed account of the cosmology of the paranoiac is vastly different than the arguments articulated by Canetti in *Crowds and Power* (1966). Freud posits an etiology of Schreber's malady, finding the roots of his paranoia in his repression of homosexual desire. Canetti is less concerned with causality; rather, he enlists the text as a paradigm of the workings of power. Instead of arguing for one reading or the other, I aim to use both of these readings to offer an analysis of the ways

technology becomes immersed and dispersed into the paranoid imagination, dislodged as hostile under the conference of the disaster. This analysis is concerned, then, with the workings of the voice in paranoia, both its power relations and its relation to sexuality.

12. In accordance with Robert's assertion about Schreber as a virtualist, it might be interesting to view Schreber as a transgressive cyborg akin to that promoted by Haraway in her "A Manifesto for Cyborgs" (1985). Haraway's cyborg, like Schreber's virtual body, defies traditional gender performances, is part machine, and is in a continual state of becoming a mode of defiance to all normatives.

13. For a discussion of the cinematic impulse before film, see Allen Weiss's "Kinomadness" in *Shattered Forms* (1992).

14. For a related treatise on the purging of God, see Artaud's radio piece "To Be Done With the Judgement of God" (1992).

Chapter Three

1. The World Trade Center attacks have also permanently changed the national character, showing the country's connections to the rest of the world in a most horrid fashion. Mainstream media now seems to refer to time as either pre- or post-"9/11." The day of the trauma becomes the marker of a new national identity that can not bear the actuality of an attack, yet can not stop bringing attention to the wounds.

2. There are current relevancies to Blanchot's insight about the distance that disaster travels. For example, the World Trade Center towers used to feel very far from my apartment, although I live below 14th street. With their collapse, and after the military locked down the area, I realized I had always lived in their shadow, and I felt their pinching absence on my skin. In New York, one felt surrounded by the disaster and its losses.

3. For a detailed history of this industry research, see Mark Bank's *History of Broadcast Audience Research* (1981).

4. Americans seem to attain ecstasy—or a sense of being-at-home—with the combination of moving and speaking/listening via acoustic technology. As a pedestrian in New York City, I am convinced that I have been witness to cell phone users in the midst of imaginary conversations.

5. For a recent history of the *Graf Zeppelin*, see Douglas Botting's *Dr. Eckener's Dream Machine: The Historic Saga of the Round-the-World Zeppelin* (2001).

6. In his recent history of role of the zeppelin in the construction of German nationalism, *Zeppelin: Germany and the Airship, 1900–1939* (2002), Guillaume de Syon argues against most histories of the relationship between zeppelin travel and German fascism. He suggests that the Nazis were in fact ambivalent about using the zeppelin as one of the symbols of German power and progress. The zeppelin was a symbol inherited from the Weimar era, and the "popularity of the machine fed in part on the old cult of Count Zeppelin." (172).

7. Perhaps the commander was also experiencing the terrifying sublime as discerned by Kant in *Observations on the Feeling of the Beautiful and Sublime* (1991:48)

8. For a theoretical treatise on witnessing in history, see Shoshana Felman and Dori Laub, *Testimony: Crises in Literature, Psychoanalysis, and History* (1992).

9. Osama bin Laden's image on video has now become the figure of disaster. He is not only the leader of al-Qaida, but our government is determined to have us believe that he is the main designer of the terrorist attack. With this framing, his somewhat gentle-looking face appears even more monstrous as we hear translations of his "evil" words.

10. The Federal Emergency Management Agency (FEMA) defines five potential categories of disaster: (1) natural; (2) technological (building implosions, nuclear accidents); (3) discrete accidents (industrial, transportation); (4) sociopolitical (assassination, hostage, terrorism); and (5) epidemics and disease (see Doane 1990; FEMA 1997a).

11. The crashing of the second plane into the tower and the subsequent fires and collapses in the World Trade Center on September 11 were captivating images that were repeatedly shown on television. For their transfixing horror and enormity, they outdid many a Hollywood disaster movie.

12. Similarly, we must remember that after the World Trade Center attacks, the networks interrupted programming and reported on the events without running commercials more than twenty-four hours. This was a clear display of their determination to report on the disaster and to keep their audience up-to-date on what was to become the beginning of a new war. In these transmissions, eyewitnessing was a key element to the broadcasts.

13. Beckett plays with interactions between live and recorded voices reporting a life in *Krapp's Last Tape* (1960). In the Beckett

film *Not I*, directed by Neil Jordan (2000), all the viewer sees is actor Julienne Moore's lips moving in the darkness; the voice is disembodied, and the lips speak without visible source–the voice is a thrown one.

Chapter Four

1. There may be ways to analyze the clipped, warbly, and slightly angry tones of George W. Bush after the terrorist attacks as performing a similar function. Rather than reassuring the American public, he reminds auditors of the possibility of further attacks and the reasons for war, thus serving to institute himself as the leader and the voice of American resolve–even as the president insists upon the danger that still exists. For as his administration repeats quite often, "they" will attack again.

2. Slavoj Žižek uses Kantorowicz's thesis in his essay "The King Is a Thing" (1991) to discuss Lenin's "two bodies," arguing, "Is not the ultimate proof of this special attitude of Leninist Communists towards the body the fact of the *mausoleum*–their obsessive compulsion to preserve intact the body of the dead Leader (Lenin, Stalin, Ho Chi Minh, Mao Zedong)? How can we explain this obsessive care if not by reference to the fact that in their symbolic universe, the body of the Leader is not just an ordinary transient body but a body redoubled in itself, an envelopment of the sublime Thing" (260).

Žižek posits that Lenin's body was doubled and the second body was "sublime, immaterial, sacred"–connected and loyal to communism and history. This is the body that is housed in the mausoleum, given to the people.

My use of Kantorowicz is different; it is applied to a particular American leader at a specific moment. Rather than doubled by a (psychic) relationship to the state and the people (or to notions of divinity), Roosevelt develops a second body via the media–and particularly by way of his voice transmitted on the radio. This body shrouds his actual, more vulnerable, always recovering corporeality.

3. Michael E. McGerr in *The Decline of Popular Politics* (1986) argues that the "advertised campaign" preceded twentieth-century media and started in the North after the Civil War. Increasingly, political techniques began to be greatly influenced by advertising and pressure groups. Ironically, one of the results of using professional methods to motivate campaigns was decreased voter turnout.

4. There were certainly many others who were suspicious of Roosevelt's speeches and their techniques. For example, see Ryan (1988).

5. I am citing the page number in the Buhite and Levy book (1991) where the speeches are transcribed; I refer to the recordings of these speeches at the Museum of Television and Radio (New York) and on audiocassette (see Roosevelt 1995).

6. Essayist E. B. White uses the word "force" to discuss the impact of radio. In 1933, he wrote of the radio usage of his rural neighbors: "People here speak of 'The Radio' in the large sense, with an overmeaning. When they say 'The Radio,' they don't mean a cabinet, an electrical phenomenon, or a man in a studio, they refer to a pervading and somewhat godlike presence which has come into their lives and homes.... One of the chief pretenders to the throne of God is Radio, which has acquired a sort of omniscience" (quoted in Lewis 1993:231).

7. Hayes (1995) notes that in listener's letters to the president, readers accented loyalty and obedience as patriotic duties rather than use of their democratic rights. This attitude, I believe, goes hand-in-hand with buttressing the power of a second body.

8. Today when users begin their cell-phone conversations, they perform a similar enunciation. They let their auditor know where they are calling from—"I'm calling from my car on the highway," and so forth. Of course, no matter where the speaker is, he is always on the phone.

9. In his essay "From Schizophrenia to Schizophonica" in *Phantasmatic Radio* (1995), Allen Weiss discusses Artaud's radio piece "To Be Done with the Judgement of God," and relates it to the "theft of the voice and the disappearance of the body" (32) that the production of recording (and relatedly, broadcasting) involves. Weiss writes that recording the voice is a risk to identity formations: "The recorded voice is the stolen voice that returns to the self as the hallucinatory presence of the voice of another" (32).

10. I refer to the game of fort-da, discussed in Freud's *Beyond the Pleasure Principle* (1961), that the child plays with a toy attached to a string; he pushes it away—a representation of his mother leaving him.

11. These changes in programming and in the public's relationship to the medium are also evident in the changes of the design for radios. During the 1920s the "Furniture Style" of radio was prevalent. Since there was no idea of what a radio for the home

should look like, sets were made to look like already existing pieces of furniture for the home (including liquor cabinets during Prohibition!). This design style persisted into the early 1930s. In 1932, sets began to be made out of Bakelite, a synthetic first patented in 1908. The English firm Ekco exploited Bakelite's molding properties but found that imitating furniture with this plastic did not make sense. Bakelite lacked the texture of wood, but Wood could not be molded into complicated curvilinear lines. In 1934, a new, smaller circular radio with two small legs was introduced. It did not appear wood-like and did not mimic any other piece of furniture. Its white dials were prominent against its sleek black surface. The loudspeaker grille was not hidden by symbolic motifs. The station band copied the circular form of the radio itself, stretching prominently at the top of the black-and-white object. This radio announced its "radio-ness" prominently. With this design, the radio no longer appeared familiar.

As communications medium and as object, radio was becoming more familiar to the public. In addition, radio prices were coming down due to increased efficiency in mass production (indeed, Bakelite helped in this) and increasing demand (J. Hill 1978:77, 78). Prices for the more opulent models in the 1920s had soared to more than $1,000. Prices adapted to the economic realities of the late 1920s and the newer models, smaller and lighter, were priced well under $100. For example, the Kadette company's 1935 Jewel model suggested retail price was $13.50; Fada's 1937 brightly colored "Coloradio" retailed at $19.99 (Collins 1987:20, 26).

By the mid-1930s, radios were taking on their own shape, enabled both by plastic and by the assembly line. The country's top industrial designers were enlisted by the more than six hundred manufacturers in business from the late 1920s to the early 1940s (Collins 1987:10). Radios were almost a staple of the home. They took on their own design identity and their own recognizability as talking objects.

The Fada "Coloradio" model of 1937 appeared in a body of bright fire-engine red plastic, with gold speaker and chrome grille work. Even when the volume is turned down, the object appears loud. It is eye-catching compared to the subtleties and grandiosity of dark wood. A Stewart Warner model of 1933, made of metal, featured the profile of a human head inlaid and partially outlined in black; this profile is also the speaker of the radio. The volume dial, also in black, is situated at the top of the brain area, and the tuner dial is located at the neck of the head. In effect, the controls of the radio are grafted onto the head of the human in this design. This suggests that the object is akin to a talking head. Indeed, on the radio's front, the head's chin is slightly turned up, and its mouth is open, appearing to be speaking. This radio model literalizes the idea of the disembodied voice and imprints it upon the frame of the object. In an almost ecstatic pose, the brainy visage serves to enunciate simultaneously with the voices that emerge from its outline.

By the mid-1930s, the ether had been secured and stabilized by governmental intervention and corporate acumen against more localized, sporadic efforts. Radios were sold in the 1930s with radio stations numbers and names already printed (or with buttons that one could push already ascribed to dial numbers). This suggested a radio world that was predictable, with profitable stations that were part of a larger corporate network. Even though the economic order was in jeopardy, the airwaves seemed fixed. The radio became a plastic, mass-produced item, and stations could be found easily on the dials.

12. An analogy could be drawn here between this popular programming and some of the fantasies of Dr. Schreber, as discussed in Chapter 2.

Chapter Five

1. A version of "War of the Worlds" was broadcast on Radio Quito in Ecuador in 1947. A similar panic broke out. When listeners were told by the station that it had been a drama, the populace was outraged. They burned the station to the ground. Two people were killed in the fire.

2. This information was found in the program for an audio exhibit at the Museum of Radio and Television, New York, entitled "The History of Radio," 1993.

3. In his history, *Advertising the American Dream* (1985), Roland Marchand argues that radio was quite a challenge to the advertising industry during its early years of commercialization. Radio was considered both *intrusive* and *intimate;* hence advertisers were unsure what tone to take when addressing the consumer, especially when it was clear that the medium was no longer "genteel."

4. For a good summary of research that examined the panic, see Lowery and DeFleur, "The Invasion from Mars: Radio Panics America" (1994); see also Hadley Cantril, *The Invasion from Mars: A*

Study in the Psychology of Panic (1940) and Howard Koch, *The Panic Broadcast: Portrait of an Event* (1970). For another nontraditional reading of the panic, see "Alien Ether" in Jeffrey Sconce's *Haunted Media* (2000).

5. For example, the magic bullet theory assumes that people in a mass society are isolated and revert to instinctual ways. They are thus vulnerable to messages from the mass media; these messages are like bullets that are aimed at each listener. These bullets affect each in similar ways. See Lowery and DeFleur (1994:14–15)

6. The Payne Fund studies were some of the first major studies that attempted to gauge media effects. Done in the early 20s, they studied how film affected children. I would argue that one of the assumptions was that mass culture was a contaminant (or an impurity) to the innocence (or the purity) of children.

7. Don Seigel's film *The Invasion of the Body Snatchers* (1956), can be seen as a depiction of Capgras' syndrome set in a paranoid cold war America. In the film, bodies are reanimated and yet are replacements of the original. The familiar body returns as an alien.

8. I use the word *doppelganger* rather than *double* because it refers to "the ghostly counterpart of a living person" and hence suggests the meaning of a dead copy of a live original.

9. The Internet came under attack by the *New York Times* for rather similar reasons. The editorial "www.internet.anarchy" in the *New York Times,* 15 August 1997 (A22) refers to the Welles incident and chides the Internet for its infantile behavior in presenting nonfacts as facts. For the editorialist, this kind of presentation of disinformation is a reckless homage to Welles.

10. I first heard reports of the attacks on the World Trade Center from listening to the radio. Like a few other people I spoke with, I thought it might be a hoax and turned on the television for verification. This might be a legacy of Welles's broadcast–radio can't be trusted–and seeing is believing.

11. Steven Connor in *Dumbstruck: A Cultural History of Ventriloquism* (2000) notes: "The word ventriloquist itself is a Latin translation of the Greek word *engastrimythos,* from *en* in, *gaster* the stomach, and *mythos* word or speech. The term referred to a particular manner of speech which gave rise to the illusion of a voice from proceeding from elsewhere than the person of the utterer" (50).

In Connor's appraisal, the Delphic oracle is ventriloquial. The oracular voice "becomes as important as it does because it invents the ecstatic voice, invents the idea of prophecy as the effect of the female voice torn apart, through a frenzied, violent, inhuman voice, a voice that at once tends and dismembers the body and yet forms out of this a new kind of vocal body, a body-in-pieces" (74).

In his history of ventriloquism, Valentine Vox too notes ancient oracles as examples of ventriloquy. From the ancient world, he also cites the Memnon Colossi, two funerary statues that were reported to have sung on certain mornings (1993:14) and the "belly prophets" who would "counterfeit spirit possession by talking in a diffused voice while engaging in certain amount of lip control" (18). Listeners were lead to believe that the voice came, not from the lips, but from the stomach of the prophet.

12. One classic example of the manic, dangerous dummy is Hugo in *The Dead of Night* (1945). Chucky (of the movie series) can be seen as a dummy who is set free; he is animated without the ventriloquist.

13. William Barlow argues in his recent history of black radio that the show *Amos 'n' Andy* was a form of minstrelsy on the air–white actors performed a radiophonic blackface. He adds that this dynamic was a form of racial ventriloquy (1999:27, 46). "Black"-sounding voices were thrown from the bodies of white actors.

14. All subsequent quotations from the script are from the edition in Cantril (1940). They will be indicated by WW, followed by the page number.

15. The broadcast's use of the verb "to take" (often used in broadcast news) suggests that the auditor travels along with the station's movements. The auditor is a silent companion to the traveling broadcast.

16. Due to an agreement in 1933 between print and broadcasting media owners, newspersons on the radio were called "commentators"; the term "reporter" was reserved for those who worked for newspapers.

17. In communications theory, this kind of use of media is called "use and gratifications" (see Lowery and DeFleur 1995:400) This particular use of the media is known as surveillance–using media to keep aware of the world around the user.

18. The actual introduction of the Emergency Broadcast System (EBS) occurred much later than the period discussed here–in 1963, in fact–but the ability to initiate an automatic government takeover of the public airwaves occurred during the Truman administration. Under the legislation that established the EBS, all

stations licensed by the FCC must install equipment that allows the president and other federal, state, or local officials to reach the public during states of emergency. As *The Emergency Broadcast System Plan* states: "[The plan] provides for utilizing the facilities and personnel of the entire non-government communications industry on a voluntary organized basis to provide the Nation with a functional emergency system to be operated by the industry under appropriate government regulations and in a controlled manner consistent with national security requirements and the Rules and Regulations of the Federal Communications Commission" (FCC 1964:1).

The system, when it is initiated by a station, "produces what is commonly called a two-tone signal (the frequencies 853Hz and 960Hz played simultaneously).... [T]his serves the dual purpose of getting the listener's attention and activating other EBS equipment in the listening area" (FEMA 1997b). With the EBS equipment activated, a station records the accompanying audio message that retransmits this message for its audience. Once a station receives the message, it must broadcast the two-tone signal and the message it records in order for the next station to receive the information. If a station does not initiate use of their EBS equipment, "the chain will be broken and a segment of the population will not receive the emergency information through EBS" (1997).

The EBS was an analog system that relied on the volunteerism of the personnel. It is now replaced by the Emergency Alert System (EAS). The EAS is digital and is not reliant on this chain of responding stations. See also Reed (1997).

19. Kant provides three different accounts of the sublime: the terrifying sublime, the noble, and the splendid. The terrifying sublime is "accompanied with a certain dread, or melancholy" (1991:47). David Nye, writing about the sublime in the American context, adds another category–"the technological sublime" (1999).

20. Another way to look at the broadcast is to use the notion of defamiliarization as defined by the Russian formalists (e.g., Shklovsky 1965). Welles's broadcast defamiliarizes the medium's programming; the program also serves to defamiliarize the object–radio–that receives the medium's broadcast. For Shklovsky, defamiliarization is an aesthetic device involving "not naming the familiar object in its description." For example, Tolstoy's description of a flogging is "made unfamiliar both by the description and by the proposal to change its form without changing its nature" (1965:13). Without using the word "flogging," Tolstoy describes the act by

including another possible means of inflicting pain (1965:13). Here, Welles describes the everyday invasiveness of radio by portraying another kind of invasion.

In addition, defamiliarization can involve describing a familiar event as if it were occurring for the first time (again, this is the case in the "War of the Worlds" broadcast–only Welles has changed the form of the invasion). Welles defamiliarized the programming of radio through its segments that have an affinity with other objects and activities. The radio's flow of informative voices and diverting sounds (its parts of storytelling and music and segue) that include program interruption, contribute to the estrangement in the overall framing of the production.

Chapter Six

1. In his pioneering book *Radio: An Art of Sound* (1971 [1936]), Rudolf Arnheim emphasizes the role of the sound of speech in radio art. He writes: "The pure sound of the word is the mother-earth from which the spoken work of art must never break loose, even when it disappears into the far heights of word-meaning" (28). Arnheim believed that since radio isolates the voice, the sound aspect of language (as opposed to the meanings of the word) is more easily discerned and has a greater effectiveness on the listener. This effectiveness harks back to an earlier pre-lingual era in human interaction. Arnheim argues that aural art reverts "to those primitive ages when, long before the invention on an actual human speech, the ... cries of living beings were understood only as sounds and only in virtue of their expressiveness" (27). For him, this emphasis on sound is a crucial factor in radio drama production. The grain of the voice signifies independently from the cognitive faculties that are involved in understanding the meaning of the enunciated words.

2. In recent theorizing on the voice and gender, I am not alone in turning to the myth of Echo as inspiration. In *Narcissus and Echo: Women in the French Récit* (1988), Naomi Segal uses the tale as an entry into discussing what she calls the confessional *récit* in French fiction, or first-person narratives written from the man's point of view in which a female character greatly influences the story. She argues for a particular reading of these texts, hinted at by Echo's story: "This means ... seeking out ... the unconscious desire embodied in speech, 'clouding' the mirror,

and looking for the female presence that pervasively echoes in the text" (18).

In *Echo and Narcissus: Women's Voice in Classical Hollywood Cinema* (1991), Amy Lawrence uses the Echo myth as a starting point for examining the treatment of female sonority in the Hollywood film.

3. The term "sonorific envelope" comes from Guy Rosolato, who argued that the maternal voice takes on spatiality. It becomes a place to be for the infant (1974).

4. I tread gingerly here. I do not want to use an ancient tale of the "West" to understand a situation in twentieth-century America without precaution. Instead, I want to reread this tale in order to see how a specific rendition of the tale is used in literature and in psychoanalysis in the last century. As I contingently mark Echo's story as one of the first instances of the disembodied voice, I am myself indulging in my own interpretation of her disembodiment as a way to speak of more recent phenomena.

5. This was an aspect of the reporting of the aftermath of the World Trade Center attack. It was important for television crews to be reporting live as close as possible to "ground zero." Mayor Guiliani's police force, though, did not allow reporters as much access as was granted to visiting celebrities. Interestingly, it became important for many people to see with their own eyes in order to really gauge the magnitude of the disaster. I think this emphasis on witnessing for oneself is as much a fascination with the destruction and the ruins as it is a realization that television reduces the immensity of the loss.

6. Freud writes in "On Narcissism": "It seems very evident that one person's narcissism has a great attraction for those others who have renounced part of their own narcissism and are seeking after object-choice; ... it is as if we envied them their power of retaining a blissful state of mind—an unassailable libido-position which we ourselves have since abandoned" (1963:70).

Freud posits a "we" (those seeking after an object-choice) and a "them" (those narcissists who appear to "retain a blissful state of mind," who seek admirers or converts to their cause of self-involvement). This explains, in part, Echo's return to Narcissus; but following the narcissistic adventure also involves the witnessing of disaster, and the ability to survive it all, albeit in an ineffectual anguish. The promise of involvement in Narcissus is to report his transition into the inanimate, or more accurately, the vegetal.

7. In his cultural history of ventriloquism, Connor (2000) entitles his chapter on modern spiritualism "A Gramophone in Every Grave." He argues that acoustic technology played a big role in early-twentieth-century practices of the séance and also that these new technologies extended an interest in locating and communicating with the dead.

8. Amy Lawrence argues that in *Sunset Boulevard* (1950:154–66) there is a reversal in the roles of Narcissus and Echo. Joe Gillis (William Holden) is treated as if his voice-over narration is female. It is always affixed to his body (a trait of the female voice-over) and never flies above the story. As a cinematically male Echo, he is unable to stop the self-destruction of the *female* Narcissan, Norma Desmond. Norma, as played by Gloria Swanson, was a great star in the silent era of cinema and was overlooked in the talkie era.

Chapter Seven

1. The introduction of television in postwar America was not accompanied by the kind of utopian rhetoric that the Internet and the radio provoked. Cultural leaders did not see television as a unifying force. I would argue that since television did not have as much popular usage before it was commercially introduced, it did not have the same mystique attached to it.

2. For further discussion on the debates and the arguments for radio as a unifier, see Susan Smulyan, *Selling Radio* (1994). Andy Warhol takes up an aspect of this argument, insisting that because Americans all watch television and drink coke, they share a commonality. See *The Philosophy of Andy Warhol* (1987).

3. For discussion of the posthuman, see Katherine Hayles's *How We Became Posthuman* (1999).

4. Shawn Wilbur argues a similar point in his essay "An Archaeology of Cyberspaces" (1997): "Whatever else Internet culture might be, it is still a largely text-based affair"(6).

5. As a user, I am beginning to lose interest in the Web and have returned to the more old-fashioned maintenance of correspondence that e-mail affords. Of course, I get a bit antsy if I go a few days without checking my e-mail, which suggests a strong emotional attachment to a connection with a system.

6. This project does not operate from the premise that listening is a passive act, of course.

7. Joy Elizabeth Hayes, in her study of Mexican radio, *Radio Nation* (2000), also uses Anderson's notions of the "imagined community" as a entry into discussing the role of radio and nationalism in Mexico during the same time.

8. To confess: I am probably a result of the production process that Poster identifies in ways I can now only partially fathom: I carry my beloved sleek Nokia mobile phone with me at all times and check my e-mail too many times a day no matter my physical location. I marvel at the instantaneous connections and relish the feeling of speedy contact. Had I been born in the early part of the twentieth century, I would no doubt have been a radio boy assembling my kit, trying to contact another in a distant region of the country.

9. Turing was an academic recruited by British military intelligence. He was also a homosexual. Unable to keep this secret, he was given female hormones by the government in an attempt to curb his sexual appetites. For more on Turing, see Ehrlich (1996).

10. Although one hears from sources originating from the communications industry that huge changes are coming in terms of new technology and that the information revolution is only beginning, I think that the situation may just be the opposite. Following Carolyn Marvin (1988) and Marshall McLuhan (1995), the information revolution began with the light bulb and may be *ending* with the Internet. All of these remarkable changes are just filling in the blank created by Edison. After all, if one opens up a computer, one of the key elements one sees is, of course, a light bulb.

11. Relatedly, Poster (2001) coined the term "underdetermined" to discuss the impact and the meaning of the Internet. As opposed to the Althusserian use of "overdetermined," underdetermined refers to the possibilities that remain, here with the use of the Internet.

12. This use of the word *chat* is reminiscent of FDR's usage in naming his radio addresses.

Bibliography

Radio programs that are referred to in the book can be found in the library at the Museum of Television and Radio in New York, N.Y.

Abed, R. T., and W. D. Fewtrell. 1990. "Delusional Misidentification of Familiar Inanimate Objects: A Rare Variant of Capgras Syndrome." *British Journal of Psychiatry* 157: 915–17.

Allison, David B., Prado de Oliveiro, Mark S. Roberts, and Allen S. Weiss, eds. 1988. *Psychosis and Sexual Identity: Toward a Post-Analytic View of the Schreber Case.* Albany: State University of New York Press.

Altman, Rick. 1980. "Moving Lips: Cinema as Ventriloquism." *Cinema/Sound; Yale French Studies* 60: 67–79.

Anderson, Benedict. 1991. *Imagined Communities: Reflections on the Origin and Spread of Nationalism.* New York: Verso.

Anderson, Laurie. 1986. *Home of the Brave.* Videorecording. Burbank, Calif.: Warner Reprise Video.

Arnheim, Rudolf. [1936] 1971. *Radio: An Art of Sound.* Translated from the German by Margaret Ludwig and Herbert Reader. London: Faber & Faber.

Artaud, Antonin. 1994. "To Have Done with the Judgement of God." Translated by Clayton Eshleman. In *Wireless Imagination,* edited by Douglas Kahn and Gregory Whithead, 309–30. Cambridge, Mass.: MIT Press.

Attali, Jacques. 1985. *Noise: The Political Economy of Music.* Translated by Brian Massumi. Minneapolis: University of Minnesota Press.

Austin, J. L. 1962. *How to Do Things With Words.* Cambridge, Mass.: Harvard University Press.

Baldwin, Neil. 1995. *Edison: Inventing the Century.* New York: Hyperion.

Ballard, J. G. 1994. *Crash.* New York: Farrar, Strauss and Giroux.

Banks, Mark James. 1981. "A History of Broadcast Audience Research in the United States, 1920–1980." Ph.D. diss., University of Tennessee.

Barlow, William. 1999. *Voice Over: The Making of Black Radio.* Philadelphia: Temple University Press.

Barthes, Roland. 1985. "The Grain of the Voice" and "Listening." In *The Responsibility of Forms,* translated by Richard Howard. Berkeley: University of California Press.

Baskerville, Barnet. 1979. *The People's Voice: The Orator in American Society.* Lexington: University of Kentucky Press.

Bataille, Georges. 1985. *Visions of Excess.* Translated by Allan Sokol. Minneapolis: University of Minnesota Press.

Baudrillard, Jean. 1983. *Simulations.* Translated by Paul Foss, Paul Patton, and Philip Beitchman. New York: Semiotext(e).

Beckett, Samuel. 1958. *The Unnamable.* New York: Grove Press.

——. 1960. *Krapp's Last Tape.* New York: Grove Press.

Beehler, Michael. 1987. "Border Patrols." In *Aliens: The Anthropology of Science Fiction.* Carbondale and Edwardsville: Southern Illinois University Press.

Benjamin, Walter. 1969. "Theses on the Philosophy of History." In *Illuminations,* 253–64. New York: Schocken Books.

Berson, Robert. 1983. "Capgras' Syndrome." *American Journal of Psychiatry* 140: 969–78.

Bhatia, M. S. 1990. "Capgras' Syndrome in a Patient with Migraine." *British Journal of Psychiatry* 157: 917–18.

Blanchot, Maurice. 1995. *The Writing of the Disaster.* Lincoln: University of Nebraska Press.

Botting, Douglas. 2001. *Dr. Eckener's Dream Machine: The Historic Saga of the Round-the-World Zeppelin.* New York: Henry Holt.

Brooks, Peter M. 1992. *Zeppelin: Rigid Airships, 1893–1940.* Washington, D.C.: Smithsonian Institution Press.

Broughtman, John. 1996. "The Bomb's Eye View." In *Cyberspace and Technology,* edited by S. Aronowitz et al. New York: Routledge.

Buhite, Russell D., and David W. Levy, eds. 1992. *FDR's Fireside Chats.* Norman: University of Oklahoma Press.

Butler, Judith. 1990. *Gender Trouble: Feminism and the Subversion of Identity.* New York: Routledge.

Canetti, Elias. 1966. *Crowds and Power.* New York: Viking Press.

Cantril, Hadley, ed. 1951. *Public Opinion, 1935–1946.* Princeton, N.J.: Princeton University Press.

Cantril, Hadley, and Gordon W. Allport. [1935] 1971. *The Psychology of Radio.* New York: Harper & Brothers.

Cantril, Hadley, with H. Gaudet and H. Herzog. [1940] 1966. *The Invasion from Mars: A Study in the Psychology of Panic, with the Complete Script of the Famous Orson Welles Broadcast.* Princeton, N.J.: Princeton University Press.

Capgras, J., and J. Reboul-Lachaux. 1923. "L'illusion des 'sosies' dans un délire systématisé chronique." *Bulletin de la Societé Clinique de Médicine Mentale* 2: 6–16.

Case, Sue-Ellen. 1989. "From Split Subjects to Split Britches." In *Feminine Focus: The New Women Playwrights,* edited by Enoch Brater, 126–46. New York: Oxford University Press.

Castillo, Pura M., and Carol Berman. 1994. "Delusional Gross Replacement of Inanimate Objects." *British Journal Of Psychiatry* 164: 693–96.

Chion, Michel. 1994. *Audio-vision: Sound on Screen.* Translated from the French by Claudia Gorbman. New York: Columbia University Press.

———. 1993. *La Voix au Cinéma.* Paris: Editions de L'Etoile.

Collins, Philip. 1987. *Radios: The Golden Years.* San Francisco: Chronicle Books.

Connor, Steven. 2000. *Dumbstruck: A Cultural History of Ventriloquism.* Oxford, U.K.: Oxford University Press.

———. 1999. "The Machine in the Ghost: Spiritualism, Technology, and the 'Direct Voice.'" In *Ghosts: Deconstruction, Psychoanalysis, History,* edited by Peter Buse and Andrew Stott. Basingstoke, U.K.: Macmillan.

Covert, Catherine. 1984. "We May Hear Too Much." In *Mass Media Between the Wars: Perceptions of Cultural Tension, 1918–1941,* edited by Catherine L. Covert and John D. Stevens. Syracuse, N.Y.: Syracuse University Press.

Culbert, David H. 1976. *News for Everyman: Radio and Foreign Affairs in Thirties America.* Westport, Conn.: Greenwoood Press.

Czitrom, Daniel. 1982. *Media and the American Mind: From Morse to McLuhan.* Chapel Hill: University of North Carolina Press.

Deleuze, Gilles, and Félix Guattari. 1983. *Anti-Oedipus: Capitalism and Schizophrenia.* Translated by Robert Hurley, Mark Seem, and Helen R. Lane. Minneapolis: University of Minnesota Press.

Derrida, Jacques. 1981. "Economimesis." *Diacritics* (June): 3–25.

——. 1994. *Specters of Marx: The State of the Debt, the Work of Mourning, and the New International.* New York: Routledge.

de Syon, Guillaume. 2002. *Zeppelin: Germany and the Airship, 1900–1939.* Baltimore: Johns Hopkins University Press.

Doane, Mary Ann. 1980. "Ideology and the Practice of Sound Editing and Mixing." In *The Cinematic Apparatus,* edited by Teresa de Lauretis and Stephen Heath. New York: St. Martin's Press.

——. 1990. "Information, Crisis, Catastrophe." In *Logics of Television: Essays in Cultural Criticism,* edited by Patricia Mellencamp. Bloomington: Indiana University Press.

Dos Passos, John. 1934. "The Radio Voice." *Common Sense* (February): 17.

Douglas, Alan. 1989. *Radio Manufacturers of the 1920s.* Vestal, N.Y.: Vestal Press.

Douglas, Susan. 1987. *Inventing American Broadcasting, 1899–1922.* Baltimore: John Hopkins University Press.

Ehrlich, Matthew. 1996. "Turing My Love." *Sexuality and Cyberspace: Women & Performance* 9 (17): 187–204.

Federal Communications Commission (FCC). 1967. *Basic Emergency Broadcast System Plan.* Washington, D.C.

Federal Emergency Management Agency (FEMA). 1997a. "About Fema." On line at <http://www.fema.gov>. 12 December 1997.

——. 1997b. "The Emergency Alert System." On line at <http://www.erh.noaa.gov>. 12 December.

Federal Radio Commission. 1933. *Annual Report of the Federal Radio Commission, 1927–33.* Washington, D.C.: F.R.C.

Felman, Shoshana, and Dori Laub. 1992. *Testimony: Crises of Witnessing in Literature, Psychoanalysis, and History.* London: Routledge.

Fine, Robert S. 1977. "Roosevelt's Radio Chatting: Its Development and Impact During the Great Depression." Ph.D. diss., New York University.

Fleming, Victor, 1939. *The Wizard of Oz.* Film produced by Mervyn LeRoy and MGM Studios.

Freud, Sigmund. 1958. "The 'Uncanny.'" In *On Creativity and the Unconscious.* Selected, with introductions and annotations by Benjamin Nelson. New York: Harper & Row.

——. [1922] 1961. *Beyond the Pleasure Principle.* New York: W. W. Norton & Co.

——. [1914] 1963. "On Narcissism: An Introduction." In *General Psychological Theory.* New York: Macmillan.

———. [1911] 1963. "Psychoanalytic Notes Upon an Autobiographical Account of a Case of Paranoia." In *Three Case Histories*. New York: Macmillan.

———. 1966. "The Libido Theory and Narcissism." In *Introductory Lectures on Psychoanalysis*, 412–30. New York: W. W. Norton.

Gallagher, Hugh Gregory. 1999. *FDR's Splendid Deception*. Arlington, Va.: Vandamere Press.

Gates, Bill. 1999. *Business @ the Speed of Thought: Succeeding in the Digital Economy*. New York: Warner Books.

Gernsback, Hugo. 1923. *Radio For All*. Philadelphia: J. B. Lippincott Company.

Gibson, William. 1984. *Neuromancer*. New York: Berkeley,

Glück, Christoph W. 1989. *Narcisse et Echo*, libretto by Theodore von Tschudi. Video directed by Claus Viller; performance directed by Herbert Wernicke and performed at the Schweitzinger Festival in 1987, 1988. Chicago: Homevision Video.

Guattari, Felix. 1980. "Becoming Woman." In *Polysexuality: Semiotexte* 10.

Hall, Stuart. 1997. *Representation: Cultural Representations and Signifying Practices*. Thousand Oaks, Calif.: Sage.

Haraway, Donna. 1985. "A Manifesto for Cyborgs: Science, Technology, and Socialist Feminism in the 1980s." In *Socialist Review* 80: 65–107.

Hartman, Geoffrey. 1979. "Words, Wish, Worth, Wordsworth." In *Deconstruction and Criticism*, edited by G. Hartman, 177–216. New York: Seabury Press.

Hayes, Joy Elizabeth. 1994. "Nationalist Discourse and the Radio Audience: Listener Responses to Roosevelt's First Fireside Chat." In *Radio Broadcasting and Nation-Building in Mexico and the United States, 1925–1945*. Ph.D. diss., University of California, San Diego, Department of Communication.

———. 2000. *Radio Nation: Communication, Popular Culture, and Nationalism in Mexico, 1920–1950*. Tucson: University of Arizona Press.

Hayhurst, J. D. 1997. "The Pneumatic Post of Paris." On line at <www.windowlink.com/jhhayhurst>. 15 April.

Hayles, Katherine N. 1999. *How We Became Posthuman: Virtual Bodies in Cybernetics, Literature, and Informatics*. Chicago: University of Chicago Press.

Heidegger, Martin. 1977. *The Question Concerning Technology and Other Essays*. Translated by William Lovitt. New York: Harper & Row.

Hill, Jonathan. 1978. *50 Years of Wireless Design.* London: Oreska Books.

Hill, Mary Louise. 1996. "Developing A Blind Understanding: A Feminist Revision of Radio Semiotics." *Experimental Sound and Radio: TDR* 40 (3): 112–20.

Hilmes, Michelle. 1997. *Radio Voices: American Broadcasting, 1922–1952.* Minneapolis: University of Minneapolis Press.

Hollander, John. 1981. *The Figure of Echo: A Mode of Allusion in Milton and After.* Berkeley: University of California Press.

Horkheimer, Max, and Theodor Adorno. 1996. "The Culture Industry: Enlightenment as Mass Deception." In *Dialectics of the Enlightenment,* 2d ed. Frankfurt: Fischer.

Jacobs, David. 1992. *Secret Life: Firsthand Documented Accounts of UFO Abductions.* New York: Simon & Schuster.

Jamieson, Kathleen Hall. 1988. *Eloquence in an Electronic Age: The Transformation of Political Speechmaking.* New York: Oxford University Press.

Kant, Immanuel. [1764] 1991. *Observations on the Feeling of the Beautiful and Sublime.* Translated by John T. Goldthwait. Berkeley: University of California Press.

Kantorowicz, Ernst. 1957. *The King's Two Bodies.* Princeton, N.J.: Princeton University Press.

Kircher, Athanasius. [1673] 1966. *Phonurgia nova* (facsimile edition). New York: Broude Brothers.

Klass, Philip. 1988. "Wells, Welles and the Martians." *New York Times Book Review,* 30 October, 1: 48–49.

Klein, Melanie. [1945] 1986. "Notes on Some Schizoid Mechanisms." In *The Selected Melanie Klein,* edited by Juliet Mitchell, 176–200. New York: Macmillan.

Koch, Howard. 1970. *The Panic Broadcast: Portrait of an Event.* Boston: Little, Brown and Company.

Kristeva, Julia. 1987. "Narcissus: The New Insanity." In *Tales of Love.* Translated by Leon Roudiez. New York: Columbia University Press.

——. 1991. *Strangers to Ourselves.* Translated by Leon Roudiez. New York: Columbia University Press.

Lacan, Jacques. 1993. *The Seminar of Jacques Lacan Book III: The Psychoses 1955–56.* New York: Norton.

Lacey, Kate. 1996. *Feminine Frequencies: Gender, German Radio, and the Public Sphere, 1923–1945.* Ann Arbor: University of Michigan Press.

Lang, Fritz. 1932. *The Testament of Dr. Mabuse.* Film produced by Nero Company.

Laplanche, Jean. 1993. *Life and Death in Psychoanalysis.* Translated by Jean Mehlman. Baltimore: Johns Hopkins University Press.

Lasch, Christopher. 1978. *The Culture of Narcissism.* New York: Norton.

Lawrence, Amy. 1991. *Echo and Narcissus: Women's Voices in Classical Hollywood Cinema.* Berkeley: University of California Press.

Lazarsfeld, Paul F. 1940. *Radio and the Printed Page.* New York: Duell, Sloan, and Pearce.

Lehmann, Ernst August. 1937. *Zeppelin, the Story of Lighter-Than-Air Craft.* New York: Longman, Green.

Lewis, Tom. 1993. *Empire on the Air: The Men Who Made Radio.* New York: Harper Collins.

Loewenstein, Joseph. 1984. *Responsive Readings.* New Haven, Conn.: Yale University Press.

Lothane, Zvi. 1992. *In Defense of Schreber: Soul Murder and Psychiatry.* Hillsdale, N.J.: Analytic Press.

Lowery, Sharon A., and Melvin L. DeFleur. 1995. "The Invasion from Mars: Radio Panics America." In *Milestones in Mass Communication Research.* Boston: Addison-Wesley.

Lovink, Geert. 1996. "Civil Society, Fanaticism, and Digital Reality: A Connection with Slavoj Žižek." *Theory.* On line at <www.Ctheory.net/text_file?pick=79>. 21 February.

Manckiewicz, Joseph. 1987. *Letter to Three Wives* (1949). Video conversion. Video Dimensions.

Marin, Louis. 1988. *Portrait of the King.* Translated by Martha Houle. Minneapolis: University of Minnesota Press.

Marchand, Roland. 1985. *Advertising the American Dream: Making Way for Modernity, 1920–1940.* Berkeley: University of California Press.

Marvin, Carolyn. 1988. *When Old Technologies Were New: Thinking About Electric Communication in the Late Nineteenth Century.* New York: Oxford University Press.

McElvaine, Robert S. 1983. *Down and Out in the Great Depression: Letters from the Forgotten Man.* Chapel Hill: University of North Carolina Press.

McGerr, Michael E. 1986. *The Decline of Popular Politics: The American North, 1865–1928.* New York: Oxford University Press.

McLuhan, Marshall. 1995. *Understanding Media: The Extensions of Man.* Cambridge, Mass.: MIT Press.

Mersenne, Marin. 1647. *Novarum observationvm physico-mathematicarvm* [microform] Marini Mersenni Minimi; tomvs III; qvibvs accessit. Aristarchvs Samivs De mvndi systemate. Paris: Sumptibus Antonii Bertier.

Miller, Laura. 1995. "Women and Children First: Gender and the Settling of the Electronic Frontier." In *Resisting the Virtual Life*, edited by J. Brook and I. A. Boal, 49–58. San Francisco: City Lights.

Morales, Carola. 1993. "Radio from Beyond the Grave." In *Radiotext(e): Semiotext(e)* 16: 330–34.

Niederland, William G. 1974. *The Schreber Case: Psychoanalytic Profile of a Paranoid Personality*. New York: New York Times Book Co.

Nye, David E. 1994. *Electrifying America: Social Meanings of a New Technology*. Cambridge, Mass.: MIT Press.

———. 1997. *Narratives and Spaces: Technology and the Construction of American Culture*. New York: Columbia University Press.

———. 1999. *American Technological Sublime*. Cambridge, Mass.: MIT Press.

Ovid. 1958. *The Metamorphoses*. Translated by Horace Gregory. New York: Viking Penguin.

Pascal, Blaise. [1670] 1967. *Pensées*. Paris: Livres de Poches.

Poster, Mark. 2001. *What's the Matter with the Internet?* Minneapolis: University of Minnesota Press.

Rameau, Jean Philippe. [1722] 1971. *Traite de 1'harmonie* [Treatise on harmony]. Translated with an introduction and notes by Philip Gossett. New York: Dover Publications.

Rank, Otto. 1971. *The Double*. Translated by Harry Tucker Jr. Chapel Hill: University of North Carolina Press.

Rastogi, S. C. 1990. "A Variant of Capgras Syndrome with Substitution of Inanimate Objects." *British Journal of Psychiatry* 156: 883–84.

Reed, Kevin. 1997. "FCC Guidelines for the Emergency Alert System." On line at <www.dlalaw.com>. 12 December.

Rheingold, Howard. 1994. *The Virtual Community: Homesteading on the Electric Frontier*. New York: Harper & Row.

Roberts, Mark. 1996. "Wired: Schreber as Machine, Technophone, and Virtualist." *Experimental Sound and Radio: TDR* 40, 3: 31–46.

Ronell, Avital. 1989. *The Telephone Book: Technology, Schizophrenia, Electric Speech*. Lincoln: University of Nebraska Press.

Roosevelt, Franklin Delano. *FDR: Fireside Chats and Speeches*. Plymouth, Mich.: Metacom, Inc., 1995. Audiocassette.

Rosendahl, Charles. "Afterword." In *Zeppelin, the Story of Lighter-Than-Air Craft*, by Ernst August Lehmann. New York: Longman, Green, and Co., 1937.

——. *What About the Airship? The Challenge to the United States*. New York: C. Scribner's & Sons, 1938.

Rosolato, Guy. "La Voix: Entre Corps et Langage." *Revue Française de Psychanalyse* 38, 1 (January 1974): 75–94.

Rutsky, R. L. *High Technē: Art and Technology from the Machine Aesthetic to the Posthuman*. Minneapolis: University of Minnesota Press, 1999.

Ryan, Halford R. *Franklin D. Roosevelt's Rhetorical Presidency*. Westport, Conn.: Greenwood Press, 1988.

Santner, Eric L. *My Own Private Germany: Daniel Paul Schreber's Secret History of Modernity*. Princeton, N.J.: Princeton University Press, 1996.

Schaeffer, Pierre. *Traité des objets musicaux: Essai interdisciplines*. Paris: Editions du Seuil, 1966.

Schreber, Daniel Paul. *Memoirs of My Nervous Illness*. Translated by I. Macalpine and R. A. Hunter. Cambridge, Mass.: Harvard University Press, 1988.

Sconce, Jeffrey. *Haunted Media: Electronic Presence from Telegraphy to Television*. Chapel Hill, N.C.: Duke University Press, 2000.

Sedgwick, Eve Kosofsky. *Between Men: English Literature and Male Momosocial Desire*, with a new preface by the author. New York: Columbia University Press, 1992.

Segal, Naomi. *Narcissus and Echo: Women in the French Récit*. Manchester, U.K.: Manchester University Press, 1988.

Shadow, The: The Original Radio Broadcasts (1937): "Society of the Living Dead" and "Poison Death." New Rochelle, N.Y.: Great American Audio Corp., 1992. Compact disc.

Shklovsky, Victor. "Art as Technique." In *Russian Formalist Criticism: Four Essays*, translated by Lee T. Lemon and Marion J. Reis, 3–24. Lincoln: University of Nebraska Press, 1965.

Silverman, Kaja. *The Acoustic Mirror*. Bloomington: Indiana University Press, 1988.

Smulyan, Susan. *Selling Radio: The Commercialization of American Broadcasting, 1920–1934*. Washington, D.C.: Smithsonian, 1994.

Sterling, Christopher. *Stay Tuned: A Concise History of American Broadcasting*. Belmont, Calif.: Wadsworth, 1978.

Stone, Allucquère Rosanne. *The War of Desire and Technology at the Close of the Mechanical Age.* Cambridge, Mass.: MIT Press, 1995.

Streeter, Thomas. *Selling the Air: A Critique of the Policy of Commercial Broadcasting in the United States.* Chicago: University of Chicago Press, 1996.

Tausk, Victor. "On the Origin of the 'Influencing Machine' in Schizophrenia." In *The Psycho-Analytic Reader,* edited by R. Fliess, 31–64. Madison, Conn.: International Universities Press, [1919] 1948.

Tenner, Edward. *Why Things Bite Back: Technology and the Revenge of Unintended Consequences.* New York: Knopf, 1996.

Theocritus. *The Greek Bucolic Poets.* Translated by J. M. Edmonds. New York: G. P. Putnam, 1929.

Toland, Roland. *The Great Dirigibles; Their Triumphs and Disasters.* New York: Dover, 1957.

Turberville, George. *Epitaphes, Epigrams, Songs, and Sonets; and Epitaphes and Sonnettes.* Facsimile with an introduction by Richard J. Panofsky. Delmar, N.Y.: Scholars' Facsimiles & Reprints, 1977 [1567; 1576].

Vox, Valentine. *I Can See Your Lips Moving: The History and Art of Ventriloquism.* North Hollywood, Calif.: Plato Publishing, 1993.

Warhol, Andy. *The Philosophy of Andy Warhol.* New York: Harcourt Brace, 1987 [1975].

Warren, Donald I. *Radio Priest: Charles Coughlin, the Father of Hate Radio.* New York: Free Press, 1996.

Weiss, Allen S. *Shattered Forms: Art Brut, Phantasms, Modernism.* Albany: State University of New York Press, 1992.

——. *Perverse Desire and the Ambiguous Icon.* Albany: State University of New York Press. 1994.

——. *Phantasmic Radio.* Durham, N.C.: Duke University Press, 1995.

——. "Radio Icons, Short Circuits, Deep Schisms." *Experimental Sound and Radio: TDR* 40, 3 (1996): 9–15.

Wells, H. G. *The War of the Worlds.* New York: Bantam Books, 1988 [1898].

Whitehead, Gregory. "Who's There? Notes on the Materiality of Radio." *Art + Text* 31 (1989):10–13.

——. "Radio Art Le Mômo: Gas Leaks, Shock Needles and Death Rattles." *Public* 4/5 (1990/91): 141–49.

——. "Holes in the Head: A Theatre for Radio Operations." *Performing Arts Journal* 39 (September 1991): 85–91.

———. "Out of the Dark: Notes on the Nobodies of Radio Art." In *Wireless Imagination: Sound, Radio, and the Avant-Garde,* edited by D. Kahn and G. Whitehead. Cambridge, Mass.: MIT Press, 1992.

Wilbur, Shawn. "The Archaeology of Cyberspaces: Virtuality, Community, and Identity." In *Internet Culture,* edited By D. Porter, 5–23. New York: Routledge, 1997.

Wilde, Oscar. *The Picture of Dorian Gray,* edited by Peter Ackroyd. Harmondsworth, UK: Penguin Books, 1988 [1890].

Williams, Raymond. *Television: Technology and Cultural Form.* Hanover, N.H.: Wesleyan University Press, 1992.

Woods, David L. *A History of Tactical Communication Techniques.* New York: Arno Press, 1974.

Woods, Lebbeus. "The Question of Space." In *Technoscience and Cyberculture,* edited by S. Aronowitz et al. New York: Routledge, 1996.

Wordsworth, William. *Selected Poems.* Edited by John O. Hayden. New York: Penguin Books, 1994.

Zimmerman, Clayton. *The Pastoral Narcissus: A Study of the First Idyll of Theocritus.* Lanham, Md.: Rowman & Littlefield, 1994.

Žižek, Slavoj. "The King Is a Thing." In *For They Know Not What They Do: Enjoyment as a Political Factor.* London: Verso Books, 1991.

———. "Against the Digital Heresy." In *On Belief.* London: Routledge, 2001.

Index

Abed, R. T., on Capgras' Syndrome, 109

Acousmatic form, 30–31; distance and, 65; radio, telephone as form of, 65

Acousmêtre, 30, 142; Chion's theory of, 5; Lamont Cranston of *The Shadow* as "sound-being," 31; "de-acousmatization" and, 31–32; Lang's *The Testament of Dr. Mabuse* and, 32–34; mechanics of, implicated in conspiracy of ruled and ruler, 40; *The Wizard of Oz* and, 34

Adorno, Theodor, 187

Aldrich, Winthrop, 55

Allport, Gordon: 1930s research into radiovoice reception, 27; research into preference for male voices, 166–67, 207n. 3

Altman, Rick: on cinema as ventriloquism, 117; on primacy of sound over image in cinema, 143; on ventriloquism in ancient Greece, 118; on voice of ventriloquist's dummy as "body voice," 118

American Airlines, 52, 62, 67, 69

American Association of Broadcast Voice Phenomena, 14, 162

American Radio Relay League, 11, 188

American Telephone & Telegraph, 11

Amos 'n' Andy (radio program), 75, 118

Anderson, Benedict, on "imagined community" and radio, 189

Anderson, Laurie, 214n. 7

Arnheim, Rudolf, 224n. 1

Artaud, Antonin, 215n. 14

Attali, Jacques, on noise, 70

Ausonius, on identification of hearing with echoing, 164

Austin, J. L.: definition of "performative utterance," 2; non-performative nature of Echo's speech and, 163

Associated Press, The, 60

Baldwin, Neil, on Edison, 211n. 1

Ballard, J. G., erotics of technological disaster in *Crash*, 67–68

Banks, Mark, on rise of audience research, 215n. 3

Barlow, William, on *Amos 'n' Andy* as radiophonic ventriloquy, 222n. 13

Barthes, Roland: on the "grain" of sound, 141; "listening speaks," 8

Baskerville, Barnet, on Fireside Chats and FDR's populist image, 77

Bataille, Georges, 68

Baudrillard, Jean, 194

Becker, Murray, photographs *Hindenburg* explosion, 60

Beckett, Samuel: on language as anguished but heroic, 73; thrown voice in *Krapp's Last Tape*, 73; *The Unnamable* and, 73

Beehler, Michael: on aliens and Freud's "The Uncanny," 136; on child's game of fort-da in Freud's "The Uncanny," 137; on the sublime and the figure of the alien, 123

Bell, Alexander Graham, 14

Bell Co., 188

Benjamin, Walter, on "states of emergency," 121

Bergen, Edgar, 116, 118

Berman, Carol, on Capgras' Syndrome and inanimate objects, 109

Berson, Robert, on Capgras' Syndrome, 109

Betty Crocker Show, The, 88

Bhatia, M. S., on Capgras' Syndrome, 109

Biltmore Agreement of 1934, 82

bin Laden, Osama, 216n. 9

Black Curtain (radio program), 26

Black Museum, The (radio program), 26

Blanc, Mel, 162

Blanchot, Maurice: on the character of disaster, 63; on amorphousness of disaster, 65, 65; on the conspiracy of passivity, 39; on disaster and distance, 49; on the self and the other 29–30, 35, 37; on spatial implications of disaster, 65

Body, the, 4

Botting, Douglas, on flights of *Graf Zeppelin,* 215n. 5

Broadcasting: as antidote to popular entertainments, 74–75; anxiety, world events, and, 121; audience research and, 51; centralization of, 191; commercialization of, and popular resistance to, 104; corporate expansion and, 51; disastrous potentiality of, 12; distance and, 12; during Depression, 82; Echo and, 154; European, in 1930s, 120; *Hindenburg* disaster and, 58, 59; impact of FDR on, 83, 88, 89; increasing news coverage in 1930s and, 50; linkage with travel networks in *Hindenburg* promotion, 53; live, and Kristeva's "signifying voice," 155; magic performance of technology and, 12; mobility and, 50; montage techniques in "War of the Worlds" and, 119; as national unifier in 1920s, 74; military frequencies and, 130; as panic-inducing, 178; "private sphere" and, 75; recruitment of amateur radio operators and, 129; unifying effects of, 75; voices and places in, 131; Williams on interruptions of flow in, 203–4; *You Are There* and, 62–63

Broadcasting, American: beginnings of, 1; criticized by *New York Times* in wake of the "War of the Worlds" broadcast, 110; disastrous events and, 13; distance and, 13; lack of variety of viewpoints and, 12; nationwide audiences for news and, 50–51; peak of cultural influence in 1930s, 1; strategies in covering disaster, 12

Broadcasting, history of: structure of, in 1930s, 108; *Hindenburg* disaster and, 48; nationwide audiences for news and, 50–51; on-the-spot reporting and, 48

Brooks, Peter, on dimensions of *Graf Zeppelin*, 54

Broughtman, John, on missiles as speech acts, 114–15, 133

Buhite, Russell D., on Fireside Chats, 77, 85

Bush, George W., compared to FDR as administrator of panic, 217n. 1

Butcher, Harry, coins term "Fireside Chat," 81

Butler, Judith, on the body, 4

Canetti, Elias: on paranoia and power, 40, 96, 214n. 11; on Schreber case and fascist ideology, 214n. 11

Cantril, Hadley: 1930s research into preference for male voice, 166–67, 207n. 3,; 1930s research into radiovoice reception, 213n. 6; on panicked response to the "War of the Worlds" broadcast, 106–7; on popularity of 1930s radio programs, 118, 121; on the "War of the Worlds," 220n. 4, 222n. 14

Capgras, J., on "l'illusion des sosies," 108

Capgras' Syndrome, 108–9

Carmen, Carl Lamson, 77–78

Carroll, Lewis, 213n. 6

Case, Sue-Ellen, 176

Castillo, Pura M., on Capgras' Syndrome, 109

Chamberlain, Neville, 120

Charlie McCarthy Show, The (radio program), 116, 118–19, 123

Chion, Michel, 5, 142; "de-acousmatization" and, 32; and maternal voice as "sonorific envelope," 144; use of terms *acousmatic* and *acousmêtre*, 30–31;

Clemens, Otto, 61

Collier's magazine, 74

Collins, Philip, on radio set design, 219n. 11

Columbia Broadcasting Service (CBS), 50, 81

Commentators: description of *Hindenburg* explosion, 59; distinction between reporters (print) and commentators (radio) in 1930s, 222n. 16; Echo as forerunner of, 178; Heatter's reporting of Lindbergh kidnapping, 50; Morrison's reporting technique, 58; NBC's Herring and, 71; Phillips's eyewitness reporting in "War of the Worlds" and, 123–25; use of in "War of the Worlds" to simulate broadcast radio news, 128

Connor, Steven: on acoustic technology and séances, 15, 211n. 7, 226n. 7; on Greek origins of ventriloquism, 222n. 11; on mediums as telephonists, 15

Conon, 150

Coolidge, Calvin, accent of, compared to FDR's, 84

Coughlin, Father: increased broadcasting of speeches of, in 1930s, 51; speaking rate compared to FDR's, 84; vocal technique of, 209n. 3

Covert, Catherine: on new communications technologies, 103–4; on listening and commercialized broadcasting, 13; on radio as "dread necessity," 10

Cranston, Lamont. *See The Shadow*

Culbert, David H., 107

Cultural studies, 2

Czitrom, Daniel, on attempts to decentralize radio, 188

Darling, female voice-over in, 172
Dead, the: activities of the American Association of Broadcast Voice Phenomena and, 14; affiliation of radio with, 103–4; airwaves as "deathly," 73; dead relatives on air, 23; as given voice by echoes, 159; Lang's *The Testament of Dr. Mabuse* and, 33; living speakers and, 15; meanings of *medium/media* and, 9; Morales on radio as site for 27; new technology as medium of, 18; 1930s radio filled with voices of, 25; return of, 26–27, 115; technologies of the home and, 23–24
DeFleur, Melvin, 222n. 17
Deleuze, Gilles, and Tausk's interpretation of influencing machines, 37–38
Depression, the, impact on radio industry, 82
Derrida, Jacques: on Freud and haunting, 24; on self-hearing and Narcissus myth, 158; on primacy of spoken voice in Western thought, 157
De Syon, Guillaume, on zeppelins, 216n. 6
Deutsche Zeppelin Reederei, 58
Dewey, Admiral, 64
Dickens, Charles, 213n. 6
Dinner Bell (WLS Chicago radio program), 58
Direct Voice, The (spiritualist journal), 15
Disaster: anthropomorphization and corporealization of, 65; Blanchot on character of, 29–30, 30,63, 65; broadcasting as potentially disastrous endeavor, 12;

construction of disastrous events, 64; distance and, 215n. 2; Echo and, 154–55; erotics of, 67–68; eyewitness and, 73; FDR's voice and, 81, 89; Federal Emergency Management Agency's classifications of, 216n. 10; figural aspects in American context, 66; *Hindenburg* explosion and, 49, 60; history of, rewritten, 64; intrinsic connection of radio with, 113; logics of 65; male narrators as survivors of, 167–68; man-made and natural, 66; media and, 215n. 1; mediation of, by government and media, 66; mediumnistic aspects of radio and, 47; necessity of covering in 1930s, 12; noise and, 70; Oklahoma City bombing and, 66; paranoid imagination, technology, and, 216n. 11; potential for, in users of radio and Internet, 185; reporting of, as threat, 113; Schreber and, 45–46; strategies of American broadcasting in covering, 12; witnessing of, 30; wordlessness of, 66
Disembodied voices: as able to transform humans into machines, 30; in Cantril and Allport, 213n. 6; Echo and, 145–46, 156; echoes and, 161; gender and, 170; Lang's *The Testament of Dr. Mabuse* and, 32; as literary device, 145; one's own voice and, 23; radio as playground for, 170; *The Shadow* and, 28; as signifiers of acoustic phenomena, 145; as virtual bodies, 157; Žižek on, 138
Disembodiment: as aberrant norm, 6; airspace and, 15; autonomy of voices in "radiospace" and, 10; in Beckett's *The Unnamable,* 73;

body in, 4, 6; defined, 5; desired
by listener, 8; Echo and, 168; as
energizing Internet space, 202–3;
erotic aspects of, 7; estrangement and, 7; female form of, 177;
Hill on female disembodiment in
radio, 141; in *Lights Out* (radio
drama), 27; listener and, 6–8;
male form of, 178; Narcissus
and, 152; non-transcendental
nature of, on radio, 6; political
power and, 8, 100; radio production and, 7; radio set design and,
218n. 11; radio vs. Internet forms
of, 5; as representation, 8; as ruling voice, 7; seduction and, 11;
as truth-telling tactic, 9; in
utopian ideas, 180; voice-over in
Hollywood cinema and, 142;
Whitehead on, 7; Žižek on the
Internet and, 183–84
Dos Passos, John, parodies Fireside Chats, 89–90, 99
Double Indemnity, male voice-over
and, 172
Douglas, Susan: on "radio boys,"
49–50, 211n. 8; on radio as
national unifier, 74; on cars and
vaudeville, 68

Echo: Addie in *Letter to Three
Wives* and, 175; in Ausonius, 164;
banished by Freud, 152; delim-
ited by narcissistic male radio
listeners, 177; as desirous of Narcissus's vocality, 155; devices in
"War of the Worlds" and, 120; as
disembodied voice, 146; disparate mythography of, 177; doubling and, 165; as drama of
voice, body, and image, 146;
echolalia of, 160; estrangement
and, 165; as eyewitness reporter,
146, 154–56, 177–78; as gendered, 171; Juno and, 146;
Lawrence on Echo and female
sonority in Hollywood cinema,143; Lawrence on voice-
over in *Sunset Boulevard* as male
Echo, 226n. 8; *Letter to Three
Wives* and, 174; Loewenstein on,
163–64; male radiovoices and,
148, 177; marginalization, survival, and, 178; as missing image
of voice, 158; narcissistic identification and, 148; narcissistic interiority and, 147; Narcissus's
death drive and, 150; Pan and,
50–51; past self and, 155; pathology and commonplaceness, 149;
perversion of the senses, 149;
radio and, 146; Rank on, 157; as
reflection in sound, 147; repetition as expressivity and, 146;
sonorous body of, 162–63; as surrogate for hearing, 157; as survivor, 156; as symbol of mimesis,
170–71; the uncanny and,
164–65; as ur-radiovoice, 165; as
virtual body, 148; as voice-over,
158; in Wernicke's version of
Glück, 169; Zimmerman on, 150
Echoes: as continuations of
speech, 161; the dead and, 159;
as disenfranchising speakers,
163; Marsenne and Kircher's
experiments with, 161–62;
supernatural qualities of,
158–59; time delay and, 160–61;
unintentional expressivity and,
162; Wordsworth on, 159–60
Edison, Thomas, 11, 42, 227n. 10;
records last words of the dying,
211n. 1
Edward VI, King, reporting of abdication of, 50
Ehrlich, Matthew, on Alan Turing,
227n. 9
Ekco (radio manufacturer),
219n. 11

Elizabethan stagecraft, 19–20. *See also Hamlet*
Emergency Alert System, 185, 222n. 18
Emergency broadcasting: Benjamin and, 121; FDR's Fireside Chats as form of, 79; imitation of style of, in "War of the Worlds," 111; simulation of military operations in "War of the Worlds" and, 127
Emergency Broadcast System, 121, 127
Eyewitness reporters: audience reactions to *Hindenburg* reporting, 62; chance and, 72; communication as narration and, 73; credibility of, 71; as democratic icons, 70–71; disastrous events and, 64, 66, 71–72, 76; Echo and, 146; failure of language and, 70; FDR and, 95; FDR as example of, 92; *Hindenburg* explosion as aesthetic event and, 59; *Hindenburg* promotional coverage and, 53; as image of audition, 74; increasing use of, in 1930s, 50–52; as intermediaries between disaster and public, 66; invisibility of, 71; Dr. Max Jordan and, 52; knowledge and, 216n. 8; mistrust of language and, 73; Morrison's reporting of *Hindenburg* disaster, 48, 58, 60–61; NBC's *You Are There* and, 62; Oklahoma City bombing and, 66; present tense and, 72; risk of being subsumed into reported event, 12, 156; sense experience and, 72; as survivors, 72; synecdochical logic and, 71; Three Mile Island disaster and, 64; visual dimension of words and, 69; the "War of the Worlds," and, 122–23, 125, 129–32; word-pictures of, as metalanguage, 70; World Trade Center disaster and, 64

Fada (radio manufacturer), 218n. 11
Federal Communications Commission (FCC), 107
Federal Emergency Management Agency (FEMA), disaster classifications of, 216n. 10
Felman, Shoshana, on witnessing, 216n. 8
Fewtrell, W. T., on Capgras' Syndrome and inanimate objects, 109
Film theory: significations of the voice and, 2; vocal disembodiment in classical Hollywood cinema, 5
Fine, Robert S., on FDR's Fireside Chats, 78
Fireside Chats: as antidote to escapist 1930s radio programming, 82; anxiety and, 87, 92, 95–96; the body politic and, 101; bring nation's political and cultural realities into home, 75; contradictory positions in, 90–91; Dos Passos's parodies of, 99; emotional state of the people and, 88; FDR as reporter in, 91; FDR's speaking rate and, 84; FDR's technique and, 78, 84–87; "imagined corporeality" of FDR and, 80; intimacy of, 78; as narrowcasting, 89; panic, threat of disorder, and, 75, 79, 87; patriotism and, 96; political power and, 77–78, 81, 83, 90; print media and, 81; pronominal shifting in, 78, 88–89; public concerns and, 88; public response to, 93–94; structure of broadcasting in 1930s and, 108; term coined by Harry Butcher of CBS, 81; verbal flaws in, 83, 92, 95
Flash Gordon (radio program), male narrating voice and, 168

Fleichsing, Dr. (Schreber's doctor), 41, 43

Fleming, Victor, 7; the *acousmêtre* in *The Wizard of Oz* and, 34

Freud, Sigmund: Beehler on, 136; Canetti and, 41; child's game of fort-da and, 218n. 10; cinematic imagery of, 151–53; concept of the alien and, 136; haunting and, 24; on *heimlich* and *unheimlich* in "The Uncanny," 21–22, 139; Klein on, 45–46; Kristeva on, 25; Laplanche on, 149; on narcissism, 148–49, 152, 225n. 6; on paranoia, 41, 44; Schreber case and, 40–41, 44; the uncanny and, 23, 25, 137–40

Frost, Stanley, 74

Gallagher, Hugh G., on FDR's disability, 79–80

Gates, Bill, 183, 194–95

German national radio, on the *Hindenburg*, 56

Gernsback, Hugo, 188

Ghosts. *See* Dead, the; *Hamlet;* Hauntings; Séances

Gibson, William, on cyberspace, 195, 197–98

Glück, Christoph, mirroring and doubling in *Echo et Narcisse,* 168–69

Graf Zeppelin, 54, 57, 59

Green Hornet, The (radio program), 113

Guattari, Félix, on influencing machines, 37–38; on Schreber, 44. *See also* Deleuze

Guiliani, Rudy, 225n. 5

Halford, Ryan R., on Fireside Chats, 77

Hall, Stuart, constructionist theory of language, 210n. 6

Hamlet: ghost in, 18–19; technology and, 18, 20

Haraway, Donna: on cyborgs, 181–82; and Schreber as cyborg, 215n. 12

Hartman, Geoffrey, on Wordsworth, 159

Hauntings: disembodiment and, 11; Echo, self-haunting, 164; Freud and, 24, 139; ghost in *Hamlet,* 18–19; in *Letter to Three Wives* and, 174; Narcissus and, 170; radio and, 25; Schreber's delusions as form of, 45; "War of the Worlds" and, 125; H. G. Wells and, 115; Whitehead on radio and, 16; Wordsworth on, 159

Hayes, Elizabeth Joy: on Fireside Chats, 78, 93–94, 218n. 7; on Mexican radio, 227n. 7

Hayhurst, J. D., on pneumatic tubes, 200

Hayles, Katherine, on the post-human, 226n. 3

Heatter, Gabriel, Lindbergh kidnapping and, 50

Heidegger, Martin, 16; on technology, 211n. 4

Heimlich: Freud on, 21–22, 139–40; 1930s radio, haunting, and, 25. *See also* Uncanny, the; *Unheimlich*

Hendrix, Jimi, 68

Herring (NBC radio reporter), 71

Hill, Mary Louise: on disembodiment, 141; on listening to radio, 171

Hilmes, Michele: on corporate control of broadcasting, 188–89; women in radio, 208n. 3

Hindenburg disaster, the, 55, 61, 65; as aesthetic event, 59; American foreign policy and, 61, 64, 121; corporate promotion and, 53, 55–56; distance and, 30, 64;

German national radio and, 56; male narrating voice and, 168; mass transit by zeppelin and, 54, 61; media responsibility and, 57; "Millionaires Flight," 55–56; mimicked in "War of the Worlds," 112, 122, 124; opulence and, 55; public response to, 62; reporting of, 48, 52, 58, 60, 62, 69, 70–73, 119, 122; structure of broadcasting and, 108, 154; as technological failure, 45, 204; time delay and, 160; the uncanny and, 63; United States government and, 54

Hitler, Adolf, 56, 120, 162
Hollander, John, on echoes, 145, 161
Hoover, Herbert, accent of, compared to FDR's, 8
Horkheimer, Max, on radio, 187

Imperialism, H. G. Wells and, 113–14
Infinite, the, Internet and, 199
Influencing machine, the: Deleuze and Guattari on, 37; schizophrenics' love objects and, 39–40; schizophrenic patients' descriptions of, in Tausk, 35–40
Inner Sanctum (radio program), 26
Internet: anthropomorphized, 186; architecture and, 201–2; "consensual hallucination," Gibson, 195; consumerism and, 184, 189–90, 198; criticized by New York Times, 221n. 9; debate surrounding, 180, 194–95; disembodiment, radio and, 3, 5, 183–84, 202–3; estrangement and, 198; governmental intervention and, 194; as imagined structure, 200; the infinite and, 199; information revolution and, 198, 202, 227n. 10; interfaces and, 186, 196–97; military ori-

gins, 191–93, 201–2; Miller on, 194; patriotism and, 179; Poster on, 182, 199n. 11; radiovoices and, 199; science fiction and, 199–200; spatiality and, 185, 197, 200–202; Stone on, 196; surveillance and 185, 191–92, 197; textuality, visuality, and, 182, 186, 195–96; Žižek on, 183–84
Internet, similarities to radio: the American home and, 205; commercialization, community interests, 11–12, 180, 184–85; democracy and, 205; disaster and, 185; disembodiment, 181; distrust of, 13, 185, 204; governmental intervention and, 180; "hackers" and amateurs, 193; mediumnistic capabilities of, 15; military origins, 11, 190; popular acceptance, 203; reporting, narration, 13; Smulyan on, 180n. 2; spatiality of 193; standard modes of communication and, 179, 185; television and, 226n. 1; textuality, visuality of, 186, 197; as unifier, 180, 189, 198, 226n. 2; utopian rhetoric, 180–81, 184–85, 193, 198
It's a Wonderful Life, male voice-over and, 172

Jacobs, David, on alien abductions, 214n. 8
Jameison, Kathleen Hall, on speeches of presidents, 85
Jordan, Dr. Max, on board Hindenburg, 52–53
Jordan, Neil, 217n. 13
Jung, Carl, 162

Kadette (radio manufacturer), 219n. 11
Kant, Immanuel, on the sublime, 123, 216n. 7

Kantorowicz, Ernst, on "second body" of monarchs, 80, 100–101

Kircher, Athanasius, echometry and, 161–62

Klass, Philip, on H. G. Wells, 111

Klein, Melanie, Freud on Schreber and, 45–46

Koch, Howard, on the "War of the Worlds" panic, 106, 116, 221n. 4

Kristeva, Julia: on Freud and the uncanny, 25; on narcissism and the signifying voice, 153–54

Lacan, Jacques, on Schreber, 41

Lacey, Kate, on development of German radio, 187

Lang, Fritz, the *acousmêtre* in *The Testament of Dr. Mabuse*, 32–34

Laplanche, Jean, on Freud and narcissism, 149, 157

Lasch, Christopher, Narcissus myth and, 145

Laub, Dori, on witnessing, 216n. 8

Lawrence, Amy: on echo and female sonority, 143; on *Sunset Boulevard*, 226n. 8; on women in radio, 166, 208n. 3

Lazarsfeld, Paul F., on popularity of 1930s radio programs, 119, 121, 167

LeHand, Missy (FDR's secretary), 99

Lehmann, Ernst (*Hindenburg* commander), 54–61

Letter to Three Wives: disembodied voices and, 173, 176; Echo and, 173–75; haunting and, 174; 1930s female radiovoices and, 174; Silverman on, 173; voice-over in, 173

Levy, David W., on Fireside Chats, 77, 85

Lewis, Tom, 218n. 6

Lewis and Clark, 193

Lights Out (radio program), 26–27

Lindbergh kidnapping, 50

Listening: broadcasting disaster, narcissism and, 155–56; commercialization and, 13; Covert on, 103; Echo and Narcissus myth and, 156; Hill on, 171; Klein on, 46; the public and, 12; radio and, 3; Schreber and, 45; severed voice and, 98; *The Shadow* and, 28; as utterance, 8, 13; Wordsworth on, 160

Loewenstein, Joseph: on Ausonius, 164; on Echo and Narcissus, 147; on Echo as analyst, 163–64; on Echo and Pan, 151; on Echo and self-haunting, 164; on Echo and speech, 163–64

London, Jack, 11, 193

Lone Ranger, The (radio program), 113

Long, Huey, 51: speaking rate of, 84; vocal technique of, 209n. 3

Lothane, Zvi, on Schreber, 43–44

Louis XIV, King, 96–97, 100

Lowery, Sharon A.: on panic after "war of the Worlds," 220n. 4; on surveillance, 222n. 17

Manckiewicz, Joseph, 173

Marchand, Roland, on intrusive/intimate radio and advertising, 220n. 3

Marconi, Guglielmo, 14, 42, 47, 64, 103

Marin, Louis: on force, 97; on representations and monarchy 80, 96–98

Marvin, Carolyn: on the body as mode of communication, 3–4; on new communications, 227n. 10

Matrix, The (film), 199–200

McElvaine, Robert S., on FDR and the public, 92–93

McGerr, Michael E., on advertising techniques and nineteenth-century politicians, 217n. 3

McLuhan, Marshall: on characteristics of media, 2–3; on the Inter-
net, 227n. 10; on media as prosthetics, 10
McVeigh, Timothy, 66
Media: the inexplicable and, 204;
Internet Gold Rush and, 179;
military and, 133; new technologies and, 182–83
Media, American: disembodiment
and, 180; utopian rhetoric and,
180
Mediums. *See* Spiritual mediums
Mercury Theater on the Air (radio
program), 106, 116, 118, 134
Mersenne, Marin, echometry and,
161–62
Microsoft Corp., 11, 21, 183, 193
Miller, Laura, on the Internet,
193–94
Moore, Julianne, 217n. 13
Morales, Carol: on the famous
dead, 162; on technology and the
dead, 14
Morrison, Herbert (WLS Chicago
reporter), 48, 58–60, 62–63, 69,
72; language in *Hindenburg*
reporting and, 69–70, 73; word-
pictures and, 69
Moschus, 151
MUDS (multiple-user domains),
200–201
Mutual Broadcasting System, 50

Narcissism: as "blissful state,"
225n. 6; broadcasting and, 155;
disembodied voices and, 157;
Freud's "ego-censor" and, 152;
Freud's visual imagery and, 151;
homosexuality and, 149; interiority and, 147–78; Laplanche on,
149; love and, 148; male radio
listeners and, 156, 177; Rank on,
150; as system of representation,
150; Weiss on, 150

Narcissus: 149–50; the body and,
152; as "disaster waiting to happen," 156; Echo, fate, 146–47,
155, 169; Glück's *Echo et Narcisse* and, 168–69; haunting and,
170; homosexuality and, 149;
Kristeva on, 153–54; Lawrence
on, 143; madness, psychoanalysis, and, 145, 150, 154; maternal
ideal and, 153; senses and, 147,
157–78, 160, 169
Narrowcasting, 11, 49, 89, 96, 113
National Broadcasting Company
(NBC), 11, 48, 71, 75; *Hindenburg*
disaster and, 52–53, 56–57, 62
New Deal, the, Fireside Chats and,
81
News reports: broadcast expansion
and, 50–51; *Hindenburg* disaster
and, 48; on-the-spot reporting
and, 48
New York Times, The: criticizes
Welles, 107, 110; criticizes the
Internet, 221n. 9
Nicole, Eugène, 101
Niederland, William, on Schreber,
43
Nietzsche, Freidrich, 162
Nye, David, on technology and the
sublime, 223n. 19

Oklahoma City bombing, the, 66
Ovid, 145, 147, 150–51, 156, 158,
162

Panic: Fireside Chats and, 75, 79,
90, 92, 103; management of, by
radio, Internet, 204; radio and,
30, 48, 64, 66, 73, 107, 110, 121,
151, 177; radiovoices and, 168,
178; *The Shadow* and, 28, 31;
structure of broadcasting and,
108; technology and, 18; "War of
the Worlds" and, 30, 106–7,
220n. 1, 220n. 4, 123, 131–32

Paramount newsreels, 60, 62
Paranoia: Canetti on, 40; Fireside
  Chats and, 96; Freud, Schreber,
  41–44; Niederland on, 43; radio
  and, 42, 47; Roberts on, 43;
  Tausk and, 39; technology and,
  213n. 11, 43
Pascal, Blaise, 199
Payne Fund, studies of effects of
  mass media, 108
Peignot, Jerome, 207n. 2
Performance studies, 2, 4
Performative utterance. *See* J. L.
  Austin
Plasmatics, The (rock band), tech-
  nological destruction and, 68
Plowden, Edmund, 100–101
Poster, Mark: on the Internet, 182,
  189, on "underdetermined"
  aspect of Internet, 227n. 11
Pruss, Max (captain of
  Hindenburg), 57–58
Psychoanalysis: anxiety, repressed
  fantasies, and, 23–24, 144;
  Beehler on, 136; Chion on, 144;
  Heidegger and, 212n. 4; Narcis-
  sus and, 145; Niederland on, 43;
  Roberts on, 42; Schreber and,
  40–44; significations of the voice
  and, 2. *See also* Freud; Influenc-
  ing Machine, the; Paranoia;
  Schizophrenia; Tausk

Radio: as acousmatic form, 65;
  advertising and, 53, 82; American cultural life and, 1, 3; as antidote to popular entertainment
  74–75; anxiety, world events,
  and, 64; Arnheim on, 224n. 1;
  Biltmore Agreement of 1934 and,
  82; Capgras' Syndrome and, 109;
  centralization, attempts at decen-
  tralization, 188; commercialization, 56, 188; corporate expansion and, 75, 188, 191; Covert on,

10; criticized by *New York Times,*
  110; disaster and, 30, 113, 167,
  204; disastrous potentiality of,
  204; disembodiment and, 5, 7,
  170; distance and, 49, 64–65; as
  domestic object, 3, 26, 30, 140; as
  doppelganger, 110; Echo and
  Narcissus myth and, 165; economy and, 166; estrangement and,
  139; FDR, political representation, and, 75, 78, 81–83, 94, 97,
  100, 187; haunting and, 125; Hill
  on 141, 176; *Hindenburg* disaster
  and, 53, 56;
  homosexuality/homosociality
  and, 167; Horkheimer and
  Adorno on authoritarian development of, 187; intrusive/intimate
  nature of, 107; Klein and, 46;
  mediumnistic aspects, 10–11;
  military and, 129–30, 190–91;
  Morales on, 27; origins, 1, 180;
  panic and, 110, 177; paranoia
  and, 47; programming in 1930s,
  26–28, 31, 50, 82, 119, 121; schizophrenia and, 40, 47; Schreber
  and, 44–45; the self and, 112, 138,
  167; spatiality and, 10; as "state
  of emergency," 121; structure of
  broadcasting and, 188; textuality,
  language, and, 2; the uncanny
  and, 8–9, 26, 140; as unifier, 10,
  74–75; utopian rhetoric and, 188;
  ventriloquism and, 117; as ventriloquist's dummy, 117; virtual
  bodies and, 71; the "War of the
  Worlds" and, 115, 125, 128–29;
  Whitehead on, 27, 112–13, 203;
  women, gender, and, 5, 166–67,
  171–72, 176; word-pictures and,
  122
Radio, Golden Era of, 105
Radio boys, 11, 49, 50
Radio set design: assembly-line
  production and, 105n. 11;

coziness of, 29; furniture style, 105n. 11; "radio craze" and, 29; Tausk's influencing machine and, 37

Radiovoices: the body and, 6, 98, 104; class and, 84; deep voices and gender, 170; Echo and, 147–48, 158; estrangement and, 12; FDR, political power, representation, 78–79, 80, 81, 83–89, 92, 95–97, 99–100; Freud and, 104; the Internet and, 199; listening and, 8; panic and, 79, 92; sonority of, 7; as "sound-beings," 5; spatiality and, 203; Whitehead and, 6, 207n. 1

Rank, Otto, on narcissism, 150, 154

Rastogi, S. C., on Capgras' Syndrome, 109

RCA, 75, 190

Reboul-Lachaux, J., on Capgras' Syndrome, 108

Reed, Kevin, on the Emergency Broadcasting System, 223n. 18

Rheingold, Howard, on Internet, 181

Roberts, Mark, 45; on Schreber, 42–43

Rockefeller, Nelson, 55

Ronell, Avital, on schizophrenia, 214n. 9

Roosevelt, Eleanor, 99

Roosevelt, Franklin D.: the American home and, 75; the body and, 79–81, 95–96, 100, 102; disaster, danger, and, 81; disembodiment and, 8, 80; eyewitness reporting and, 91–92, 95; "fourth wall" and, 89; governing techniques of, 79, 87, 92, 96, 102; language and, 8n. 6; panic and, 79, 92; political representation and persuasiveness of, 8, 77–78, 80–82, 88, 92, 97, 100–101, 204; props and, 79; public response to, 88–89, 93–94,

103; radio programming in 1930s and, 83; *The Shadow* and, 95, 99, 102; spatiality and, 99; speaking rate of, 84; speaking style of, 78, 83–87, 89–91, 95; structure of broadcasting and, 83, 108; "War of the Worlds" and, 127–28

Rosendahl, Charles (*Hindenburg* commander), 58–61

Rosolato, Guy, term "sonorific envelope and," 225n. 3

Roy Rogers in the 21st Century (radio program), 113

Rutsky, R. L., on technology, 16–17

Ryan, Halford R., on Fireside Chats, 84, 86, 86n. 4

Santner, Eric, on Schreber, 41

Sarnoff, David, 47

Schaeffer, Pierre, 5n. 2

Schizophrenia: as conspiracy of ruled and ruler, 40; Deleuze and Guattari on, 37–38; influencing machines and, 35–40; narcissism and, 39; radio and, 47; radiovoices and, 6–7; schizophrenics as exploited workers, 40; Tausk on, 35–40; Whitehead on, 6–7

Schreber, Daniel Paul: Canetti on, 41; discursive will and, 44; end of the world and, 46; human frame and, 44; importance of 40, 214n. 11; "mechanistic ordering" and, 43; "picturing" abilities of, 43–44; radio and, 45, 47, 105; Roberts on, 43; Santner on, 41; technology and, 42; thrown voices and, 47; voices and, 45

Schweitzinger Festival, 168

Science fiction, 114, 199–200

Sconce, Jeffrey, 221n. 4

Séances: Connor on, 15, 211n. 7; living speakers and, 15; technology and, 15

Segal, Naomi, on Echo and literature, 224n. 2

Seggio, Lori, coins term "Oz Effect," 210n. 5

Seigel, Don, *The Invasion of the Body Snatchers* as depiction of Capgras' Syndrome, 221n. 7

Shadow, The (radio program), 9, 26–29, 32, 95, 99, 101, 103, 105, 113, 168

Shklovsky, Victor, on defamiliarization, 223n. 20

Silverman, Kaja: and Chion, 144–45; on female embodiment in classic Hollywood cinema, 5; on female vs. male voice-over in classic Hollywood cinema, 142–44, 172–73; on Narcissus, 153

Smulyan, Susan: on pre-broadcasting amateur radio, 49–50; on radio as unifier, 226n. 2

Spanish Civil War, 50

Speck, Willy (*Hindenburg* radio officer), 58–59

Spiritual mediums: Connor on, 15, 211n. 7, 226n. 7; the dead and, 9–10; FDR and, 102; media and, 9, 204; in nineteenth century, 9; radio and, 16, 26, 46, 103, 112, 162; *The Shadow* and, 28; technology and, 14

Star Trek, 197

Sterling, Christopher, 28, 50

Stone, Allucquère Roseanne: on interfaces as metaphor, 196; on interfaces and pleasure, 186

Sublime, the: *Hindenburg* explosion and, 216n. 7; Kant on, 223n. 19; Nye on, 223n. 19; "War of the Worlds" and, 123

Sunset Boulevard, 226n. 8

Surveillance: DeFleur on, 222n. 17; in *Hamlet,* 20; the Internet and, 192; Lowery on, 222n. 17; military's use of radio and, 105; narcissism and, 152; in the "War of the Worlds," 115

Suspense (radio program), 26

Tausk, Victor, on schizophrenia and influencing machines, 35–40

Technē: Heidegger on, 16; understanding of, in ancient Greece, 16, 67. *See also* Rutsky.

Technology: aesthetics and, 17, 69; Laurie Anderson's *Home of the Brave* and, 214n. 7; Ballard's *Crash* and, 67–68; Broughtman on, 114; commercialization and corporatization of, 16–17, 21, 30, 179, 181, 184; Connor on spiritualism and, 211n. 7, 226n. 7; the dead and, 14; the disaster and, 67, 214n. 11,; eroticism and, 67–68; failure of, 49, 204; FDR and, 78; German nationalism and, 57; Gibson on, 198; in *Hamlet,* 19–20; Haraway on, 181–82; Heidegger on, 16; *Hindenburg* disaster and, 49, 204; imperialism and, 114; in Lang's *The Testament of Dr. Mabuse,* 32–33; language and, 182; magic and, 12; military and, 190; nature and, 67; Nye on, 225n. 19; paranoia and, 214n. 11; promise of, 20, 49; public response to, 103; radio dramas and, 14–15, 26; Rutsky on, 16–17; schizophrenia and, 35–36; science fiction and, 114; the sublime and, 223n. 19; technological destruction, 67–69; Tenner on, 213n. 5; the uncanny and, 24; understanding of, in ancient Greece, 16–17; utopian rhetoric surrounding, 184; violence and, 21, 67–68, 213n. 5; "War of the Worlds" and, 115, 171, 204

Tenner, Edward, on technology, 185, 213n. 5
Tesla, Nikola, 14
Testament of Dr. Mabuse, The, 32–33, 40
Theocritus, on Echo and Pan, 151
Three Mile Island disaster, the: construction of disastrous events and, 64; human mismanagement of technology and, 67
Titanic, The, congressional legislation spawned by, 129–30
Toland, Robert, on *Hindenburg* disaster, 54, 58–62
Tolstoy, Leo, defamiliarization and, 223n. 20
Transmitted voices: American culture and, 3; child's game of fort-da and, 137–38; FDR and, 80, 89–90, 98; Lang's *The Testament of Dr. Mabuse* and, 33–34; listener and, 1; on-the-spot reporting and, 51; political power, control, 30, 34, 98; Schreber and, 44; spatiality and, 102; Whitehead on, 98; *The Wizard of Oz* and, 7, 34
Tuberville, George, 164
Turing, Alan, 192
2001: A Space Odyssey, 199

Uncanny, the: Laurie Anderson's *Home of the Brave* and, 214n. 7; computers and, 23; corporate interests and, 205; the dead and, 23; as double of the self, 136; Echo and, 146, 158, 164; estrangement and, 137; Freud on fictive uncanny effects, 24–25; Freud on multiple uncanny effects, 138–39; Freud on substitutional logic of, 23; German connotations, 21, 25; in *Hamlet,* 19–20; Kristeva on, 25; language and, 21, 25, 158, 164; radio

drama and, 23, 25–26, 28–29, 46, 103; radio set design and, 26, 29; repression and, 22; *The Shadow* and, 28; technology and, 19–20, 23–24; the "War of the Worlds" and, 136; zeppelins and, 63. *See also Unheimlich*
Unheimlich, before-and-after story of, 136; as origin of opposite, 140; simultaneity and, 140
United States government, *Hindenburg,* disaster and, 54, 61
United States Navy, 11; control over radio, 129, 193

Ventriloquism: Altman on, 117–18, 143; in ancient Greece, 118; *The Charlie McCarthy Show* and, 116; child's game of fort-da and, 137; Connor on, 221n. 11; radio and, 116–18; 131; Žižek on, 138, 207n. 4
Ventriloquist's dummy: child's game of fort-da and, 138; computer interfaces and, 196–97; dangerous examples of, 222n. 12; as doppelganger, 118; radio and, 117–18; the uncanny and, 24; the "War of the Worlds" and, 133
Voice-over: the body and, 142, 172; Echo and, 158; in Hollywood cinema, 120, 143–44; in *Letter to Three Wives,* 175; as metafictional voice, 142; Silverman on, 172; visuality and, 142; writers and, 144
Voices: child's game of fort-da and, 137–38; Derrida on, 157; in *Hamlet,* 18; influencing machines and, 40; narrative and, 143; as "object-choices," 157; Roberts on, 45; schizophrenia and, 40; Schreber and, 45; Silverman on, 143; spiritualism and, 46; supernatural radio and, 3, 27,

120, 131; "War of the Worlds" and, 125; Whitehead on, 16; writers and, 143–44. *See also* Radiovoices

Voices, tone: Father Coughlin, Huey Long, and, 209n. 3; Welles and, 134, 213n. 6

Voices, words per minute: Father Coughlin, Huey Long, and, 209n. 3, FDR's speeches and, 84

Vox, Valentine, on ventriloquism, 222n. 11

"War of the Worlds," 8, 65, 106, 119, 123, 125, 132–33, 156, 171; broadcast techniques and, 111, 119, 122, 128; Capgras' Syndrome and, 109, 136; commentators in, 131; criticism of, 110; distance and, 30; Echo and, 165; emergency broadcasting and, 111; fear of invasion and, 63–64, 128–29, 133–34; *Hindenburg* disaster and, 112, 124; listening and, 156; male domination of radio and, 166, 170; military tactics and, 127, 129, 133, 139; narrative and, 126, 129, 131–32, 168; as performative utterance, 2; Russian formalists' notions of defamiliarization and, 223n. 20; technological failure and, 204; technology and, 133; the uncanny and, 138–39; ventriloquists' dummies and, 133; voices and, 127, 138

Warhol, Andy, 226n. 2

Watson, Thomas A. (Alexander Graham Bell's assistant), 15

Weiss, Allen S.: on cinematic impulse before film, 215n. 13; on narcissism, 150; on radio, 101; on voice in Artaud, 218n. 9;

Welles, Orson, 2, 27, 106, 111, 112, 120, 134–35, 165; alienation of characters, 112, 135; aliens and, 115; apology of, 107; caricatures invasiveness of radio, 115; criticized by *New York Times*, 110; forms of radio and, 113, 116; Klass on, 111; military tactics, communications, and, 130; narrative framing and, 116; radio system and, 113, 133–34; H. G. Wells and, 115, 134

Wernicke, Herbert, 168–70

White, E. B., 217n. 6

Whitehead, Gregory, 6, 7, 113, 203; on bodies, radio, 27, 98; coinage of term "radiovoice" and, 207n. 1; on listening as utterance, pleasure, 8; on ontology of radio, 112; on radio as afterlife, 15–16, 104; on radio as necropolis, 125; on radio as séance, 15

Wilbur, Shawn, on cyberspace as text-based, 226n. 4

Wilde, Oscar, 150

Williams, Raymond, 51, 203–4

Wired magazine, 190

Witches Tale, The (radio program), 26

Wizard of Oz, The, 7; as *acousmêtre,* 34

WLS Chicago (radio station), 58–59

Woods, David L., on military uses of radio, 129, 133

Woods, Lebbeus, 202

Word-pictures: in Beckett's *The Unnamable,* 73; the disaster and, 76; Echo and Narcissus and, 156; eyewitness reporters and, 12, 70, 72; Fireside Chats and, 91; *Hindenburg* disaster and, 62, 69; inexpressibility as form of, 69, 73; in "War of the Worlds", 122, 124

Wordsworth, William: on inspirational qualities of echoes, 160; on synesthetic listening, 160; "Yes, It Was the Mountain Echo," 159

World Trade Center disaster, the, 13, 216n. 12; as aesthetic event, 216n. 11; construction of disastrous events and, 64; eyewitnessing and, 72, 225n. 5; syllogistic logic and, 65

You Are There (radio program): fictional witnessing and, 63; simulation of historic events and, 62

Zeppelins, 54, 63, 122; broadcasting and, 56; distance and, 53; German nationalism and, 216n. 6, 63; *Hindenburg* explosion and, 52, 56–57, 60–61; as uncanny objects, 63; United States government and, 61

Zimmerman, Clayton, on Echo and Narcissus myth, 145, 150

Žižek, Slavoj: bodies of leaders and, 80n. 2; cyberspace theorizing and, 183–84, 210n. 4; disembodiment and, 210n. 4, 183–84; estrangement and, 138; on the Internet, 183–84; ventriloquism and, 210n. 4